# *Tearoom Trade*

OBSERVATIONS
A series edited by Howard S. Becker
Northwestern University

# *Tearoom Trade*

## *Impersonal Sex in Public Places*

*Enlarged Edition with a Retrospect on Ethical Issues*

Recipient of the C. Wright Mills Award
of the Society for the Study of Social Problems

LAUD HUMPHREYS

ALDINE PUBLISHING COMPANY
chicago

TO MY WIFE, NANCY, AND MY CHILDREN, CLAIR AND DAVID, WHOSE ENCOURAGEMENT AND LOVE MADE THIS RESEARCH POSSIBLE

**About the Author**

Laud Humphreys received his divinity degree from Seabury-Western Theological Seminary and spent fourteen years in the ministry of the Episcopal Church. After returning to graduate school, he received his Ph.D. in sociology from Washington University in 1968. He has taught at Southern Illinois University and is presently associate professor of sociology at Pitzer College in Claremont, California.



First published 1970 by
Aldine Publishing Company
529 South Wabash Avenue
Chicago, Illinois 60605

Enlarged edition published 1975

ISBN 0-202-30282-2 clothbound edition
ISBN 0-202-30283-0 paperbound edition

Library of Congress Catalog Number 74-22642

Printed in the United States of America

# Contents

# Foreword

*Tearoom Trade* brings together a number of sociological traditions in a unique study that contributes toward establishing the sociology of sexual behavior on a theoretically and methodologically sound basis. But this study has broader relevance than is implicit in its content, which deals with sexual behavior, more specifically homosexual behavior.

In the tradition of studies of city life that continues into the present from such beginnings as Henry Mayhew's *London Labour and the London Poor,* Laud Humphreys contributes to our understanding of the city as a place where people with special tastes, needs, interests, and problems work out a niche in which they can express themselves among like-minded and supportive people. Mayhew's work is replete with examples of the multiple use of locales in the city and of the overlapping use of city places by both conforming and deviant persons. Thus an advertisement for the fourth volume of his monumental study said:

The class of the individuals treated of in this volume are the Non-Workers, or in other words, the Dangerous Classes of the Metropolis . . . Their favorite haunts, and the localities in London wherein they chiefly congregate, as well as their modes of existence, are accurately described; in addition to which have been inserted very many deeply interesting autobiographies, faithfully transcribed from their own lips, which go far to unveil the intricate schemes of villainy and crime that abound in the metropolis and prove how much more rational and effective are preventative measures than such as are merely correctional. Every phase of vice has been investigated and treated of in order that all possible information that can prove interesting to the moralist, the philanthropist, and the statist as well as to the general public, might be afforded. In a word, the veil has been raised, and the skeleton exposed to the view of the public.

Sociologists have long been fascinated by the variety and complexity of social patterns in the city, and by the ability of differing groups and disparate activities to exist side by side. Anselm Strauss has observed that urban sociologists are intrigued with cities as places that facilitate the creative use of privacy by their inhabitants, which he sees as the obverse of the much discussed urban anomie. Strauss comments:

People who seek escape from the confines of their small towns or from their equally oppressive urban families have traditionally flocked to those sections of cities known as "villages," "tower towns," "near north sides," and other bohemian and quasi-bohemian areas. Here are found the people who wish privileged privacy: prostitutes, homosexuals, touts, criminals, as well as artists, cafe society, devotees of the arts, illicit lovers—anybody and everybody who is eager to keep the small town qualities of the metropolis at a long arm's length.

Humphreys' research expands those sociological interests beyond the traditional concern with residential locales or specialized establishments, such as honky-tonk districts or gay bars, and highlights another aspect of many city institutions. The use of ordinary park restrooms as sites for impersonal homosexual contacts illustrates one way city places may be used by varying clienteles for varying and sometimes morally contradictory purposes. The sociologist's contribution to this commonplace observation is to show how socially constructed patterns of use of time, space, technological resources, information, and interpersonal contacts make possible this common but at first glance unlikely result. Previous studies have shown how particular settings change their clientele at different times of the day, for instance, a bar that is a working man's tavern during the day and a bohemian hang-out at night. But Humphreys' contribution is perhaps unique in applying the microsociological techniques developed by sociologists like Becker, Goffman, and Garfinkel to analyze a situation in which two institutions, one devoted to the mundane necessity for places of sanitary elimination in parks and the other to the need for covert homosexual gratification, alternate over a period of minutes in an area of a hundred square feet, and yet do not conflict in their everyday operation. The contrast is particularly dramatic because his study deals with stigmatized behavior. But the principles that underlie this highly structured operation are much broader in their implications for our understanding of urbanity.

A second area of large significance has to do with the social psychology of interaction and adult socialization. The "tearoom" is a focused gathering (in Goffman's sense), a place where people have certain kinds of business to transact and where during the process of that transaction they must accept certain costs and risks for the gains they seek. Analysis of the highly structured patterns that arise in this particular situation increases our understanding of the more general rules of interaction by which people in routine encounters of all kinds manage their identities, create impressions, move toward their goals, and control information about themselves, minimizing the costs and risks in concerted action with others. Humphreys shows how the participants bargain to establish a mode of interaction in which each protects himself and the other, and establish roles that both provide them with gratification and serve the needs of others. In short, he shows us how the tearoom encounter is structured as a positive sum game for the participants and how a normative structure develops in these encounters to insure that the outcome of the game is positive rather than zero or negative.

The analysis highlights one aspect of all interaction: the protection of the identities of the participants in the gathering. The silence and impersonality of these events are understandable when we perceive their function as a way of protecting other identities the participants value (husband, father, respected member of the community, masculine person). As with all interaction, this social process is structured to avoid overinvolvement by the participants, some of whom have needs defined as inappropriate to the situation, which they might be tempted to gratify if the norms of interaction did not discourage them.

We also learn about the impact of societal definitions, even on such a secret and anonymous activity as the tearoom. Humphreys shows us that the structure of interaction there is adapted to the proscribed nature of the conduct that takes place and to the threats of the outside world (police, wise teenagers, or unsuspecting passers-by). We discover that the highly constrained interaction within the tearoom is a function not only of the desires of the participants to limit their involvement but also of stigmatization of their activity. Activity in the tearooms is organized to make what is highly stigmatized seem matter of fact and taken for granted. So long as there is no conversation and little gestural communication, the participants can mask the varying interpretations each privately makes of what is going on. One suspects that if the participants talked freely about what they were doing they would not find it easy to maintain the gathering as a positive sum game. Evelyn Hooker has observed how even in an interview situation with rapport built up over a long period of time, homosexuals find it difficult to discuss in detail their specifically sexual behavior and their feelings about it.

Just as the study's careful analysis of the tearoom as a focused gathering contributes to our understanding of the interaction processes, Humphreys' analysis of the characteristics of the participants outlines the career socialization of this group of homosexuals. The information presented in Chapters 6 and 7 gives us examples of socialization into a variety of identities concealed under the overly simplistic label "homosexual." In the tradition of Everett Hughes and Howard Becker, the study performs the essential sociological task of relating the identities discovered to social structural factors (marital status and independent/dependent occupations) that operate as constraints on the development of the individual's homosexual identity. It shows that the particular stance the individual takes toward his sexual behavior is adaptive to the particular structural position he finds himself in, much as the occupational identities of the business executive or army officer or factory worker are adaptive to their particular social structural situation. In short, Humphreys' study teaches us about the processes of adult socialization that establish a kind of recreational identity, using the same methods that Hughes and his students have used for studying occupational identities. His work reminds us that much of the literature on deviant behavior (particularly on drug use) can be seen as the study of particular kinds of hobbyists. Perhaps we need systematic comparisons between the situations of hobbyists whose hobbies are legal (like fishermen, hunters, or photographers) and those whose hobbies are shady (sexual deviants, drug users, pornography consumers, weekend hippies, and the like).

This study obviously represents most directly a contribution to our knowledge of the sociology of deviant behavior. It is in the tradition of much of the work over the last fifteen years, which seeks to examine the routine grounds of deviant behavior rather than treating such behavior as esoteric or ineffably arcane. Such a perspective has become commonplace in the sociological study of more familiar forms of deviant behavior: crime, juvenile delinquency, and drug and alcohol use. There has been persistent tendency, however, to treat sexual deviance as somehow special, not subject to analysis in terms of the ordinary principles of social behavior. Along with such writers as Evelyn Hooker, John Gagnon, Albert J. Reiss, and William Simon, Humphreys introduces a necessary emphasis on the social comprehensibility of the behavior he studies.

When he began his studies, Humphreys was interested in carrying out a broad sociological study of homosexual behavior, an interest stimulated by his work with parishioners whose homosexual problems brought them to him for counseling. He began his study in what has become the usual way for students of deviant behavior who are "going into the field." He started, that is, with the most socially visible gathering places for the group he was interested in—in this case, with the gay bars. This kind of start is very easy for the sociologist interested in studying homosexual behavior, for there are published guidebooks listing the major gay bars in most cities of the country. For several months Humphreys' field work proceeded in the usual way: he got to know a few informants and became acquainted with less visible gathering places (for example, a coffee house that was a point of contact between hustlers and homosexuals). In the process of this field work he began to understand the stratification of gay places and gay cliques in the city that was his research locale. Had he continued along this line, Humphreys would in all likelihood have produced a traditional study of a deviant subculture, a type of study for which there are many excellent models in the sociological literature. A "traditional" study would have been no mean accomplishment with respect to the particular form of deviance in which he was interested, since only Evelyn Hooker's work gives us anything approaching a detailed empirical study of this subculture.

However, in our discussions of his research as it progressed both he, because of his extensive knowledge of different kinds of homosexuals, and I, with some ideas developed from Albert J. Reiss's important paper on hustling and the novels of John Rechy, were dissatisfied with the idea of a study of the conventional kind. We observed that while Reiss's paper provides an excellent analysis of the teenage hustler subculture, it tells us almost nothing about the homosexuals who provide consumer demand for that culture. For all the visibility of homosexual hustler gathering places, such as the Times Square and the Griffith Park of Rechy's novels, the literature told us almost nothing about the men who used these facilities as individuals but were not participants in the gay or hustler worlds. These were the invisible men of the literature on homosexuality.

This state of sociological knowledge is typical for empirical research on deviant behavior. Sociologists find it easier and more congenial to study a particular kind of deviant individual, the type Erving Goffman has called the social deviants, "who are seen as declining voluntarily and openly to accept the social place accorded them and who act irregularly and somewhat rebelliously in connection with our basic institutions," and who further come together into a subcommunity or milieu to form a deviant community. Goffman would be content to have the field of inquiry called "deviance" limited to such groups, but the scholarly goals of those who study deviant behavior are obviously broader and should include all individuals whose deviance is apparent even if they do not form special communities or subcultures. Probably the least explored area of the sociology of deviant behavior is exactly that of deviance that is organized, important to the individuals who engage in it, and strongly structured socially, but is not subcultural.

It seemed to us that concentration on this latter kind of individual rather than on the gay world could make a useful contribution. For a while, therefore, Humphreys sought to develop methods for moving from male hustlers to their clients and had some small success. However, as we discussed the results of his preliminary forays into the tearooms, we both came to realize that they provided an even better starting point from which to move away from a focus on the gay world, for the initial estimates of activity in the tearooms suggested that many more individuals made use of them than sought out hustlers for sexual partners. It appeared, in short, that the professionals were considerably outnumbered by the amateurs in this market for impersonal homosexual experience. Our decision was also influenced by the fact that the tearoom seemed to be a unique social setting in the high degree of structure maintained through nonverbal means, and this aspect of the situation seemed worthy of study in itself.

When all the data were in and analyzed, it developed that the tearoom setting was not as devoid of subcultural influences as we would have liked; the patrons varied a great deal in the extent to which they participated in the gay world. But for a very significant number, the tearooms seem to represent their only contact with a deviant sexual setting, and these individuals could not be considered social deviants in Goffman's sense. Humphreys was successful, then, in carrying out a study of a group of people engaged in deviant behavior for whom deviance was highly individual but, as the analysis demonstrates, no less social on that account.

The analysis of this group, both of their behavior in the tearoom setting and of their management of their discreditable status, presents us with a new picture. One hopes its results will encourage sociologists to seek out other unstructured collectivities of persons engaged in deviant behavior to study how that behavior is organized and sustained with minimal subcultural supports, and why. It is likely that in any such study, the researcher, like Humphreys, will have to make flexible use of a variety of methods, moving from observational to archival to conversational interviewing to questionnaires, as dictated by the kinds of questions to which answers must be found.

For all Humphreys' success in moving beyond the limits of homosexuality as a subculturally grounded behavior, there is one important omission in his study, an omission necessitated by his particular methodological approach, which required protecting all but a few of the randomly selected respondents from the anxiety that might have been caused them by the researcher announcing his interest to them. This study does not seek to analyze in any detail the personal significance to the participants of their homosexual behavior. It says little about why they engage in the behavior, what role it plays in their inner psychic life or in the maintenance of their ego identity. This aspect of the social psychology of homosexuality represents an important area for future research. Humphreys' success in acquiring the sub-sample he calls "the intensive dozen" suggests that such a study would be possible were the researcher able to give his respondents sufficient assurance of anonymity, and were he sensitive enough in his contacts with them to avoid threatening the balance by which they maintain a "straight" stance away from the homosexual setting. Investigation of these aspects of homosexual behavior up until now has been very much the province of psychological investigators, particularly psychiatrists and other therapeutically oriented professionals. The growing sociological literature casts doubt on the portrait of the "homosexual" in this therapeutically oriented literature and suggests that adequate understanding of the personal significance of this kind of sexual behavior for the large and varied group subject to the label "homosexual" can come only from psychological studies not dependent on a therapeutic screen for sample selection.

Even without a clear picture of motivational factors, Humphreys' research has much to recommend it to those policy makers who are concerned with homosexual behavior and the tearoom particularly as a locale of public impersonal sexual behavior. Persons whose experience exposes them principally to sophisticated cosmopolitan settings, where homosexuality no longer carries its traditionally destructive label, can easily underestimate the extent to which communities can be made to respond with distress and anger to exposures of homosexual activity. We can thank John Gerassi for a thorough journalistic study of one community (Boise, Idaho) in which excessive public attention to the dangers of homosexuality proved destructive not only to the lives of individuals but to community more generally. In a less dramatic but endemic way, the moral enterprise of the police in many cities across the country does unnecessary damage to individuals and subtracts from the law enforcement resources available for dealing with behavior that represents a much greater threat to public order and to citizens' personal security.

*Tearoom Trade* makes an important contribution in exploding many myths on which police moral enterprise directed toward tearooms and other homosexual gathering places is based. Humphreys demonstrates that tearooms represent neither the moral danger to unsuspecting youth nor the simple public nuisances of which they have been accused. His careful analysis of the controlled interaction process by which the contract for the sexual act is made, and of its fragility, shows that there is none of the aggressiveness and flaunting of homosexual behavior on which the moral entrepreneurs who encourage and apologize for police crackdowns rely in their support of such crusades.

In summary, *Tearoom Trade* makes an important contribution to our understanding of one particular form of deviant sexual behavior. I hope it will play a role in pointing toward more flexible research approaches to sexual behavior, to deviance more generally, and to the social psychological study of city locales. I hope also that it will contribute a useful social science base to efforts of those who are striving to formulate a more rational and less destructive social policy toward homosexual activity.

Lee Rainwater
Harvard University

# Acknowledgments

LEE RAINWATER has exercised the greatest influence on this study. Among his other fine qualities as a research director, he manifests an ability not to hear when a researcher says he is ready to give up. His typical response to despair is, "Well, then, let's add *this* to the research design." His suggestions, support, and intelligent direction enhanced every stage of the study. I also want to express special appreciation to Howard S. Becker, editor of the Observations series, for his patience and excellent criticisms.

Others who have contributed greatly to the research by taking time to read and criticize parts of this work include Rodney M. Coe, John H. Gagnon, Gilbert Geis, Erving Goffman, Jules Henry, Martin Hoffman, Evelyn Hooker, Irving L. Horowitz, Joseph A. Kahl, John I. Kitsuse, William H. Masters, David J. Pittman, and William Simon.

To Daniel V. Grobelny, my data processor and factotum, I owe special thanks for the countless ways he has helped in this project. Without his assistance, I seriously doubt that the research could have been brought to fruition. Of the other students who have helped in a number of ways, Henry Korman and Edelle Waller deserve special mention for their assistance in data analysis, as does Byron Dee Snider for his textual advice.

From most of my respondents, I can only beg pardon for intrusion into their secret lives. I have tried to be as protective and unobtrusive as possible and trust that none will be worse off for the experience. To the "intensive dozen," whose cooperation gave another dimension of depth to the data, I extend my gratitude. If such willingness to expose their moral careers helps others gain an intelligent understanding of a segment of the rich spectrum of human behavior, the courage of these men will be rewarded.

The National Institute of Mental Health has earned my thanks —as well as the appreciation of my wife and children—for their generosity. This study was supported, in part, by Pre-doctoral Research Fellowships 1-F1-MH-34,177-01 (BEH-A) and 2-F8-MH-34,177-02 (CUAN) from the N.I.M.H., Division of Public Health of the Department of Health, Education, and Welfare.

Finally, the deepest gratitude is earned by those who provide shelter in a storm. I am thus indebted to the members of the sociology faculty at the Edwardsville campus of Southern Illinois University. They provided a berth for me and encouraged me with kindness and research funds when all three were greatly needed.

Although all of the above were helpful, none should be held responsible for the errors, conclusions, or consequences of this study.

# *Chapter 1*. Public Settings for "Private" Encounters

While the agreements resulting in "one-night-stands" occur in many settings–the bath, the street, the public toilet–and may vary greatly in the elaborateness or simplicity of the interaction preceding culmination in the sexual act, their essential feature is the expectation that sex can be had without obligation or commitment.[1]

AT SHORTLY after five o'clock on a weekday evening, four men enter a public restroom in the city park. One wears a well-tailored business suit; another wears tennis shoes, shorts, and teeshirt; the third man is still clad in the khaki uniform of his filling station; the last, a salesman, has loosened his tie and left his sports coat in the car. What has caused these men to leave the company of other homeward-bound commuters on the freeway? What common interest brings these men, with their divergent backgrounds, to this public facility?

They have come here not for the obvious reason, but in a search for "instant sex." Many men–married and unmarried, those with

1. Evelyn Hooker, "Male Homosexuals and Their 'Worlds,'" in Judd Marmor, ed., *Sexual Inversion* (New York: Basic Books, 1965), p. 97.

heterosexual identities and those whose self-image is a homosexual one—seek such impersonal sex, shunning involvement, desiring kicks without commitment. Whatever reasons—social, physiological, or psychological—might be postulated for this search, the phenomenon of impersonal sex persists as a widespread but rarely studied form of human interaction.

There are several settings for this type of deviant activity—the balconies of movie theaters, automobiles, behind bushes—but few offer the advantages for these men that public restrooms provide. "Tearooms," as these facilities are called in the language of the homosexual subculture,[2] have several characteristics that make them attractive as locales for sexual encounters without involvement.

According to its most precise meaning in the argot, the only "true" tearoom is one that gains a reputation as a place where homosexual encounters occur. Presumably, any restroom could qualify for this distinction, but comparatively few are singled out for this function at any one time. For instance, I have researched a metropolitan area with more than ninety public toilets in its parks, only twenty of which are in regular use as locales for sexual games. Restrooms thus designated join the company of automobiles and bathhouses as places for deviant sexual activity second only to private bedrooms in popularity.[3] During certain seasons of the year—roughly, that period from April through October that midwestern homosexuals call "the hunting season"—tearooms may surpass any other locale of homoerotic enterprise in volume of activity.

Public restrooms are chosen by those who want homoerotic activity without commitment for a number of reasons. *They are ac-*

2. Like most other words in the homosexual vocabulary, the origin of *tearoom* is unknown. British slang has used "tea" to denote "urine." Another British usage is as a verb, meaning "to engage with, encounter, go in against." See John S. Farmer and W. E. Henley, *A Dictionary of Slang and Colloquial English* (London: George Rutledge & Sons, 1921).

3. It is not possible to know how many sexual acts are performed in the various types of settings. Writers on the homosexual subculture agree, in general, on the relative popularity of these locales. For general surveys of the homosexual scene, see especially Evelyn Hooker, "The Homosexual Community," in *Personality Research* (Copenhagen: Monksgaard, 1962), pp. 40–59; and Maurice Leznoff and William A. Westley, "The Homosexual Community," *Social Problems,* Vol. 3, No. 4 (April, 1965), pp. 257–263.

*cessible, easily recognized by the initiate, and provide little public visibility.* Tearooms thus offer the advantages of both public and private settings. They are available and recognizable enough to attract a large volume of potential sexual partners, providing an opportunity for rapid action with a variety of men. When added to the relative privacy of these settings, such features enhance the impersonality of the sheltered interaction.

## Availability

In the first place, tearooms are readily accessible to the male population. They may be located in any sort of public gathering place: department stores, bus stations, libraries, hotels, YMCA's, or courthouses. In keeping with the drive-in craze of American society, however, the more popular facilities are those readily accessible to the roadways. The restrooms of public parks and beaches —and, more recently, the rest stops set at programmed intervals along superhighways—are now attracting the clientele that, in a more pedestrian age, frequented great buildings of the inner cities. As will be explained in Chapter 2, my research is focused on the activity that takes place in the restrooms of public parks, not only because (with some seasonal variation) they provide the most action but also because of other factors that make them suitable for sociological study.

It is a function of some societies to make these facilities for elimination available to the public. Perhaps the public toilet is one of the marks of "civilization," at least as perceived by European and post-European culture. I recall a letter from a sailor stationed in North Africa during World War II in which he called the people "uncivilized" because they had no public restrooms and used streets and gutters for the purpose of elimination.

For the cultural historian, American park restrooms merit study as physical traces of modern civilization. The older ones are often appended to pavilions or concealed beneath the paving of graceful colonnades. One marble-lined room in which I have done research occupies half of a Greek temple-like structure, a building of beautiful lines and proportions. A second type, built before the Great

Depression, are the toilet facilities located in park administration buildings, maintenance shops, or garages. For the most part, these lack the artistic qualities of the first type. Partly because they are not as accessible from the roads and partly because they are too easily approached by supervisory personnel and other interfering "straights," these restrooms enjoy homosexual popularity only during the months when other outlets are closed.

With the depression of the 1930's a new variety of public toilet appeared on the park scene. Ten of the twelve tearooms in which I made systematic observations (see Chapter 2) were of this category. Although the floor plans and building materials used vary from city to city, the majority of restrooms I have seen were constructed during this period. These have been built by the Work Projects Administration and, in any one community, seem to have been stamped from the same die. In the city where most of my research took place, they are constructed of a native white stone with men's and women's facilities back-to-back under one red roof. They have heavy wooden doors, usually screened from public view by a latticework partition attached to the building's exterior. In most of these doors, there is an inset of opaque French panes.

Each of the toilet facilities in the building has two windows of the same opaque glass, situated at either side of the room. The outside of these apertures is always covered with heavy screen. Against the blank wall opposite the door there are (from left to right) three urinals and two stalls, although smaller restrooms may provide only two urinals and one stall. Some of the facilities still have wash basins intact, situated in the corner to the left as one enters the door, but few of these are in working order. There is an occasional wastebasket. Paper towels are seldom provided, and there are no other furnishings in the rooms (see Figure 1.1).

Few park restrooms date back to the 1940's, when the nation was concerned with building those other major outlets for homosexual activity, the military posts. Apparently, most public construction in the 1950's was connected with the rush to provide more athletic facilities–swimming pools, golf courses, skating rinks, and the like.

The past decade has witnessed the construction of new, functional, cement-block facilities. Most of these structures are located along the expressways, but a number are appearing in the parks and playgrounds of our cities. These relief stations may be viewed as an expression of the current interest in urban planning: some replace buildings no longer fit for use; others are located on the newly created urban playgrounds; and the bulk accompany the nation's answer to problems of mass transportation. However one may interpret the new construction as a reflection of the course of American history, it should be a boon to the tearoom customers. Most of the newly built restrooms are isolated structures with ready access to the roads and thus meet the prime requisites of tearoom activity.

*Figure 1.1*
*Diagram of Typical Public Park Restroom*

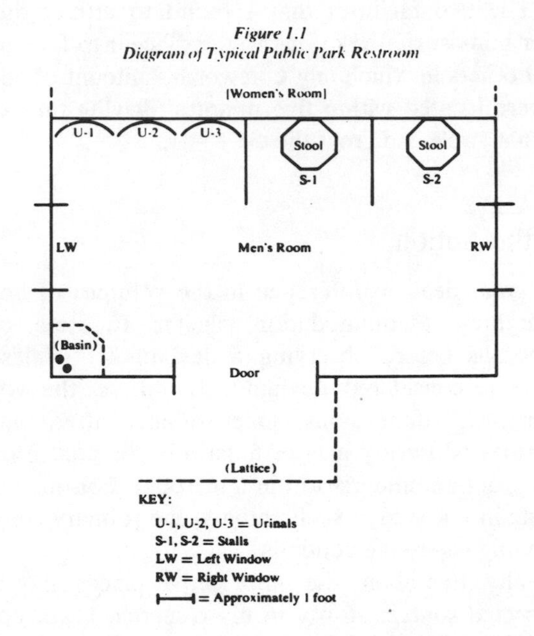


According to some older respondents, the real turning point for the tearoom trade arrived with the WPA. One man, who has been active in the homosexual subculture for more than forty years, puts it this way:

I suppose there has been such activity since the invention of plumbing. I first started out in one of those pavilion places. But the real fun began during the depression. There were all those new buildings, easy to reach, and the automobile was really getting popular about then. . . . Suddenly, it just seemed like half the men in town met in the tearooms.

Not all of the new buildings were easy to reach, but those that were soon found popularity for homosexual activity. Tearoom ecology, like that of society at large, is highly affected by the location of transportation routes. Whether by accident or design, most large city parks are located close to major thoroughfares and freeways. Because the activity in tearooms reaches its peak at the close of the workday (see Figure 2.1), restrooms will draw more customers if located near principal commuting routes of the metropolitan area. The two facilities that I found to attract the greatest numbers for homosexual relations were adjacent to four-lane traffic arteries. All others in which any noteworthy amount of activity was observed were located within five minutes' driving time of the expressways that circle and cross the city.

## Locating the Action

There is a great deal of difference in the volumes of homosexual activity that these accommodations shelter. In some, one might wait for months before observing a deviant act (unless solitary masturbation is considered deviant). In others, the volume approaches orgiastic dimensions. One summer afternoon, for instance, I witnessed twenty acts of fellatio in the course of an hour while waiting out a thunderstorm in a tearoom. For one who wishes to participate in (or study) such activity, the primary consideration is one of finding where the action is.

Occasionally, tips about the more active places may be gained from unexpected sources. Early in my research, I was approached by a man (whom I later surmised to be a park patrolman in plain clothes) while waiting at the window of a tearoom for some patrons to arrive. After finishing his business at the urinal and exchanging some remarks about the weather (it had been raining), the man came abruptly to the point: "Look, fellow, if you're looking for sex, this isn't the place. We're clamping down on this park because of trouble with the niggers. Try the john at the northeast corner of [Reagan] Park. You'll find plenty of action there." He was right. Some of my best observations were made at the spot he recommended. In most cases, however, I could only enter, wait, and watch–a method that was costly in both time and gasoline. After surveying a couple of dozen such rooms in this way, however, I became able to identify the more popular tearooms by observing certain physical evidence, the most obvious of which is the location of the facility. During the warm seasons, those restrooms that are isolated from other park facilities, such as administration buildings, shops, tennis courts, playgrounds, and picnic areas, are the more popular for deviant activity. The most active tearooms studied were all isolated from recreational areas, cut off by drives or lakes from baseball diamonds and picnic tables.

I have chosen the term "purlieu" (with its ancient meaning of land severed from a royal forest by perambulation) to describe the immediate environs best suited to the tearoom trade. Drives and walks that separate a public toilet from the rest of the park are almost certain guides to deviant sex. The ideal setting for homosexual activity is a tearoom situated on an island of grass, with roads close by on every side. The getaway car is just a few steps away; children are not apt to wander over from the playground; no one can surprise the participants by walking in from the woods or from over a hill; it is not likely that straight people will stop there at all. According to my observations, the women's side of these buildings is seldom used.

Active tearooms are also identifiable by the number of automobiles parked nearby. If two or more cars remain in front of a relatively isolated restroom for more than ten minutes, one may be reasonably certain that homosexual activity is in progress inside. This sign that the sexual market is in operation is an important one to the participants, who seldom enter a park restroom unless the presence of other unoccupied cars indicates that potential partners are inside. A lone arriver will usually wait in his auto until at least one other has parked nearby. That this signal is obscured when a golf course, zoo, or other facility that draws automobiles is located in close proximity may help explain the popularity of the isolated restroom.

Another means of recognizing the active tearoom requires closer inspection. Here, I refer to the condition of the windows and doors. Men who play the tearoom game must be able to know when someone is approaching. A door that squeaks or sticks is of great assistance; however, the condition of the windows is even more important. If they are of opaque glass, are nailed shut, or have no broken panes, the researcher may presume that the facility is seldom used for homosexual encounters.

In a western city, I have observed an exception to this rule. One of the popular meeting places there was a restroom located beneath the pavement of a colonnade. There were vents but no windows. The only access to this tearoom, however, was by means of a circular, metal stairway, and clanging footfalls could be heard well before the intruder was far enough down to see into the room. Normally, popular tearooms have at least one pane broken from each window, unless the windows have been opened. Fragments of glass that remain between the window frame and an outside screen are indicative of destruction that was initiated from within the restroom rather than by outside vandals. As the account of a teen-age attack in Chapter 5 indicates, occasional damage to the buildings comes from outside. But one of the first acts of participants after the spring opening or renovation of a facility is to break out a few carefully selected panes so that insiders can see who is approaching.

Graffiti were expected to provide some indication of restroom usage for deviant activity. On the basis of quantity alone, however, inscriptions vary most directly with the time since the latest repainting or cleansing of the walls or with the type of wall covering used. There also seems to be a relationship between the quantity of such markings and the neighborhood in which the facility is situated. Restrooms in lower class and commercial neighborhoods or close to schools tend to invite more of such writings than those in middle class or residential areas.

The *type* of graffiti found does correlate with use of the room for homosexual purposes. In the more active tearooms, I have often noticed inscriptions such as: "show hard—get sucked," "will suck cocks—10/12/66—all morning," or "I have eight inches—who wants it?" One respondent says that the presence of recent markings such as these reassures him that he has come to the right place for action. Active homosexual locales are conspicuously lacking in initials, sketches of nude females, poetry, and certain of the more classic four-letter words. Writings on the walls of the true tearooms are straightforward, functional messages, lacking the fantasy content of the graffiti in most men's rooms. Moreover, this research suggests that involvement in homosexual encounters may preclude the leisure time necessary for some of the more creative types of graffiti production.

## Volume and Variety

The availability of facilities they can recognize attracts a great number of men who wish, for whatever reason, to engage in impersonal homoerotic activity. Simple observation is enough to guide these participants, the researcher, and, perhaps, the police to active tearooms. It is much more difficult to make an accurate appraisal of the proportion of the male population who engage in such activity over a representative length of time. Even with good sampling procedures, a large staff of assistants would be needed to make the observations necessary for an adequate census of this mobile population.[4] All that may be said with some degree of certainty is that the percentage of the male population who participate in tearoom sex in the United States is somewhat less than the 16 per cent of the adult white male population Kinsey found to have "at least as much of the homosexual as the heterosexual in their histories." [5]

4. By estimating (*a*) the average daily frequency of sex acts in each of twenty restrooms observed and (*b*) the average number of automobiles suspected of having been parked by participants near restrooms in five different parks, I have concluded that approximately 5 per cent of the adult male population of the metropolitan area under study are involved in these encounters in a year's time. The imprecision of the methods used in obtaining this "guesstimate" does not warrant elaboration.

5. Alfred C. Kinsey and others, *Sexual Behavior in the Human Male* (Philadelphia: Saunders, 1948), pp. 650–651. See also William Simon and John H. Gagnon, "Homosexuality: The Formulation of a Sociological Perspective," *Journal of Health and Social Behavior,* Vol. 8, No. 3 (September, 1967), p. 180: "About one half [of the male homosexuals studied] reported that sixty percent or more of their sexual partners were persons with whom they had sex only one time. Between ten and twenty percent report that they often picked up their sexual partners in public terminals, and an even larger proportion reported similar contacts in other public or semipublic locations."

Participants assure me that it is not uncommon in tearooms for one man to fellate as many as ten others in a day. I have personally watched a fellator take on three men in succession in a half hour of observation. One respondent, who has cooperated with the researcher in a number of taped interviews, claims to average three men each day during the busy seasons.

I have seen some waiting turn for this type of service. Leaving one such scene on a warm September Saturday, I remarked to a man who left close behind me: "Kind of crowded in there, isn't it?" "Hell, yes," he answered. "It's getting so you have to take a number and wait in line in these places!"

There are many who frequent the same facility repeatedly. Men will come to be known as regular, even daily, participants, stopping off at the same tearoom on the way to or from work. One physician in his late fifties was so punctual in his appearance at a particular restroom that I began to look forward to our daily chats. This robust, affable respondent said he had stopped at this tearoom every evening of the week (except Wednesday, his day off) for years "for a blow-job." Another respondent, a salesman whose schedule is flexible, may "make the scene" more than once a day—usually at his favorite men's room. At the time of our formal interview, this man claimed to have had four orgasms in the past twenty-four hours.

According to participants I have interviewed, those who are looking for impersonal sex in tearooms are relatively certain of finding the sort of partner they want . . .

> You go into the tearoom. You can pick up some really nice things in there. Again, it is a matter of sex real quick; and, if you like this kind, fine—you've got it. You get one and he is done; and, before long, you've got another one.

. . . when they want it:

> Well, I go there; and you can always find someone to suck your cock, morning, noon, or night. I know lots of guys who stop by there on their way to work—and all during the day.

It is this sort of volume and variety that keeps the tearooms viable as market places of the one-night-stand variety.

Of the bar crowd in gay (homosexual) society, only a small percentage would be found in park restrooms. But this more overt, gay bar clientele constitutes a minor part of those in any American city who follow a predominantly homosexual pattern. The so-called closet queens and other types of covert deviants make up the vast majority of those who engage in homosexual acts—and these are the persons most attracted to tearoom encounters (see Chapter 6).

Tearooms are popular, not because they serve as gathering places for homosexuals but because they attract a variety of men, a *minority* of whom are active in the homosexual subculture. When we consider the types of participants, it will be seen that a large group of them have no homosexual self-identity. For various reasons, they do not want to be seen with those who might be identified as such or to become involved with them on a "social" basis.

## Privacy in Public

I have mentioned that one of the distinguishing traits of an active tearoom is its isolation from other facilities in a park. The addition of four picnic tables close to a once popular restroom all but eliminated that facility for research purposes. This portion of a tape, made as I toured the parks in search of action one April Sunday, is indicative of this ecological pattern:

> This [park] is really dead! The tremendous volume of picnickers in all of the parks. . . . It seems like every family in the city is out today. It is a beautiful day, very warm, very pleasant. And everyone is out with their children. . . . The one facility in this park which is most active consistently is just completely surrounded by picnickers, and this would kill any gay activity. . . .

At this stage in the development of American culture, at least, some sort of privacy is requisite for sex. Whether deviant or "normal," sexual activity demands a degree of seclusion. Even orgies, I am told, require darkness or a minimum of light. When, as is the case with fellatio, the form of sexual engagement is prohibited, privacy decreases risk and is even more valued.

This constitutes a dilemma for those who would engage in impersonal sex of this type: how to find a setting that is accessible and identifiable, that will provide the necessary volume and variety of participants, while preserving at least a minimum of privacy? The trysting place must not be too available for the undesired. It must not be identifiable by the uninitiated. The potential participant passing by should be able to perceive what is taking place inside, while those playing baseball across the way should remain ignorant of the sexual game behind tearoom walls.

Ecological factors, the tearoom purlieu, that separate these facilities from other activity in the public park, have already been discussed. The presence of walls and stalls and opaque windows also help preserve the needed privacy. But there is another aspect of the tearoom encounters that is crucial to the maintenance of privacy in public settings. I refer to the silence of the interaction.

Throughout most homosexual encounters in public restrooms, nothing is spoken. One may spend many hours in these buildings and witness dozens of sexual acts without hearing a word. Of fifty encounters on which I made extensive notes,[6] only fifteen included vocal utterances. The fifteen instances of speech break down as follows: Two were encounters in which I sought to ease the strain of legitimizing myself as lookout by saying, "You go ahead—I'll watch." Four were whispered remarks between sexual partners, such as, "Not so hard!" or "Thanks." One was an exchange of greetings between friends.

The other eight verbal exchanges were in full voice and more extensive, but they reflected an attendant circumstance that was exceptional. When a group of us were locked in a restroom and attacked by several youths, we spoke for defense and out of fear. (See Chapter 5 for an account of this siege.) This event ruptured the reserve among us and resulted in a series of conversations among those who shared this adventure for several days afterward. Gradually, this sudden unity subsided, and the encounters drifted back into silence.

6. Although I made fifty systematic observations of tearoom encounters, fifty-three acts of fellatio were observed at those times. The sexual acts sometimes occur in such rapid succession that it is impossible to report them as involving separate encounters. See the explanation of such "series encounters" in Chapter 4.

Barring such unusual events, an occasionally whispered "thanks" at the conclusion of the act constitutes the bulk of even whispered communication. At first, I presumed that speech was avoided for fear of incrimination. The excuse that intentions have been misunderstood is much weaker when those proposals are expressed in words rather than signalled by body movements. As research progressed, however, it became evident that the privacy of silent interaction accomplishes much more than mere defense against exposure to a hostile world. Even when a careful lookout is maintaining the boundaries of an encounter against intrusion, the sexual participants tend to be silent. The mechanism of silence goes beyond satisfying the demand for privacy. Like all other characteristics of the tearoom setting, it serves to guarantee anonymity, to assure the impersonality of the sexual liaison.

Tearoom sex is distinctly less personal than any other form of sexual activity, with the single exception of solitary masturbation. More will be said of this in the concluding chapter of the book. For now, let me indicate only what I mean by "less personal": simply, that there is less emotional and physical involvement in restroom fellatio–less, even, than in the furtive action that takes place in autos and behind bushes. In those instances, at least, there is generally some verbal involvement. Often, in tearoom stalls, the only portions of the players' bodies that touch are the mouth of the insertee and the penis of the insertor; and the mouths of these partners seldom open for speech.

Only a public place, such as a park restroom, could provide the lack of personal involvement in sex that certain men desire. The setting fosters the necessary turnover in participants by its accessibility and visibility to the "right" men. In these public settings, too, there exists a sort of democracy that is endemic to impersonal sex. Men of all racial, social, educational, and physical characteristics meet in these places for sexual union. With the lack of involvement, personal preferences tend to be minimized.

If a person is going to entangle his body with another's in bed–or allow his mind to become involved with another mind–he will have certain standards of appearance, cleanliness, personality, or age that the prospective partner must meet. Age, looks, and other external variables are germane to the sexual action. As the amount of anticipated contact of body and mind in the sex act decreases, so do the standards expected of the partner. As one respondent told me:

> I go to bed with gay people, too. But if I am going to bed with a gay person, I have certain standards that I prefer them to meet. And, in the tearooms, you don't have to worry about these things—because it is just a purely one-sided affair.

Participants may develop strong attachments to the settings of their adventures in impersonal sex. I have noted more than once that these men seem to acquire stronger sentimental attachments to the buildings in which they meet for sex than to the persons with whom they engage in it. One respondent tells the following story of his roommate's devotion to a particular restroom:

> (We had been discussing the relative merits of various facilities, when I asked him: "Do you remember that old tearoom across from the park garage—the one they tore down last winter?")
>
> Do I ever! That was the greatest place in the park. Do you know what my roommate did last Christmas, after they tore the place down? He took a wreath, sprayed it with black paint, and laid it on top of the snow—right where that corner stall had stood. . . . He was really broken up!

The walls and fixtures of these public facilities are provided by society at large, but much remains for the participants to provide for themselves. Silence in these settings is the product of years of interaction. It is a normative response to the demand for privacy without involvement, a rule that has been developed and taught. Except for solitary masturbation, sex necessitates joint action; and impersonal sex requires that this interaction be as unrevealing as possible. In a number of ways, the structure of tearoom encounters has been developed, refined, and communicated. The primary task of this book is to describe for the reader the social structure of impersonal sex, the mechanisms that make it possible.

How, then, does such an operation work? What rules govern it? What roles may people play in it? What sort of ritual sustains the action? What are the risks—to players and others—of such activity? What kinds of people find the tearooms inviting for sexual experience, and how do they relate this behavior to the rest of their lives? These questions remain to be answered; but, before I can reply to them, it is important for the reader to know how I found these answers. Answers become clear only when we are aware what questions were asked and how conclusions were reached.

# *Chapter 2.* Methods: The Sociologist as Voyeur

IN THE summer of 1965, I wrote a research paper on the subject of homosexuality. After reading the paper, my graduate adviser raised a question, the answer to which was not available from my data or from the literature on sexual deviance: "But where does the average guy go just to get a blow job? That's where you should do your research." I suspected that the answer was "to the tearooms," but this was little more than a hunch. We decided that this area of covert deviant behavior, tangential to the subculture, was one that needed study.

Stories of tearoom adventures and raids constantly pass along the homosexual grapevine. There is a great deal of talk (usually of a pejorative nature) about these facilities in gay circles. Most men with whom I had conversed at any length during my brief research admitted to "tricking" (engaging in one-time sexual relationships) in tearooms from time to time.

Sociologists had studied bar operations [1] and the practice of male prostitution by teen-age gang members,[2] but no one had tackled the scenes of impersonal sex where most arrests are made. Literature on the subject indicates that, up to now, the police and other law enforcement agents have been the only systematic observers of homosexual action in public restrooms. In some localities, these agents have been very busy with such observations. For example, of the 493 charges of felony for supposed homosexual conduct made during a recent four-year period in Los Angeles County, California, 56 per cent were against persons arrested in public restrooms.[3]

Social scientists have avoided this area of deviant behavior, perhaps due to the many emotional and methodological problems it presents–some of which are common to any study of a deviant population. Ethical and emotional problems, I suspect, provide the more serious obstacles for most prospective researchers. As Hooker points out, "Gaining access to secret worlds of homosexuals, and maintaining rapport while conducting an ethnographic field study, requires the development of a non-evaluative attitude toward all forms of sexual behavior." [4] Such an attitude, involving divorce from one's socialization, is not easy to come by. No amount of intellectual exercise alone can enable the ethnographer to make such emotional adjustments, and ethical concerns (see the Postscript for a full discussion) serve to complicate the task.

I am inclined to agree with Polsky when he says: "Most difficul-

1. In this connection, Evelyn Hooker, "The Homosexual Community," in *Personality Research* (Copenhagen: Monksgaard, 1962) is important. See also Sherri Cavan, *Liquor License: An Ethnography of Bar Behavior* (Chicago: Aldine, 1966), especially pp. 211–226.

2. Albert J. Reiss, Jr., "The Social Integration of Queers and Peers," *Social Problems,* Vol. 9, No. 2 (Fall, 1961), pp. 102–120.

3. These arrests for felonious homosexual offenses in Los Angeles County, from 1962–64, were analyzed in Jon J. Gallo and others, "The Consenting Adult Homosexual and the Law: An Empirical Study of Enforcement and Administration in Los Angeles County," *UCLA Law Review,* 13 (March, 1966), p. 804. A number of references to public restrooms in this excellent study constitute nearly all the literature on this subject. Outside of occasional comments in gay novels and other works on the subject of homosexuality that tearooms provide "one of the known sexual outlets" for the homosexual, there is no other mention to be found.

4. Hooker, "The Homosexual Community," p. 40.

ties that one meets and solves in doing field research on criminals are simply the difficulties one meets and solves in doing field research."[5] The obstructions encountered in the course of this study—insurmountable as some appeared at the time—are, for the most part, shared with other ethnographers, particularly those who take on deviant populations.

Unless one intends to study only that beleaguered, captive population, the students in our college classrooms, the first problem is one of locating subjects for research. In his study of the Negro street corner man, Elliot Liebow found that "he is no more at home to the researcher than he is to the case worker or the census taker."[6] The refreshingly human account of Whyte's "first efforts" at research in *Street Corner Society* underscores this point.[7] Masters and Johnson turned to prostitutes for respondents who were "knowledgeable, cooperative, and available for study" in the early stages of their investigation of human sexual response.[8]

As indicated in the preceding chapter, my initial problem was one of locating the more popular tearooms. Once I could find where the "action" was, I knew that potential research subjects would be involved. This is the advantage of studying a population defined only by their participation in a specific sort of interaction. To observe those involved in race track society, the scientist goes to the race tracks.[9] To study "homosexuals" or "schizophrenics," however, one must first overcome the vague, stereotypical generalizations to which even social science falls victim in order to define (much less isolate and sample) the population.

This is not a study of "homosexuals" but of participants in homosexual acts. The subjects of this study have but one thing in common: each has been observed by me in the course of a homosexual act in a public park restroom. This is the activity, and these are the actors, that I set out to study in 1965. The physical traces

5. Ned Polsky, *Hustlers, Beats, and Others* (Chicago: Aldine, 1967), p. 126.
6. Elliot Liebow, *Tally's Corner* (Boston: Little, Brown, 1967), p. 7.
7. William Foote Whyte, *Street Corner Society* (Chicago: University of Chicago Press, 1943), pp. 288–298.
8. William H. Masters and Virginia E. Johnson, *Human Sexual Response* (Boston: Little, Brown, 1966), p. 10.
9. An interesting example of precisely this sort of study is Marvin B. Scott, *The Racing Game* (Chicago: Aldine, 1968).

that helped lead me to such performers and performances are discussed in Chapter 1. When a researcher is able to engage participants in conversation outside the tearooms, he may be directed to some of the more active spots of a city. In the early stages of research, however, such measures as location, surroundings, and the number of cars parked in front are very helpful in locating the more profitable places for research.

## Other Tearooms—Other Variables

There are, of course, other tearooms, not located in parks, that might have been studied. Those in the Y's and transportation facilities have received the greatest publicity.[10] My study, however, has been focused upon the park facilities for two reasons. First, the latter have the greatest notoriety in the homosexual subculture. Second, I wanted to control the ecological and demographic variables as much as possible. All but two of the restrooms in which I conducted systematic observations were of the same floor plan, and all shared common environmental conditions. Of greater importance is the "democratic" nature of outdoor facilities. Parks are much more apt to draw a representative sample of the population.

In the same city, there is a well-known tearoom in a courthouse, another in a large department store, and a third in the basement of a class B movie theater. Each caters to a different clientele, is subject to different influences from the physical surroundings, and is supervised by different forces of social control. In the department store tearoom, most of the men wear neckties. Participants venture there during lunch hour from their nearby offices. This is a white collar facility, patrolled by the store's detectives. Word has it that an apprehended offender is taken to the office of the store manager, who administers reprimands and threats and then pronounces sentence: he revokes the guilty man's credit card! I once spent an hour counselling a distraught participant who was contemplating suicide in apprehension of what his wife might be told if she tried to charge

10. Perhaps the most famous tearoom arrest in America was that of a presidential assistant in the restroom of a Washington YMCA in 1964.

anything at this popular store, where her husband had been caught in an act of fellatio.

Although I have made informal observations of tearoom activity in New York, Chicago, St. Louis, Kansas City, Des Moines, Tulsa, Denver, Los Angeles, and San Francisco, the greater part of the research was concentrated in one metropolitan area. Admittedly, there are a number of factors that cast doubt on the applicability of these findings to other regions of the United States, much less to other nations and cultures.

One feature of the toilet stalls in the city where my research was concentrated constitutes an important variable: there are no doors on the stalls in the public parks. Signals from the stalls, therefore, are all of the bodily motion variety—gestures of the head or hands. One social scientist questioned an earlier paper of mine that had omitted reference to other types of signaling:

> You don't say anything about men who go into a stall, close the door and then make contact with the chap in the next stall by means such as foot-tapping or passing notes. I presume that, given the layout of the restrooms you surveyed, this was not common practice, but it is certainly done widely here. As a matter of fact, the University recently removed the doors from *every other* stall in several of the larger men's rooms on campus in order to cut down on this activity.[11]

In tearooms where there were doors on the stalls, I *have* observed the use of foot-tapping as a means of communication. What the university authorities mentioned above apparently failed to realize, however, is that doors on the stalls serve as hindrances rather than aids to homoerotic activity. Certainly, the passing of notes would cause inconvenience and place the actor in greater jeopardy.

Other variables such as climate, availability of parks, the nature of police surveillance, amount of newspaper publicity accorded offenders, or relative popularity of other sexual outlets could result in wide variations in the volume of tearoom activity.[12] My conten-

11. In a letter from Martin Hoffman, M.D., School of Criminology, University of California, Berkeley, August 2, 1967.

12. For instance, informants tell me that the policy of Denver's daily newspapers to publish names, addresses, and places of employment of all men arrested on charges of homosexual behavior has caused a decrease of tearoom activity in the city—with a corresponding rise in the popularity of other homosexual outlets.

tion, however, is that the basic rules of the game–and the profile of the players–are applicable to any place in the United States.

This much may be said with certainty: there is probably no major city in the nation without its tearooms in current operation. These facilities constitute a major part of the free sex market for those in the homosexual subculture–and for millions who might never identify with the gay society. For the social scientist, these public toilets provide a means for direct observation of the dynamics of sexual encounters *in situ;* moreover, as will be seen, they facilitate the gathering of a representative sample of secret deviants, for most of whom association with the deviant subculture is minimal.

## Neatness versus Accuracy

I employed the methods described herein not because they are the most accurate in the sense of "neatness" or "cleanness" but because they promised the greatest accuracy in terms of faithfulness to people and actions as they live and happen. These are strategies that I judged to be the least obtrusive measures available–the least likely to distort the real world.

My biases are those that Bruyn attributes to the participant observer, who "is interested in people as they are, not as he thinks they ought to be according to some standard of his own." [13] To employ, therefore, any strategies that might distort either the activity observed or the profile of those who engage in it would be foreign to my scientific philosophy and inimical to my purposes.

Some methods, then, have grown quite naturally from the chromosomal messages of a particular "school" of sociology. Others are mutations resulting from interaction with my research environment. As obstacles developed, means were devised to circumvent them. Unusual difficulties call for unusual strategies. Although I have employed a number of "oddball measures," as they are called by Webb and his associates, these research methods

13. Severyn T. Bruyn, *The Human Perspective in Sociology* (Englewood Cliffs, N. J.: Prentice-Hall, 1966), p. 18.

are actually only uncommon applications of such tested measures as physical traces, the running record, and simple observation.[14]

My concern in this study has been with the description of a specific style of deviant behavior and of the population who engage in that activity. Beyond such systematic, descriptive analyses, I have tried to offer, in the light of deviance theory, some explanation as to why and how these people participate in the particular form of behavior described. I have not attempted to test any prestated hypotheses. Such an approach tends to limit sociological research to the imagery of the physical sciences. It seems to me equally valid to apply a number of measures to one population or one type of social interaction for the purpose of describing that encounter and its participants.

Hypotheses should develop *out of* such ethnographic work, rather than provide restrictions and distortions from its inception. Where my data have called for a conceptual framework, I have tried to supply it, sometimes with the help of other social scientists. In those cases where data were strong enough to generate new theoretical approaches, I have attempted to be a willing medium. The descriptive study is important, not only in obtaining objective and systematic knowledge of behavior that is either unknown or taken for granted, but in providing the groundwork for new theoretical development. If the social scientist is to move back and forth between his data and the body of social theory, the path of that movement should not be restricted to a set of predestined hypotheses.[15]

The research in which I engaged, from the summer of 1965 through the winter of 1967–68, may be broken down into two distinct stages, each with its subcategories. The first was an ethnographic or participant-observation stage. This part of the research extended over two years on a part-time basis (I was also involved in graduate study at the time).

The second half involved six months of full-time work in administering interview schedules to more than one hundred respondents

14. Eugene J. Webb and others, *Unobtrusive Measures: Nonreactive Research in the Social Sciences* (Chicago: Rand McNally, 1966). All of these measures are described in some detail in this work.

15. For a description of theory development at its best, see C. Wright Mills, *The Sociological Imagination* (New York: Grove Press, 1959), p. 73.

and in attempting to interview another twenty-seven. Another year has been devoted to analysis of the resulting data.

## Preparing for the Field

As an ethnographer, my first task was to acquaint myself with the homosexual subculture. Because of my pastoral experience, I was no total stranger to those circles. While a seminarian, I was employed for two years in a parish that was known in the homosexual world as Chicago's "queen parish"—a place to which the homosexuals could turn for counsel, understanding priests, good music, and worship with an aesthetic emphasis. I soon came to know the gay parishioners and to speak their language. Seminarians who worked there called on people who lived in unbelievable squalor and in houses of prostitution, so it was nothing for us to seek the flock in gay bars as well. One of the faithful churchmen was bartender and part-time entertainer in one of the more popular spots, and he always looked after the seminarians and warned us of impending raids.

This particular part of my education was supplemented in the summer of 1953, when I spent three months in clinical training at the State University of Iowa's psychiatric hospital. This was a model institution, operated primarily for research and training purposes, and (in line with research interests of the Head of Staff) was well stocked that summer with male homosexual patients. That training provided me with a background in psychoanalytic theory regarding homosexuality.

From 1955 to 1965, I served parishes in Oklahoma, Colorado, and Kansas, twice serving as Episcopal campus chaplain on a part-time basis. Because I was considered "wise" and did not attempt to "reform" them, hundreds of homosexuals of all sorts and conditions came to me during those years for counselling. Having joined me in counselling parishioners over the coffee pot for many a night, my wife provided much understanding assistance in this area of my ministry.

The problem, at the beginning of my research, was threefold: to become acquainted with the sociological literature on sexual deviance; to gain entry to a deviant subculture in a strange city where

I no longer had pastoral, and only part-time priestly, duties; and to begin to listen to sexual deviants with a scientist's rather than a pastor's ear.

## Passing as Deviant

Like any deviant group, homosexuals have developed defenses against outsiders: secrecy about their true identity, symbolic gestures and the use of the eyes for communication, unwillingness to expose the whereabouts of their meeting places, extraordinary caution with strangers, and admission to certain places only in the company of a recognized person. Shorn of pastoral contacts and unwilling to use professional credentials, I had to enter the subculture as would any newcomer and to make contact with respondents under the guise of being another gay guy.[16]

Such entry is not difficult to accomplish. Almost any taxi driver can tell a customer where to find a gay bar. A guide to such gathering places [17] may be purchased for five dollars. The real problem is not one of making contact with the subculture but of making the contact "stick." Acceptance does not come easy, and it is extremely difficult to move beyond superficial contact in public places to acceptance by the group and invitations to private and semiprivate parties. This problem has been well expressed by a team engaged in homosexual research at the University of Michigan:

> An outsider–be he a novitiate deviant, police officer, or sociologist–finds it necessary to cope with a kind of double closure one confronts around many kinds of subcultural deviance; to wit, one may gain entrance into the deviant enterprise only if he has had previous connection with it, but he can gain such connections only if he has them.[18]

16. My reticence at admitting I was a sociologist resulted, in part, from the cautioning of a gay friend who warned me that homosexuals in the community are particularly wary of sociologists. This is supposedly the result of the failure of a graduate student at another university to disguise the names of bars and respondents in a master's thesis on this subject.

17. *Guild Guide* (Washington: Guild Press, 1968).

18. Donald J. Black and Maureen A. Mileski, "Passing as Deviant: Methodological Problems and Tactics," unpublished working paper available through the Department of Sociology, University of Michigan, Ann Arbor, pp. 4–5.

On one occasion, for instance, tickets to an after-hours party were sold to the man next to me at a bar. When I asked to buy one, I was told that they were "full up." Following the tip of another customer, I showed up anyway and walked right in. No one questioned my being there. Since my purpose at this point of the field study was simply to "get the feel" of the deviant community rather than to study methods of penetrating its boundaries, I finally tired of the long method and told a friendly potential respondent who I was and what I was doing. He then got me invited to cocktail parties before the annual "drag ball," and my survey of the subculture neared completion.

During those first months, I made the rounds of ten gay bars then operating in the metropolitan area, attended private gatherings and the annual ball, covered the scene where male prostitutes operate out of a coffee house, observed pick-up operations in the parks and streets, and had dozens of informal interviews with participants in the gay society. I also visited the locales where "instant sex" was to be had: the local bathhouse, certain movie theaters, and the tearooms.

From the beginning, my decision was to continue the practice of the field study in passing as deviant. Although this raises questions of scientific ethics, which will be dealt with later, there are good reasons for following this method of participant observation.

In the first place, I am convinced that there is only *one* way to watch highly discreditable behavior and that is to pretend to be in the same boat with those engaging in it. To wear a button that says "I Am a Watchbird, Watching You" into a tearoom, would instantly eliminate all action except the flushing of toilets and the exiting of all present. Polsky has done excellent observation of pool hustlers because he is experienced and welcome in their game. He is accepted as one of them. He might also do well, as he suggests, in interviewing a jewel thief or a fence in his tavern hangout. But it should be noted that he does not propose watching them steal, whereas my research required observation of criminal acts.[19]

The second reason is to prevent distortion. Hypothetically, let us assume that a few men could be found to continue their sexual

19. Polsky, *Hustlers, Beats, and Others,* p. 127.

activity while under observation. How "normal" could that activity be? How could the researcher separate the "show" and the "cover" from standard procedures of the encounter? Masters and Johnson might gather clinical data in a clinical setting without distortion, but a stage is a suitable research site only for those who wish to study the "onstage" behavior of actors.

## Serving as Watchqueen

In *Unobtrusive Measures,* the authors refer to the participant observation method as one of "simple observation." [20] This is something of a misnomer for the study of sexually deviant behavior. Observation of the tearoom encounters—far from being simple—became, at some stages of the research, almost impossibly complex.

Observation is made doubly difficult when the observer is an object of suspicion. Any man who remains in a public washroom for more than five minutes is apt to be either a member of the vice squad or someone on the make. As yet, he is not suspected as being a social scientist. The researcher, concerned as he is in uncovering information, is unavoidably at variance with the secretive interests of the deviant population. Because his behavior is both criminal[21] and the object of much social derision, the tearoom customer is exceptionally sensitive to the intrusion of all strangers.

Bruyn points out three difficulties attendant to participant observation: "how to become a natural part of the life of the observed," "how to maintain scientific integrity," and "problems of ethical integrity." [22] Each of these problems is intensified in the observation of homosexual activity. When the focus of an encounter is specifically sexual, it is very difficult for the observer to take a

20. Webb and others, *Unobtrusive Measures,* p. 49.

21. The Revised Statutes of the state under study, for instance, read on this wise: H563.230. *The abominable and detestable crime against nature—penalty.*—Every person who shall be convicted of the detestable and abominable crime against nature, committed with mankind or with beast, with the sexual organs or with the mouth, shall be punished by imprisonment in the penitentiary not less than two years.

22. Bruyn, *Human Perspective*

"natural part" in the action without actual involvement of a sexual nature. Such involvement would, of course, raise serious questions of both scientific and ethical integrity on his part. His central problem, then, is one of maintaining both objectivity and participation (the old theological question of how to be *in,* but not *of,* the world).

In their excellent and comprehensive paper on the subject of passing as deviant, Black and Mileski outline ways "by which the social organization itself can be mobilized by the investigator in the interests of his research."[23] Unfortunately, this paper had not been written when I needed it; nevertheless, my preliminary observations of tearoom encounters led to the discovery of an essential strategy–the real methodological breakthrough of this research–that involved such mobilization of the social organization being observed.

The very fear and suspicion encountered in the restrooms produces a participant role, the sexuality of which is optional. This is the role of the lookout ("watchqueen" in the argot), a man who is situated at the door or windows from which he may observe the means of access to the restroom. When someone approaches, he coughs. He nods when the coast is clear or if he recognizes an entering party as a regular.

The lookouts fall into three main types. The most common of these are the "waiters," men who are waiting for someone with whom they have made an appointment or whom they expect to find at this spot, for a particular type of "trick," or for a chance to get in on the action. The others are the masturbaters, who engage in autoerotic behavior (either overtly or beneath their clothing) while observing sexual acts, and the voyeurs, who appear to derive sexual stimulation and pleasure from watching the others. Waiters sometimes masturbate while waiting–and I have no evidence to prove some are not also voyeurs. The point is that the primary purpose of their presence differs from that of the pure mastubater or voyeur: the waiters expect to become players. In a sense, the masturbaters are all voyeurs, while the reverse is not true.

In terms of appearances, I assumed the role of the voyeur–a

23. Black and Mileski, "Passing as Deviant," p. 2.

role superbly suited for sociologists and the only lookout role that is not overtly sexual. On those occasions when there was only one other man present in the room, I have taken a role that is even less sexual than that of the voyeur-lookout: the straight person who has come to the facility for purposes of elimination. Although it avoids sexual pressure, this role is problematic for the researcher: it is short-lived and invariably disrupts the action he has set out to observe. (See Chapter 3 for discussion of this role and others.)

Before being alerted to the role of lookout by a cooperating respondent, I tried first the role of the straight and then that of the waiter. As the former, I disrupted the action and frustrated my research. As the latter—glancing at my watch and pacing nervously from window to door to peer out—I could not stay long without being invited to enter the action and could only make furtive observation of the encounters. As it was, the waiter and voyeur roles are subject to blurring and I was often mistaken for the former.

By serving as a voyeur-lookout, I was able to move around the room at will, from window to window, and to observe all that went on without alarming my respondents or otherwise disturbing the action. I found this role much more amenable and profitable than the limited roles assumed in the earlier stages of research. Not only has being a watchqueen enabled me to gather data on the behavioral patterns, it has facilitated the linking of participants in homosexual acts with particular automobiles.

During the first year of observations—from April of 1966 to April 1967—my field research notes were made with the aid of a portable tape recorder, concealed under a pasteboard carton on the front seat of my automobile. Research efforts during this time were directed toward comprehensiveness. I attempted to survey all of the active tearooms in one city and to extend my observations, whenever possible, to other communities across the country. My concern was to observe the activity across a representative range of times and places.

The park restrooms first become active as sexual outlets between 7:30 and 8:30 A.M., when the park attendants arrive to unlock them. The early customers are men who meet on their way to work. After 9:00, the activity drops off sharply until lunch time. During the first two hours of the afternoon, there is another abrupt increase in activity from those who spend their lunch breaks in the park, followed by a leveling-off until about 4:00 P.M. From this time until about 7:00 in the evening, the great bulk of tearoom participants arrive. Most participants stop off in the park restrooms while driving home from work. As one respondent stated, he tries to make it to a tearoom "nearly every evening about 5:30 for a quick job on the way home."

A few of these facilities remain open until as late as 9:00 P.M., but most are locked up by 7:30. On Saturdays and Sundays, the over-all volume of activity is much greater, reaching its peak between 4:00 and 4:30 P.M. I have observed a drop in tearoom action on the weekends immediately after lunch time, a period that coincides with the greatest amount of picnic activity. Otherwise, the curve is roughly bell-shaped, rising to the late afternoon peak. There are, of course, variations in these patterns from park to park and during different seasons of the year. The "hunting season" is described in Chapter 1, but I estimate that the months of greatest sexual volume in the park restrooms are from July through October.

My interest, then, was in distributing observation time throughout these periods of varying activity—and in different parks and different seasons. In all, during this first year, I observed some 120 sexual acts in nineteen different men's rooms in five parks of the one city. Not including the time spent outdoors, in driving, or engaged in informal interviews with participants, I spent close to sixty hours in the tearooms in this first stage of the observations. This time was broken into segments of an hour or less (averaging about twenty minutes), between which periods I drove to other tearooms or parks, sat in my automobile, talked with the few men I could involve in conversations outdoors, or simply stood outside.

This excerpt from one of the tapes I made in October, 1966, may communicate to the reader an idea of my observational techniques at that stage of the research:

> I was in this facility about five minutes, during that time the Negro in his thirties, neatly dressed, who had the [Ford], stood constantly at the urinal and masturbated, making no attempt to hide what he was doing. There was a young Negro in there at the same time—very neat, very

well dressed, in his late teens I would gather–with glasses, student type. He stood at the window throughout the time and said nothing. I stood near him at the window, and he made no approach. I went to the other window, and he made no move. As I was leaving, the man from the white Chevrolet left his car and went in. . . . Now, as I describe the two Negroes, I know the one man was alone in his car. The younger man obviously came on foot to this facility. All right, on to some other places. It is now 4:47, traffic is very heavy, much distraction. . . . I'm now approaching the facility again and there's not much point going there, because there are no cars out front–so I'll move on to Hillside.

My purpose in this "time and place sampling" was to avoid the research errors outlined by Webb and others–particularly the danger "that the timing of the data collection may be such that a selective population periodically appears before the observer, while another population, equally periodically, engages in the same behavior, but comes along only when the observer is absent. Similarly, the individual's behavior may shift as the hours or days of the week change." [24]

## Sampling Covert Deviants

Hooker has noted that homosexuals who lead secret lives are usually available for study "only when caught by law enforcement agents, or when seeking psychiatric help."[25] To my knowledge, no one has yet attempted to acquire a *representative* sample of *covert* deviants for any sort of research. Polsky's efforts to secure a representative sample of "beats," in order to effect a survey of drug use among them, is a possible exception to this generalization, although I question that Village beats could be called *covert* deviants.

Following Rainwater's suggestion, I gathered a sample of the tearoom participants by tracing the license plates of the autos they drive to the parks. I have already indicated ways in which automobiles provide observable traces of their drivers' movements (see Chapter 1). Operation of one's car is a form of self-presentation that tells the observant sociologist a great deal about the operator.

24. Webb and others, *op. cit.*, p. 136.
25. Hooker, *op. cit.*, p. 169.

For several months, I had noted fluctuations in the number of automobiles that remained more than fifteen minutes in front of the sampled tearooms. My observations had indicated that, with the sole exception of police cars, autos that parked in front of these public restrooms (which, as has been mentioned, are usually isolated from other park facilities) for a quarter of an hour or more invariably belonged to participants in the homosexual encounters. The same is true for cars that appeared in front of two or more such facilities in the course of an hour.

These variations in frequency were recorded for half-hour periods from 11:00 A.M. to 7:00 P.M., each day of the week, for each of four parks observed during the summer months. Averages of these volumes were calculated for each thirty-minute time period, the weekdays and weekends being separated for control purposes. Although the original calculations were made separately for each park, no major differences were observed in the over-all traffic pattern thus recorded. These data were then collapsed into the graphs that appear as Figures 2.1 and 2.2.

In September of 1966, then, I set about to gather a sample in as systematic a manner as possible under the circumstances. With the help of the tape recorder, I took the license numbers of as many cars during each half-hour period as equalled approximately 10 per cent of the average volume of "likely" autos at that time on that day of the week. At least for the largest park (which represents roughly half of the observed homosexual activity of this sort in the city), the results were fairly representative on a time basis. Random selection cannot be claimed for this sample: because of the pressures of time and possible detection, I was able to record only a portion of the license plates of participating men I saw at any one time, the choice of which to record being determined by the volume and flow of traffic and the position in which the autos were parked.

I also noted, whenever possible, a brief description of both the car and its driver. By means of frequent sorties into the tearooms for observation, each recorded license number was verified as belonging to a man actually observed in homosexual activity inside the facilities. Sometimes the numbers were taped prior to my entrance, in anticipation of what I would find inside. In most cases, however, I observed the activity, left the tearoom, waited in my car

*Figure 2.1*
*Illustrating Volume of Autos Observed at Restrooms and Sampling Method (Averaged from Data Gathered on Weekdays)*

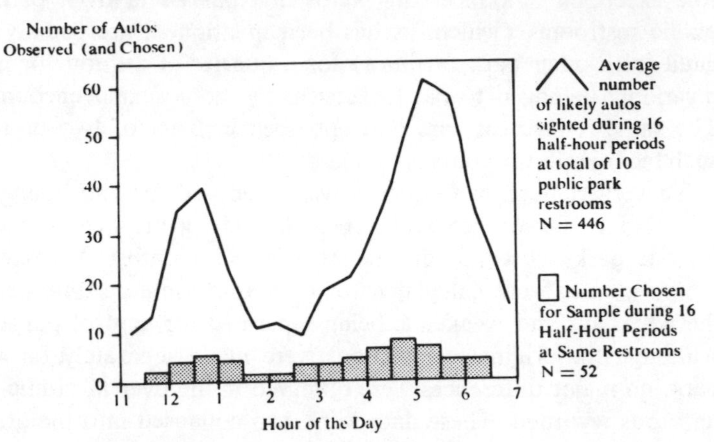


*Figure 2.2*
*Illustrating Volume of Autos Observed at Restrooms and Sampling Method (Averaged from Data Gathered on Weekends)*

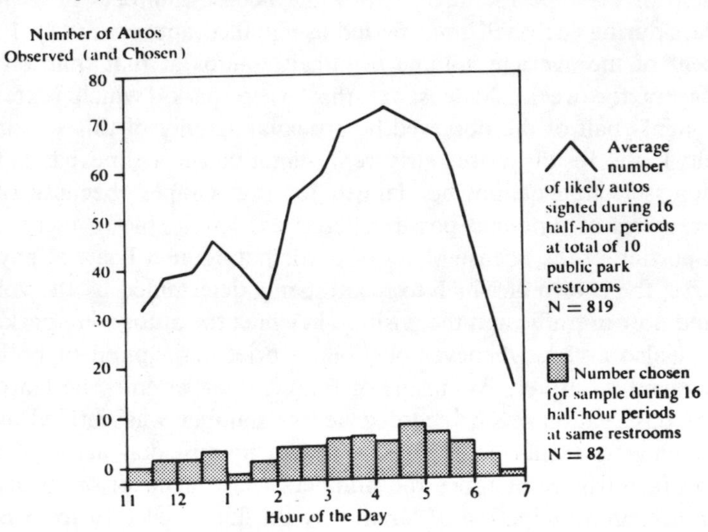

for the participants to enter their autos—then recorded the plate numbers and brief descriptions. For each of these men but one I added to the data the role he took in the sexual encounter.

The original sample thus gained was of 134 license numbers, carefully linked to persons involved in the homosexual encounters, gathered from the environs of ten public restrooms in four different parks of a metropolitan area of two million people. With attrition and additions that will be described later, one hundred participants in the tearoom game were included in the final sample.

## Systematic Observation

Before leaving the account of my observation strategies to consider the archival measures employed during the first half of my research, I want to describe the techniques employed in "tightening up" my data. Following the preliminary observations, I developed a "Systematic Observation Sheet" on which to record my observations. This form—used by myself in describing fifty encounters and by a cooperating participant in the recording of thirty others—helped to assure consistent and thorough recording of the observed encounters.

Figure 2.3 is a reproduction of an actual Systematic Observation Sheet, as filled out by me immediately upon return to my office one summer afternoon. Only the date, place, and description of an auto have been blanked out in order to avoid incrimination. This was the first, and briefest, of a series of three successive encounters observed in that popular restroom in the course of thirty-five minutes. After they were concluded, I drove to another part of the park and, with the use of a clipboard, filled in the diagrams and made written notes. As a left-hander, I find writing difficult; so I waited until I could use a typewriter to add the running commentary at the bottom.

As may be seen, this report sheet includes places for recording the time and place involved; a description of the participants (their age, attire, auto, and role in the encounter); a description of weather and other environmental conditions; a diagram on which movements of the participants could be plotted, along with location of the places of contract and fellatio; as well as a complete description of the progress of the encounters and reactions of the observer.

Such care was taken for several reasons. My first concern has been for objective validity—to avoid distortion of the data either by my presence or my presuppositions. I have also desired to make future replications and comparative studies possible, by being as systematic as possible in recording and gathering data.

Finally, I wanted to make the best of a rather unique opportunity for participant observation. The tearooms are challenging, not only because they present unusual problems for the researcher but because they provide an extraordinary opportunity for detailed observation. Due to the lack of verbal communication and the consistency of the physical settings, a type of laboratory is provided by these facilities—one in which human behavior may be observed with the control of a number of variables.

The analysis of the encounters that follows in Chapters 3 and 4 is based, primarily, on the fifty systematic observations I made between March and August, 1967. The numerous informal observations I made previously—and the thirty systematic observations made by a cooperating respondent—have served mainly as checks against this systematic portion of my research. Although I can think of no way in which my earlier observations run counter to these detailed ones, their greatest value was as preparation for this stage of the participant observation. Those of the respondent were also in general agreement with mine. Perhaps because he was frequently a sexual participant in the encounters he observed, however, he tended to concentrate more on the details of the sexual acts and less on the interaction leading to them. It is also interesting to note that his estimate of the age of participants was lower than mine. It is not possible to say whether this discrepancy resulted from a tendency on his part to view others as potential sexual partners or from a parallel difference in our own ages. Anyway, it is doubtful that the populations we observed differed greatly.

*Figure 2.3*

SYSTEMATIC OBSERVATION SHEET — Date: — Day: Sat

O = Observor (1) (2) — General Conditions: Weather & temp. 80° - partly cloudy - beautiful

X = Principal Aggressor — # & type of people in parks: moderate #, few picnickers, most engaged in sports

Y = Principal Passive Partisipant — est. volume of gay activity: heavy 8 in 35 minutes

A - N = Other Participants — Place:

Z = Law Enforcement Personnel

Time Began: 3:20 (Encounter A)

Time Ended: 3:30

Participants: [include symbol, est. age, attire, other distinguishing characteristics, type of auto driven]

X: 40 - black hair, pants & shoes - pink sport shirt - tanned

Y: 45 - balding — tall, dark pants, blue & tan checked sport shirt

Others: A - 20 - Negro, tan slacks — white sport shirt

(F) = Fellatio performed

(C) = Contract made

Description of Action: [note: when possible, indicate: delays in autos, etc., before entering tearoom...manner of approaches...types of sexual roles taken... nature of interruptions and reaction to them...ANYTHING WHICH MAY BE SPOKEN... any masturbation going on...actions of lookout(s)...REACTION TO TEENAGERS AND ANY PARTICIPATION BY THEM...reactions to observor...length of time of sexual acts...spitting, washing of hands, wiping, etc.]

X was standing at right window & A seated on stool when O entered. O went to first urinal. X moved into third urinal, unzipped pants but did not urinate. He began to look at me. I zipped pants and moved in front of left window. X went back to opposite window. I saw Y get out of car and approach tearoom. He went to third urinal as soon as entered. In about 2 minutes, X moved into center urinal and began to cruise Y. By then, Y had an erection - X reached over and began to masturbate him with right hand, himself with left. I moved over to the far window. A looked at me. I smiled and nodded. X and Y walked together to stal # 1. X lowered pants and sat down. Y, standing in front with pants still unzipped and erection showing, continued to masturbate for another minute, then he inserted penis in X's mouth. He reached clima-x in about 3 minutes, having clasped hands behind X"s neck. He then went to basin, washed hands & left.

## The Talk Outside

A sociologist without verbal communication is like a doctor without a stethoscope. The silence of these sexual encounters confounded such research problems as legitimation of the observer and identification of roles. As indicated above, however, it has certain advantages in limiting the number of variables that must be observed, recorded, and evaluated. When action alone is being observed and analyzed, the patterns of behavior themselves acquire meaning independent of verbalization. "The method of participant observation," Bruyn states, "is a research procedure which can provide the basis for establishing adequacy at the level of meaning." [26] What verbal research is possible through outside interviews then becomes an independent means of verifying the observations.

Despite the almost inviolate silence within the restroom setting, tearoom participants are neither mute nor particularly taciturn. Away from the scenes where their sexual deviance is exposed—outside what I shall later discuss as the "interaction membrane"—conversation is again possible. Once my car and face had become familiar, I was able to enter into verbal relationships with twelve of the participants, whom I refer to as the "intensive dozen." Eight of these men are included in the final sample. Four others, although engaged in dialogue near the tearooms where I observed them, were not included in the sample. Of the eight in the sample, five (including the two "walkers," who had walked rather than driven to the tearooms) were contacted after leaving the scene of an encounter, and three became cooperating respondents as a result of relationships that developed from the formal interviews.

After the initial contacts with this intensive dozen, I told them of my research, disclosing my real purpose for being in the tearooms. With the help of some meals together and a number of drinks, all agreed to cooperate in subsequent interviewing sessions. A few of these interviews were taped (only two men were sufficiently unafraid to allow their voices to be recorded on tape—and I don't blame the others) but most were later reconstructed from notes.

26. Bruyn, *op. cit.*, p. 179.

Apart from the systematic observations themselves, these conversations constitute the richest source of data in the study.

Some may ask why, if nine of these cooperating respondents were obtained without the formal interviews, I bothered with the seemingly endless task of acquiring a sample and administering questionnaires—particularly when interviews with the intensive dozen provided such depth to the data. The answer is simple: these men are not representative of the tearoom population. I could engage them in conversation only because they are more overt, less defensive, and better educated than the average participant.

This suggests a problem for all research that relies on willing respondents. Their very willingness to cooperate sets them apart from those they are meant to represent. *Tally's Corner* and *Street Corner Society* stand high among the classics of social science—and rightly so—but I wonder sometimes how well Tally and Doc represent the apathetic, alienated, uninvolved men of the street corners. When authors such as Liebow and Whyte strive to compensate for this by extending their research throughout the friendship networks, great ethnography results. But the saddest works in the name of social science are those that barrage the reader with endless individual case studies and small samples from private psychiatric practices, few of which can be representative of the vast numbers of human beings who are supposed to be "understood" in terms of these deviant deviants.

## Archival Evidence

The unobtrusive measures of participant observation and physical traces, combined with a limited use of open-ended interviews for purposes of correction and validation, enabled me to describe the previously unexplored area of tearoom encounters. The preliminary description of the participant population, however, began only after the establishment of a verified sample. For this stage of the study, I turned to archival measures, "the running record."[27]

Identification of the sample was made by using the automobile

27. Webb and others, *op. cit.*, pp. 53–87.

license registers of the states in which my respondents lived. Fortunately, friendly policemen gave me access to the license registers, without asking to see the numbers or becoming too inquisitive about the type of "market research" in which I was engaged. These registers provided the names and addresses of those in the sample, as well as the brand name and year of the automobiles thus registered. The make of the car, as recorded in the registers, was checked against my transcribed description of each car. In the two cases where these descriptions were contradictory, the numbers were rejected from the sample. Names and addresses were then checked in the directories of the metropolitan area, from which volumes I also acquired marital and occupational data for most of the sample.

Geographic mobility and data gaps plague the researcher who attempts to use the city directory as a source of information. Fortunately, however, new directories had been issued just prior to my need for them. Somewhat to my surprise, I had another advantage due to residential stability on the part of the population under study. Only 17 per cent of the men in the sample were not listed in these directories. Occupational data were not given for 37 per cent of the men (including those not in the directories).

In those few cases where addresses in license registers did not correspond with those in the city and county directories, I took advantage of still another archival source: the telephone company's index of numbers by street addresses, which had been published more recently than either of the other archival sources. By the time my sample had been verified and identified, none of the archival measures employed was over a year old, and the most recent had been published only the week before completion of this stage of the research.[28]

For fear of eliminating variables that might profitably be studied at a later date, I did not scrub from my sample those for whom the archives provided no marital or occupational data. These men, I

28. Because identification of the city in which this research was conducted might result in pressure being brought to bear on law enforcement agencies or respondents, it has been necessary for me to omit references to the archival volumes used. The name of the city, county, or state appears in the title of each of these sources.

felt, might represent either a transient or secretive portion of tearoom participants, the exclusion of which would have distorted the population.

Other biases were not avoidable; however, where possible, I have attempted to compensate for them. In the first place, I did not record the license numbers of automobiles from states not represented in the metropolitan area. My estimate is that about 5 per cent of the cars driven by participants in these homosexual encounters bore such out-of-state plates. The majority of these autos also had stickers that identified the owners as armed forces personnel from nearby military installations. This fact is important for indicating (*a*) that a very small percentage of the participants are tourists or salesmen who travel from a great distance, and (*b*) that the military should have a larger representation in my sample than the 2 per cent indicated by the available occupational data. If the archives and local license plates are biased against any one segment of the population, it is members of the armed forces. When compensation for this bias has been made, the indications (including those gained from interviews) are that some 10 per cent of tearoom participants will be armed forces personnel. This factor, however, should vary with the proximity of parks to large military installations. There are no such bases within a twenty-mile radius of the parks in this study.

Other license numbers were excluded from the sample because they precluded research. Because these may have produced a bias, they will be mentioned. First, eighteen were eliminated because they were not listed in the license registers. (The police attribute such gaps in their data to clerical error.) Seven men resided outside the metropolitan area under study. Another five were driving leased or company cars. For two, the automobile description in the registers did not fit my description. Finally, the license registers listed two nonexistent addresses. Other adjustments were made before I reached the final sample of 100. Two men were dropped from the sample for identity reasons. To replace them, I added two young men who had walked to the tearooms and were included in my intensive dozen. I had estimated that a small percentage of the participants walked to their favorite tearooms and thought it important to have representation from the pedestrian population.

If one may disregard for a moment the strong possibility that most of these exclusions may have resulted from errors on the part of clerks, printers, or myself, one other factor may be hidden behind these omissions. Is it not possible that some of these unidentifiable plates may have been switched, counterfeited, or acquired by other illegitimate means? Some men might have leased cars or given false addresses in order to preserve their anonymity. I know of no unobtrusive way to test the degree of deliberate deception. If deception were the motive in these instances, it was successful.

## A View from the Streets

Like archives, park restrooms, and automobiles, the streets of our cities are subject to public regulation and scrutiny. They are thus good places for nonreactive research (nonreactive in that it requires no response from the research subjects). Having gained addresses for every person in my sample, I spent a Christmas vacation on the streets and highways. By recording a description of every residence and neighborhood represented in the sample, I was able to gain further data on my research subjects.

The first purpose of this survey of homes was to acquire descriptions of the house types and dwelling areas that, when combined with occupational data gleaned from the archives, would enable me to use Warner's Index of Status Characteristics (I. S. C.) for a socioeconomic profile of my population.[29] Generally speaking, this attempt was not successful: job classifications were too vague and large city housing units too difficult to rank by Warner's criteria.

As physical evidence, however, homes provide a source of data about a population that outweighs any failure they may have as a status index. Swing sets and bicycles in the yards indicate that a family is not childless. A shrine to Saint Mary suggests that the resident is Roman Catholic in religious identification. Christmas decorations bespeak at least a nominal Christian preference. A boat

29. See W. Lloyd Warner and others, *Social Class in America* (Chicago: Science Research Associates, 1949).

or trailer in the driveway suggests love of the outdoor life. "For Rent" signs may indicate the size of an average apartment and, in some cases, the price. The most important sign, however, was the relative "neatness" of the house and grounds. Some implications of this information are pointed out in Chapter 7.

## Obtrusive Measures

Realizing that the majority of my participant sample were married —and nearly all of them quite secretive about their deviant activity —I was faced with the problem of how to interview more than the nine willing respondents. Formal interviews of the sample were part of the original research design. The little I knew about these covert deviants made me want to know a great deal more. Here was a unique population just waiting to be studied—but I had no way to approach them. Clearly, I could not knock on the door of a suburban residence and say, "Excuse me, I saw you engaging in a homosexual act in a tearoom last year, and I wonder if I might ask you a few questions." Having already been jailed, locked in a restroom, and attacked by a group of ruffians, I had no desire to conclude my research with a series of beatings.

Perhaps I might have had some success by contacting these men at their work, granted that I could obtain their business addresses. This strategy would have precluded the possibility of seeing their homes and meeting their wives, however, and I believed these confrontations to be important.

About this time, fortunately, I was asked to develop a questionnaire for a social health survey of men in the community, which was being conducted by a research center with which I had been a research associate. Based on such interview schedules already in use in Michigan and New York, the product would provide nearly all the information I would want on the men in my sample: family background, socioeconomic factors, personal health and social histories, religious and employment data, a few questions on social and political attitudes, a survey of friendship networks, and information on marital relationships and sex.

With the permission of the director of the research project, I added my deviant sample to the over-all sample of the survey, making certain that only one trusted, mature graduate student and I made all the interviews of my respondents. Thus legitimized, we set out to interview. Using a table of random numbers, I randomized my sample, so that its representativeness would not be lost in the event that we should be unable to complete all 100 interviews.

More will be written later of the measures taken to safeguard respondents; the important thing to note here is that none of the respondents was threatened by the interviews. My master list was kept in a safe-deposit box. Each interview card, kept under lock and key, was destroyed with completion of the schedule. No names or other identifying tags were allowed to appear on the questionnaires. Although I recognized each of the men interviewed from observation of them in the tearooms, there was no indication that they remembered me. I was careful to change my appearance, dress, and automobile from the days when I had passed as deviant. I also allowed at least a year's time to lapse between the original sampling procedure and the interviews.

This strategy was most important—both from the standpoint of research validity and ethics—because it enabled me to approach my respondents as normal people, answering normal questions, as part of a normal survey. They *are* part of a larger sample. Their being interviewed is not stigmatizing, because they comprise but a small portion of a much larger sample of the population in their area. They were not put on the spot about their deviance, because they were not interviewed as deviants.

The attrition rate for these interviews was high, but not discouragingly so. Attempts were made at securing seventy-five interviews, fifty of which were completed. Thirty-five per cent were lost by attrition, including 13 per cent who refused to cooperate in the interviews. In addition to the fifty completed schedules, three fathers of participants consented to interviews on the social health survey, as did two fathers of the control sample.

Because of the preinterview data obtained by the archival and observational research previously described, it was possible to learn a great deal even from the losses. As should be expected, the residue of men with whom interviews were completed are slightly overrepresentative of the middle and upper classes; they are suburbanites, more highly educated men. Those who were lost represent a more transient group (the most common reason for loss was that the subject had moved and left no forwarding address), employed in manual jobs. From preinterview information it was learned that the largest single occupational class in the sample was the truck drivers. Only two members of this class remained among those interviewed.

The refusals also indicated some biases. These men, when pinpointed on a map, clustered around the Italian and working class German areas of the city. Of the ten lost in this manner, three had Italian names and five bore names of distinctly Germanic origin.

Once these interviews were completed, preparations could be made for the final step of the research design. From names appearing in the randomly selected sample of the over-all social health survey, fifty men were selected, matched with the completed questionnaires on the following four characteristics: I. S. C. occupational category, race, area of the metropolitan region in which the party resided, and marital status. The loss here was not from refusals or lost addresses but from those who, when interviewed, failed to correspond with the expected characteristics for matching. Our precedure, in those cases, was simply to move on to another name in the larger sample.

These last fifty interviews, then, enabled me to compare characteristics of two samples—one deviant, one control—matched on the basis of certain socioeconomic characteristics, race, and marital status. Although I made a large proportion of these interviews, and nearly all of the deviant interviews, I found it necessary to hire and train two graduate students to assist with interviewing the control sample. A meeting was held with the assistant interviewers immediately following the completion of each schedule—and all coding of the questionnaires was done by us in conference.

There were a number of open-ended questions in the interview schedules, but the majority included a wide range of precoded answers, for the sake of ease in interviewing and economy in analysis. In addition, the interviewers were trained to make copious marginal notes and required to submit a postinterview questionnaire with each schedule. The median time required for administering the interview schedules did not differ greatly between the two samples:

one hour for the deviants, fifty-five minutes for the "straights." Even the days of the week when respondents were interviewed showed little variation between the two samples: Sunday, Tuesday, and Saturday, in that order, being the more popular days.

## Summary

From a methodological standpoint, the value of this research is that it has employed a variety of methods, each testing a different outcropping of the research population and their sexual encounters. It has united the systematic use of participant observation strategies with other nonreactive measures such as physical traces and archives. The exigencies of research in a socially sensitive area demanded such approaches; and the application of unobtrusive measures yielded data that call, in turn, for reactive methods.

Research strategies do not develop *ex nihilo*. In part, they are the outgrowth of the researcher's basic assumptions. Special conditions of the research problem itself also exercise a determining influence upon the methods used. This chapter has been an attempt to indicate how my ethnographic assumptions, coupled with the difficulties inhering in the study of covert deviants and their behavior, have given rise to a set of strategies.

With the help of "oddball" measures, the outlines of the portrait of participants in the homosexual encounters of the tearooms appeared. Reactive strategies were needed to fill in the distinguishing features. They are human, socially patterned features; and it is doubtful that any one method could have given them the expressive description they deserve.

# *Chapter 3.* Rules and Roles

Well, let's start off with one fellow in there—just all by his lonesome—he's the only one in there, and he is standing at the window, watching. He sees somebody at the water fountain first. He sees them coming up; he sees what they look like; he's got a few seconds. He scoots around to the urinal; and he usually stands at one of the two ends—not in the middle, one of the two ends—and this is the strange thing about it.[1]

WHAT IS described here is the beginning of a human encounter both problematic and consequential: problematic because it involves decision making, the choice of strategies; consequential, not only because it may conclude with a sexual payoff but because this payoff has the capacity "to flow beyond the bounds of the occasion in which it is delivered and to influence objectively the later life of the bettor." [2] The players are about to engage in a game of chance,

1. From a taped interview with a cooperating respondent.

2. Throughout this chapter, Erving Goffman's writings on face-to-face interaction have provided me with vocabulary and an approach to conceptualization. Because in many ways I take leave from his systematic presentations, he is not to be held responsible for the conclusions I have reached. For the context of this quotation, see his *Interaction Ritual* (Chicago: Aldine, 1967), pp. 159–160.

risk-taking action of the type Goffman would call "fateful activity."[3]

Like other games of chance, deviant sexual encounters focus on an eventual reward. The tactics are determined by the players' calculations of how best to maximize profit, the primary reward being sexual pleasures under preferred circumstances and the chief cost being possible exposure to a hostile community. The consequentiality of such action is of two sorts: the immediate, sought-after payoff and the long-range contingencies, which may or may not be desired.

It is not merely the counterposition of possible success or failure in the immediate "settlement" of play that makes sex games exciting but the potential for future gain or loss as well. The data of this study indicate that some tearoom participants dream of finding a relatively permanent friend or sexual partner among their restroom contacts. All of them fear such possible adjuncts as arrest, abuse, or loss of reputation:

*Respondent:*

I don't know why I go to the tearooms—they're so fucking dangerous! But I've been pretty lucky so far.

*Interviewer:*

No trouble?

*Respondent:*

No trouble—yet; but I've had some pretty close scrapes. Lots of excitement!

Other risk-taking actions of a sexual nature involve like contingencies. Flirtation, adultery, wife-swapping, whoring, or "tricking" of any sort may produce long-range consequences, most of which are on the negative end of any scale of expectations. The following is a press report of the realization of one such negative contingency:

The heavens forbid and the firmament displayed its romantic unveiling as Mrs. [Rider] was aroused from her slumber at 4 A.M. She did hear a noise in the basement. She investigated and surely enough she did see with her own eyes her husband and a young man lying absolutely nude on the basement floor.[4]

3. *Ibid.*, p. 164.

4. From a front-page banner news story in the *St. Louis Evening Whirl*, Vol. 29, No. 74 (January 9, 1968).

If the prospective player can cope with these contingencies (by using such devices as "hope," a belief in "providence" or "luck," or confidence in his own skills), he will experience excitement in the action. Such coping mechanisms both heighten the rewards of the game of chance and lower its costs, thus increasing profit. Goffman quotes Michael Balint in this connection: "This mixture of fear, pleasure, and confident hope in face of external danger is what constitutes the fundamental element of all thrills." [5]

In this way, tearoom action is not unlike a great many other gaming encounters.[6] The tactics employed are all aimed at (1) maximizing rewards and (2) minimizing risks (and other costs such as fatigue). The *rules* of the game are generally directed to the second of these goals ("Thou shalt not . . ."); *strategies* look toward the first, while keeping an eye on the second. I have gained the impression that rules are more universal than strategies. Whereas the latter will vary widely, rules do not change from one encounter to another within the same sport.

The homosexual games of cruising for the one-night-stand exhibit the universal and protective nature of rules, which are standard for all situations:

1. Avoid the exchange of biographical data.
2. Watch out for chicken [teen-agers]–they're dangerous game.
3. Never force your intentions on anyone.
4. Don't knock [criticize] a trick [sex partner]–he may be somebody's mother [homosexual mentor].
5. Never back down on trade agreements. ["Trade" are "tricks" who do not, as yet, consider themselves homosexual. This group includes most of the male prostitutes, "hustlers." Trade agreements, then, include paying the amount promised, if a financial transaction is involved, and no kissing above the belt, because most "trade" think kissing is "queer."] The only change in basic rules for the tearoom scene involves a tightening of rule (1) to the point of silence, a modification resulting, in part, from the more public nature and higher turnover of the tearoom market. Under these conditions, greater caution in preserving anonymity must be exercised.

5. Goffman, *Interaction Ritual*, pp. 196–197.
6. Erving Goffman, *Encounters* (Indianapolis: Bobbs-Merrill, 1961), p. 68.

Even more important, however, is the function of silence in keeping these encounters impersonal.

Unlike rules, strategies vary considerably from car to bar to bathhouse, coffeehouse, or tearoom. Bar tactics involve more skill in conversation and much less use of body movements than do restroom tactics. Although display of physiques and bulges suggestive of sexual equipment may have strategic use in all settings, only in the baths and tearooms does open display of sexual organs have tactical importance. For example, a simplified expression of the primary tearoom strategy is frequently inscribed on the walls: "Show hard–get sucked." To follow this strategy in a gay bar would result in instant expulsion.

Tearoom strategies, as ritual means of achieving collective action with minimum revelation, will be discussed in the next chapter. The rules above provide a protective code, a set of norms common to all ephemeral encounters of a homosexual nature, which no ritual performance may violate.

## Role Flexibility

Another aspect of the normative structure of tearoom games is found in the roles that participants play. I refer to parts taken not only by participants in the sexual acts as such but by all who enter public facilities during an encounter. A man who knows nothing of the homosexual game in progress may enter a restroom, spend a minute urinating, and leave, unwittingly playing an important role in a tearoom encounter.

For those who are aware of and willing to play the game, however, the exigencies of these encounters demand a great deal of role flexibility. The consequences of being caught performing the central, sexual roles are so great that those roles are made manifest only in the final moments of the game. Furthermore, because tearoom encounters occur under a great deal of time pressure, participants must be able to step in and out of the parts at will. The demands of speed and secrecy, then, result in a highly standardized and flexible set of roles, such as are described in the catalogue below.

### A Catalogue of Participant Roles in Tearoom Encounters

*Players:*

*Insertee.* The fellator, the "cock-sucker"; man into whose orifice the penis of another is inserted.

*Insertor.* One who is being "blown" or "sucked" (in anal intercourse, the "fucker"); man who inserts his penis into the orifice of another.

*Lookouts (Watchqueens):*

*Waiters.* Men who are waiting for (1) a particular person, (2) a particular type of "trick," or (3) for a chance to get in on the action.

*Masturbaters.* Those who either (1) are present just to masturbate, or (2) engage in masturbation while being *Waiters.*

*Voyeurs.* Those who "get their kicks" out of watching others engage in sex; these men are sometimes also *Masturbaters.*

*Straights:*

Persons who do not participate in the action. This role is usually short lived (three minutes or less) or may "melt" over time into one of the other roles. It is hypothesized that these men are either too heterosexually oriented or too inhibited to take part in the game. Unless "wise," these men may suffer embarrassment and may react negatively to the scene.

*Teenagers (Chicken):*

*Straights.* See above.

*Enlisters.* Youths who want to get in on the action (and thus are *Waiters* but poor *Lookouts*); they watch to learn strategies but are generally too feared to be allowed in on the action.

*Toughs.* Youths who harass other tearoom participants, sometimes by physical attacks such as "rolling."

*Hustlers.* *Enlisters* who demand payment for serving as *Insertors.* If payment is refused, they tend to become *Toughs.*

*Agents of Social Control:*

Social control agents of three general types: (1) vice squad members, (2) park policemen, or (3) other park employees.

To minimize revelation, the roles of persons involved in these games of chance become increasingly manifest as the encounter approaches what Goffman calls its settlement phase. "Finally there is the *settlement phase,* beginning when the outcome has been disclosed and lasting until losses have been paid up and gains collected." [7] Only after the game has ended in payoff or disaster can others label most of the participants. The "walk-on" role of a

7. Goffman, *Interaction Ritual,* p. 154.

straight is the general exception, this role being recognizable immediately upon exit of the actor.

The players (insertees and insertors) are identifiable only in the sex act; waiters—and even straights—may be transformed into players; chicken may turn out to be hustlers, toughs, straights, or participants; social control agents (nearly always in plain clothes) are generally identifiable only when disaster strikes. Perhaps it is this ambiguity in early role identification that enables pool hustlers, narcotics agents, and other con men to operate in their games. Notice, in Polsky's account, how the "fish" can be defined only during the settlement phase of a series of pool games:

As we have noted, the ideal kind of sucker is the "fish" who doesn't realize he can never win and makes himself available on other days for return matches, much like the sort of mark whom con men call an "addict." In order to reinforce any propensity his victim might have for being or becoming a fish, the hustler tries to win the last game of a match by only a small margin even though he *knows* it is the last game, i.e., knows that after he beats the sucker the latter will quit because he is cleaned out or unwilling to risk the small amount he may have left. On very rare occasions, to the hustler's surprise and delight, when the sucker is thus cleaned out he may not end the match but instead become a sort of instant fish (my term, not used by hustlers): he may have the hustler wait while he (the sucker) runs out to get more cash and comes back with same.[8]

This is what I mean when I say that a role unfolds, becoming evident only as the action approaches showdown. Are not drama, suspense stories—perhaps all of fictional literature—constructed on this foundation? In this type of "living theater," even the actor may not know his role until the action is finished. In the tearooms, a waiter may have begun an encounter with the intention of being an insertor, only to end up as a masturbater. Or, as in the following transcript, the man who intends to be an insertee may agree to take the insertor role:

I've run into this a couple of times: "Let me do you. I don't want to be done." Well, maybe I'll say yes, and maybe I won't—it depends—because, if I've been done myself, I'm finished for the afternoon. I might

8. Ned Polsky, *Hustlers, Beats, and Others* (Chicago: Aldine, 1967), pp. 63–64.

as well pack up and go home. I'm no good for anything . . . after that. Because I simply can't do it again, that's all—unless I have two or three hours separating them. So, what determines the role? Perhaps it's personal preference. I don't know.

It has been my practice throughout the analysis of the research data to discuss developing concepts and theories with cooperating respondents. (I consider this sort of inside evaluation one of the more valuable means of validation.) After I had gone over the preceding pages of this chapter with the member of the intensive dozen quoted above, he paused for a moment, then said: "Yes, I think that's right—that explains lots of things. You might even say that this is how you know the game is really over—once the roles are defined."

If we may view role performance as shaped by the end of the action and identifiable only in terms of the payoff, it may help us to understand the difficulties sex researchers have with applying traditional, psychologically oriented analyses of gender identity to actual patterns of homosexual performance:

For the majority of the individuals in my particular sample there is no apparent correspondence between a conscious sense of gender identity and a preferred or predominant role in sexual activity. Except for a small minority the sexual pattern cannot be categorized in terms of a predominant role, and the consciousness of masculinity or femininity appears to bear no clear relation to particular sexual patterns.[9]

Until Dr. Hooker called my attention to it, this research had been hindered by preconceptions that did not fit the observations. I had fallen victim to the danger against which she warns, having allowed the common ascription of sex status to influence description of the major roles in the encounters. As may be seen in the reproduction of a Systematic Observation Sheet in the previous chapter, I referred to the principal players as the Aggressor and the Passive Participant. In a later paper, it was my own ambivalence (more than that of the players themselves) that showed in the use of a "feminine-aggressive/masculine-passive" dichotomy. In only a

9. Evelyn Hooker, "An Empirical Study of Some Relations Between Sexual Patterns and Gender Identity in Male Homosexuals," in John Money, ed., *Sex Research: New Developments* (New York: Holt, Rinehart & Winston, 1965), p. 50.

strictly physical sense is there anything more masculine about the man who inserts his penis in the mouth or anal cavity of another; and the other, into whose orifice the organ is inserted, is not necessarily the more feminine.

Moreover, my original impressions of the encounters–reinforced, no doubt, by my own ideas of "homosexual roles"–led me to think of the "sucker" as the aggressor and the man "being blown" as the passive participant. (Note that passive tense is used for the insertor in the argot of straight society.) Again, this is not supported by the data. Of fifty-three acts of fellatio that I observed systematically, later analysis indicated that the insertee was the "aggressor" in twenty, the insertor was the "aggressor" in twenty-seven, the two seemed equally aggressive in two cases, and the data were insufficient for determination in four of the acts. The "aggressor" was defined as the player who first made an irrevocable commitment, an unmistakable overture. As I point out in the next chapter, there are aggressive or "active" systems of strategy, and there are relatively passive ones, but not aggressive or passive players.

By adopting the insertee/insertor terminology that Hooker had borrowed from another study,[10] I was able to liberate my analysis for a more objective and adaptable approach to the action. When bound to the ascribed masculine/feminine, aggressive/passive labels, I had found it difficult to conceptualize the switching of roles that occurs in some of the encounters. The point is that insertee and insertor are not sex roles as such, but parts into which actors step as they approach the payoff of a sexual encounter.

The following account, taken verbatim from one of my Systematic Observation Sheets, illustrates well the flexible nature of the tearoom roles (O is the observer; A, B, C, D, X, and Y are the other participants; bracketed comments are added now).

X followed O from car and entered with him. Urinals and stalls (except for center urinal) were already taken, so O stood by door looking around. B and C were exchanging glances at urinals. D was standing in stall # 1 and apparently masturbating, facing back wall. . . . [D, then, is apparently a masturbater. All other roles remain unassigned.]

10. Irving Bieber and others, *Homosexuality* (New York: Vintage, 1962), pp. 238–239.

A was standing at entrance to stall #2, facing out into the room. X moved from near wash basin to in front of window and motioned to O to come over and stand by him. O ignored invitation and moved to opposite window and looked out toward street. D zipped up pants and, still showing signs of an erection, went over to stand by door. C left urinal and went to basin, eyeing D. B left the tearoom. For about two minutes, everyone just stood looking at each other. C then went to first stall, lowered pants and sat on stool and began to masturbate quite openly with all parties watching. . . . [Is C also a masturbater?]

In about two minutes, D left. C got up very fast, zipped pants and left in pursuit of D. I watched out the window as each got into his VW and C followed D up the street. . . . [No, C had more important things on his mind than just masturbation. The act on the stool must be interpreted as a signal, especially directed to D.]

A left just as Y entered. . . . [Since everyone waited around too long to be classified as straight, we may now identify A, B, C, and D as waiters.]

Y was very tough looking. . . . [Is he a hustler, a tough, or a straight?]

He went into second stall, unzipped pants and began to masturbate with his back to me. I went to door (which was stuck open with the humidity) and peered out. X moved swiftly and Y turned around to facilitate X's masturbating him. . . . [Now we can identify some players, but which is the insertee and which is the insertor?]

X sucked Y, after unfastening his pants and pulling them down so that his stomach, pubic hair, and testicles were exposed, for about five minutes. [This is the payoff. X is the insertee–Y the insertor.]

Watching through the crack in the door, I saw a park department truck drive over the curb and up on the grass directly in front of the facility. (Two police cars and a "roving patrol cycle" had stopped.) Y pulled back, pulled his pants up and zipped them. He left the tearoom immediately and I followed. X followed me out. [We might have had police involved; but, since there was no disaster to conclude this encounter, they must remain unidentified.]

It should be possible to see from the foregoing account how the possibilities for role identification narrowed as the gaming encounter approached the payoff stage. In the early minutes of the game, there were six of us who *could* have filled almost any of the possible participant roles. Although it is impossible to read the thoughts and intentions of these men, their actions indicate that some were eventually cast in undesired roles: A, B, C, and D might have preferred to be insertees or insertors but wound up as waiters. (Perhaps C and D were more successful elsewhere—but that would have been a different encounter.)

It should also be noted that departure from the scene of the action has the same effect as the payoff in enabling the observer to identify an individual's role performance. For any participant, extrusion through what Goffman labels the interaction membrane is the equivalent of the settlement phase.[11] In poker a departing player "settles up" whenever he leaves, regardless of whether the game continues after his exit or not. So it is with other gaming encounters. Within the boundaries of the game, one world of rules, roles, strategies, and goals is in operation; outside the membrane, another world is in effect. Arrival through the membrane constitutes a "birth" into a new world of action; departure from this world constitutes a "death" to the world of the encounter and a payoff stage for the participant who passes on.

As Goffman indicates, use of the membrane metaphor is simply a more organic, "psychobiological" way of referring to tension management or boundary maintenance. It is far more suitable than other forms of conceptualization for describing the tearoom scene. In the case of the tearooms—along with most other locales of sexual games (the satyric activity of bush and beach providing the exception)—a physical boundary encloses the action, thus taking care of much of the need for tension management or boundary maintenance. The physical traces discussed in Chapter 1—the tearoom purlieu, broken windowpanes—are the result of a process of selection and adaptation aimed at providing the most suitable physical properties for the interaction membrane.

Next to the physical setting itself, the lookout plays the most important part in maintaining the boundaries of the tearoom encounter. He signals when intrusion is about to occur and serves to legitimate those who enter. (See pp. 27–28 for a full account of the

11. Goffman, *Encounters,* pp. 65–66. For a discussion of the "interaction membrane," see *idem,* p. 32.

lookout's role.) An excerpt from one of my observations illustrates both of these sentry functions:

> I saw A coming up walk and coughed. X and Y broke–Y sat down–X moved back to window. A entered and I recognized him. He went to first stall, lowered pants and sat down. I nodded to X and Y, who resumed fellating position.

## Role Instability

It appears that, during the career of any one participant, the role of insertor tends to be transposed into that of insertee. (Chapter 6 includes a discussion of the "aging crisis" of tearoom players.) Where a role structure is teleological, as in sexual games, the role that produces the payoff may be said to be most stable. The ultimate, base role of tearoom encounters is that of insertee.

The more generalized, nonspecific roles in a gaming encounter—judged to be more stable by the outside world—evidence instability within the encounter. By "instability" of a role, I mean its observed tendency to melt, slip, fuse, or drift into another of the standard roles. This tendency is manifested regardless of who may take up that role in the course of an encounter. The role of the "straight" is transient. In a deviant encounter, this label is not adhesive; it does not stick to a person for an extended period of time.

What I am describing here is a phenomenon that, it seems to me, may be seen in many social situations: the less specific, more moderate roles are generally unstable; interaction tends to polarize actors into black-and-white, clearly defined extremes; neutrality becomes threatening; doubt is defined as heresy; depending on the predominant viewpoint of the group, the liberal is labeled as either "a servant of the Establishment" or "a fellow-traveler of the Communists"; the tendency of any group is to classify all those present into a dichotomy of "those with us" and "those against us." In the long run, participants in a homosexual encounter will drift into roles that are either functional to the game or that constitute a threat and annoyance.

By its very nature, the deviant game tends to exalt roles that are considered perverse in the value system of the dominant culture.

Liebow discusses the same sort of transformation of externally based attributes in his study of street corner Negro men:

> There, on the streetcorner, public fictions support a system of values which, together with the value system of society at large, make for a world of ambivalence, contradiction and paradox, where failures are rationalized into phantom successes and weaknesses magically transformed into strengths.[12]

Attributes valued within the tearooms may receive a negative evaluation outside the membrane of the encounter. I have interviewed whites who want blacks only as servants in their private clubs yet prefer them as sexual partners in their public restrooms.

As we recede from the payoff roles–from those on which the game focuses and which are definable only in the ultimate phase of the action–and move toward roles that may be valued by straight society, the instability of the roles increases. The parts of the straights, waiters, and teen-agers tend to melt into more clearly defined roles. The crucial variable here is one of time exposure. If men remain exposed "too long" to the action, they cease to operate as straights.

Such role drift may be observed during the brief span of a single encounter. When viewed from a different perspective, however, the central tendency of any man to play a particular part in the encounters may also be seen to drift. Within any one encounter, the less stable roles tend to drift toward the extremes of friend and enemy. With repeated exposure, however, the drift is toward the basic roles of the sexual encounter, those of the insertor and insertee. Similarly, where some communication continues to exist, parents tend to be "turned-on" by their pot-smoking offspring. Spectators tend to be drawn into mob action, and kibitzers into card games. Even police may adopt the roles they are assigned to eliminate:

> It is a well-known phenomenon that when officers are left too long on the vice squad–the maximum allowable at any one time being four to five years–they begin to "go over," adopting the behaviorisms and mores of the criminals with whom they are dealing, and shifting their primary allegiance. The same holds true for probation officers working with gangs.[13]

12. Elliot Liebow, *Tally's Corner* (Boston: Little, Brown, 1967), p. 214.
13. Robert Conot, *Rivers of Blood, Years of Darkness* (New York: Bantam, 1967), p. 165.

Ten of the twelve cooperating respondents in my research claim to have had, at one time or another, vice squad members who became favorite customers for their sexual services.

Such role drift, and not active recruitment, is the phenomenon reported in the common subcultural phrase: "Today's trade is tomorrow's competition." One of my respondents provided an account of some observations in this area:

> Last year there was a fellow. I saw him, I guess, at the beginning of the hunting season, which would be really about the middle of May, when it really gets going in full swing. I saw him in there one Saturday —very straight, all the symptoms of being straight as can be. And, about one week later, I saw him in there again. And this went on, until finally—I guess about mid-July—he wasn't straight anymore. . . . He finally decided—I think he got so curious that he had to try it and see what it was like. And I've seen this happen, too. But it is really funny, because he kept coming back and coming back till it got to the point where he was there every day. . . . It got to the point where everybody actually ignored him. He would come in and go to the urinal and not do a damn thing. He'd stand there—and then he would walk away and stand over against that window, the one by the urinal. He'd just stand there for a while, watching what was going on. He'd never make a move; he'd never move out of his tracks. He'd just stand there just as intent as could be, really interested. And eventually, I guess, his curiosity got the better of him.

The gaming careers of tearoom participants might be analyzed by tracing the procession of individuals, over time, through a number of the standard roles. Some begin as enlisters, become waiters with age, and move on to the insertor and insertee roles. Hustlers may step in and out of the role of toughs before moving on as insertors. Still others, having received a verbal education in tearoom strategies from the homosexual subculture, will appropriate the insertee role in their first encounter. From extensive interviewing, I know that these career patterns (along with many others) do occur; furthermore, as will be explained when we consider the participant types, such career patterns will vary with certain social characteristics. What is needed by way of future research is longitudinal data on the in-game careers—data that are not dependent on the memories of respondents.

Without both elasticity and standardization, the role structure of these encounters would not be workable. Operating under pressures to maintain secrecy and to curtail the time involved, those who seek sex in the tearooms must be able to move quickly through mutually understood identities as they select appropriate strategies. Such social organization is essential for collective action, at least when that action is illegitimate.

# *Chapter 4.* Patterns of Collective Action

O.K., here goes—no self-respecting homosexual in his right mind should condone sex in public places, but let's face it, it's fun. . . . The danger adds to the adventure. The hunt, the cruise, the rendezvous, a great little game. Then more likely than not, "instant sex." That's it.[1]

THE NATURE of sexual activity presents two severe problems for those who desire impersonal one-night-stands. In the first place, except for masturbation, sex necessitates collective action; and all collective action requires communication. Mutually understood signals must be conveyed, intentions expressed, and the action sustained by reciprocal encouragement. Under normal circumstances, such communication is ritualized in those patterns of word and movement we call courtship and love-making. Verbal agreements are reached and intentions conveyed. Even when deception is in-

1. Letter in "Open Forum: Sex in Public Places," edited by Larry Carlson in *Vector,* Vol. 3, No. 6 (May, 1967), p. 15. In my opinion, *Vector* is the best of the homophile journals. It is published monthly by the Society for Individual Rights, 83 Sixth Street, San Francisco, California.

volved in such exchanges, as it often is, self-revelation and commitment are likely by-products of courtship rituals. In the search for impersonal, anonymous sex, however, these ordinary patterns of collective action must be avoided.

A second problem arises from the cultural conditioning of Western man. For him, sex is invested with personal meanings: interpersonal relationship, romantic love, and an endless catalogue of sentiments. Sex without "love" meets with such general condemnation that the essential ritual of courtship is almost obscured in rococo accretions that assure those involved that a respectable level of romantic intent has been reached. Normal preludes to sexual action thus encourage the very commitment and exposure that the tearoom participant wishes to avoid. Since ordinary ways reveal and involve, special ritual is needed for the impersonal sex of public restrooms.

Both the appeal and the danger of ephemeral sex are increased because the partners are usually strangers to one another. The propositioning of strangers for either heterosexual or homosexual acts is dangerous and exciting–so much so that it is made possible only by concerted action, which progresses in stages of increasing mutuality. The special ritual of tearooms, then, must be both noncoercive and noncommital.

## Approaching

The steps, phases, or general moves I have observed in tearoom games all involve somatic motion. As silence is one of the rules of these encounters, the strategies of the players require some sort of physical movement: a gesture with the hands, motions of the eyes, manipulation and erection of the penis, a movement of the head, a change in stance, or a transfer from one place to another.

The approach to the place of encounter, although not a step within the game, resembles moves of the latter sort. Although occurring outside the interaction membrane, the approach may affect the action inside. An automobile may circle the area a time or two, finally stopping in front of the facility. In what I estimate to be about a third of the cases, the driver will park a moderate distance away from the facility—sometimes as far as 200 feet to the side or in back, to avoid having his car associated with the tearoom.

Unless hurried (or interested in some particular person entering, or already inside, the facility), the man will usually wait in his auto for five minutes or longer. While waiting, he looks the situation over: Are there police cars near? Does he recognize any of the other autos? Does another person waiting look like a desirable partner? He may read a newspaper and listen to the radio, or even get out and wipe his windshield, invariably looking up when another car approaches. The purpose here is to look as natural as possible in this setting, while taking the opportunity to "cruise" other prospective players as they drive slowly by.

Sometimes he will go into the restroom on the heels of a person he has been watching. Should he find the occupant of another auto interesting, he may decide to enter as a signal for the other man to follow. If no one else approaches or leaves, he may enter to see what is going on inside. Some will wait in their autos for as long as an hour, until they see a desirable prospect approaching or sense that the time is right for entry.

From the viewpoint of those already in the restroom, the action of the man outside may communicate a great deal about his availability for the game. Straights do not wait; they stop, enter, urinate, and leave. A man who remains in his car while a number of others come and go—then starts for the facility as soon as a relatively handsome, young fellow approaches—may be revealing both his preferences and his unwillingness to engage in action with anyone "substandard."

Whatever his behavior outside, any man who approaches an occupied tearoom should know that he is being carefully appraised as he strides up the path. While some are evaluating him from the windows, others may be engaged in "zipping the fly."

## Positioning

Once inside the interaction membrane, the participant has his opportunity to cruise those already there. He will have only the brief time of his passage across the room for sizing-up the situation.

Once he has positioned himself at the urinal or in a stall, he has already begun his first move of the game. Even the decision as to which urinal he will use is a tactical consideration. If either of the end fixtures is occupied, which is often the case, an entering party who takes his position at the center of the three urinals is "coming on too strong." This is apt to be the "forward" sort of player who wants both possible views. Should both ends be occupied, it is never considered fair for a new arrival to take the middle. He might interrupt someone else's play. For reasons other than courtesy, however, the skilled player will occupy one of the end urinals because it leaves him more room to maneuver in the forthcoming plays.

If the new participant stands close to the fixture, so that his front side may not easily be seen, and gazes downward, it is assumed by the players that he is straight. By not allowing his penis to be seen by others, he has precluded his involvement in action at the urinals. This strategy, followed by an early departure from the premises, is all that those who wish to "play it straight" need to know about the tearoom game. If he makes the positioning move in that manner, no man should ever be concerned about being propositioned, molested, or otherwise involved in the action. (For defecation, one should seek a facility with doors on the stalls.)

A man who knows the rules and wishes to play, however, will stand comfortably back from the urinal, allowing his gaze to shift from side to side or to the ceiling. At this point, he may notice a man in the nearest stall peer over the edge at him. The next step is for the man in the stall (or someone else in the room) to move to the urinal at the opposite end, being careful to leave a "safe" distance between himself and the other player.

My data indicate that those who occupy a stall upon entering (or who move into a stall after a brief stop at the urinal) are playing what might be called the Passive-Insertee System. By making such an opening bid, they indicate to other participants their intention to serve as fellator. In the systematic observation of fifty encounters ending in fifty-three acts of fellatio, twenty-seven of the insertees opened in this manner (twenty-five sitting on stools, two standing). Only two insertors opened by sitting on stools and four by standing in stalls.

Positioning is a far more "fateful" move for those who wish to be insertees than for others. In sixteen of the observed encounters, the fellator made no further move until the payoff stage of the game. The strategy of these men was to sit and wait, playing a distinctly passive role. Those who conclude as insertors, however, are twice as apt to begin at the urinals as are the insertees. A few of each just stood around or went to a window during the positioning phase of the game.

## Signaling

The major thesis of Scott's work on horse racing is that "the proper study of social organization is the study of the organization of information." [2] To what extent this holds for all organizations is not within my realm of knowledge. For gaming encounters, however, this is undoubtedly true, with "skill" inhering in the player's ability to convey, interpret, assimilate, and act upon the basis of information given and received. Every move in the gaming encounter is not only a means of bettering one's physical position in relation to other participants but also a means of communication.

Whereas, for most insertees, positioning is vital for informing others of their intentions, about half of the eventual insertors convey such information in the signaling phase. The primary strategy employed by the latter is playing with one's penis in what may be called "casual masturbation."

*Respondent:*

> The thing he [the potential insertee] is watching for is "handling," to see whether or not the guy is going to play with himself. He's going to pretend like he is masturbating, and this is the signal right there. . . .

*Interviewer:*

> So the sign of willingness to play is playing with oneself or masturbation?

*Respondent:*

> Pseudomasturbation.

2. Marvin B. Scott, *The Racing Game* (Chicago: Aldine, 1968), p. 3.

The willing player (especially if he intends to be an insertor) steps back a few inches from the urinal, so that his penis may be viewed easily. He then begins to stroke it or play with the head of the organ. As soon as another man at the urinals observes this signal, he will also begin autoerotic manipulation. Usually, erection may be observed after less than a minute of such stimulation.

The eyes now come into play. The prospective partner will look intently at the other's organ, occasionally breaking his stare only to fix directly upon the eyes of the other. "This mutual glance between persons, in distinction from the simple sight or observation of the other, signifies a wholly new and unique union between them." [3] A few of the players have been observed to move directly from positioning to eye contact, but this seems to happen in only about 5 per cent of the cases.

Through all of this, it is important to remember that showing an erection is, for the insertor, the one essential and invariable means of indicating a willingness to play. No one will be "groped" or otherwise involved in the directly sexual play of the tearooms unless he displays this sign. This touches on the rule of not forcing one's intentions on another, and I have observed no exceptions to its use. On the basis of extensive and systematic observation, I doubt the veracity of any person (detective or otherwise) who claims to have been "molested" in such a setting without first having "given his consent" by showing an erection. Conversely, anyone familiar with this strategy may become involved in the action merely by following it. He need not be otherwise skilled to play the game.

Most of those who intend to be insertors will engage in casual masturbation at a urinal. Others will do so openly while standing or sitting in a stall. Rarely, a man will begin masturbation while standing elsewhere in the room and then only because all other facilities are occupied.

In about 10 per cent of the cases, a man will convey his willingness to serve as insertee by beckoning with his hand or motioning with his head for another in the room to enter the stall where he is

3. From George Simmel, *Soziologie,* as quoted in Goffman, *Behavior in Public Places* (New York: The Free Press, 1963), p. 93. For a thorough discussion of the use of eye contact in face-to-face engagements, see pp. 91–96 of Goffman's book.

seated. There are a few other signals used by men on the stools to attract attention to their interests. If there are doors on the stalls, foot-tapping or note-passing may be employed. If there is a "glory hole" (a small hole, approximately three inches in diameter, which has been carefully carved, at about average "penis height," in the partition of the stall), it may be used as a means of signaling from the stall. This has been observed occurring in three manners: by the appearance of an eye on the stool-side of the partition (a very strong indication that the seated man is watching you), by wiggling fingers through the hole, or by the projection of a tongue through the glory hole.

Occasionally, there is no need for the parties to exchange signals at this stage of the game. Others in the room may signal for a waiting person to enter the stall of an insertee. There may have been conversation outside the facility—or acquaintance with a player—which precludes the necessity of any such communication inside the interaction membrane. This was the case in about one-sixth of the acts I witnessed.

## Maneuvering

The third move of the game is optional. It conveys little information to other players and, for this reason, may be skipped. As the Systematic Observation Sheets show, twenty-eight of the eventual insertees and thirty-five of the insertors (out of fifty-three sexual acts) made no move during this phase of the interaction. This is a time of maneuvering, of changing one's position in relation to other persons and structures in the room. It is important at this point in the action, first, because it indicates the crucial nature of the next move (the contract) and, second, because it is an early means of discerning which men wish to serve as insertees.

Twenty of the thirty-three players observed in motion during this stage of the encounter later became insertees. Two-thirds of these used the strategy of moving closer to someone at the urinal:

> X entered shortly and went to third urinal. Y entered in about a minute and went to first urinal. . . . O stood and watched X and Y. Y was masturbating, as was X. X kept looking over shoulder at me. I

smiled and moved over against far wall, lit cigarette. *X moved to second urinal* and took hold of Y's penis and began manipulating it. I moved to door to observe park policeman (in plain clothes with badge), who was seated on park bench. Then I went back to position by wall. By this time, X was on knees in front of urinals, fellating Y. I went back to door, saw A approaching, and coughed loudly.

Others may use this stage to move closer to someone elsewhere in the room or to move from the urinal to an unoccupied stall. All of these strategies are implemental but nonessential to the basic action patterns. The restroom's floor plan, I have found, is the strongest determinant of what happens during this phase of the game. If there are only two urinals in the facility, the aggressor's maneuver might be no more than to take a half-step toward the prospective partner.

## Contracting

Positions having been taken and the signals called, the players now engage in a crucial exchange. Due to the noncoercive nature of tearoom encounters, the contract phase of the game cannot be evaded. Initially, participants have given little consent to sexual interaction. By means of bodily movements, in particular the exposure of an erect penis, they have signaled such consent. Now *a contract must be agreed upon,* setting both the terms of the forthcoming sexual exchange and the expression of mutual consent.

Eighty-eight per cent of the contracts observed are initiated in one of two ways, depending upon the intended role of the initiator. One who wishes to be an insertee makes this move by taking hold of his partner's exposed and erect penis. One who wants to be an insertor under the terms of the contract steps into the stall where the prospective insertee is seated. If neither of these moves is rejected, the contract is sealed.

Manipulation of the other's organ is reciprocated in about half of the cases. Some respondents have indicated that they appreciate this gesture of mutuality, but it is not at all essential to the agreement reached. The lack of negative response from the recipient of the action is enough to seal the contract. It is interesting, in this connection, to note that such motions are seldom met with rejection (only one of my systematic observations records such a break in the action). By moving through gradual stages, the actors have achieved enough silent communication to guarantee mutuality.

In the positioning and signaling phases of the game, the players have already indicated their intentions. This stage, then, merely formalizes the agreement and sets the terms of the payoff. One should note, in this connection, that a party's relative aggressiveness or passivity in this phase of the game does not, in itself, indicate the role to be acted out at the climax of the interaction. In connection with the positioning of the first move, however, it does provide an indication of future role identification: the man who is seated in the stall *and* is the passive party to the contract will generally end up as an insertee; the man who stands at the urinal *and* is passive in the contract stage, however, will usually be an insertor at the payoff. The more active insertees play from the urinal and initiate the contract by groping, but active insertors play from the urinal (or elsewhere in the room) and initiate the contract by entering the stall of a passive insertee (see Table 4.1).

The systems of strategy illustrated in Table 4.1 account for 77 per cent of the patterns of play for the insertees observed and for 68 per cent of the insertors' moves. (Again, the insertee role seems to be most stable in the encounters.) The Active-Insertee and Passive-Insertor Systems have already been illustrated and discussed in detail. An illustration from the systematic observation reports of the other two systems follows:

[This was the fourth encounter observed in this tearoom within an hour. The man here identified as X had been the fellator in the second of these actions and had remained seated on the stool throughout the third. I estimated his age at about fifty. He was thin, had grey hair, and wore glasses. Y was about thirty-five, wearing white jeans and a green sport shirt, and was described as "neat." He was well-tanned, had black hair, was balding, and drove up in a new, luxury-class automobile.]

Saw Y approaching tearoom from bridge, so I got into room just before him. I stood at first urinal for a minute, until he began to masturbate at other one–then I moved to the window and looked out on the road. I could see X peering through glory hole at Y when I was at the urinal. Y moved to opposite window and looked out. He then

*Table 4.1 Major Strategy Systems in Tearoom Encounters. (Source: systematic observations of 48 encounters ending in fellatio.)*

| | *Insertee* | *Insertor* |
|---|---|---|
| *Active* | position: urinal<br>signal: casual masturbation<br>contract: manipulates partner's penis<br><br>(27%)* | position: urinal<br>signal: casual masturbation<br>contract: steps into partner's stall<br><br>(41%)** |
| *Passive* | position: sits in stall<br>signal: masturbation (sometimes beckoning)<br>contract: accepts partner's entry<br><br>(50%)* | position. urinal<br>signal: masturbation<br>contract: accepts partner's manipulation<br><br>(27%)** |
| Totals | N = 37 (77%)* | N = 33 (68%)** |

* Percentage of total insertees.

** Percentage of total insertors.

Note: Eleven insertees (23%) and fifteen insertors (32%) followed a variety of minor strategy systems, combining elements of the major systems with idiosyncratic moves.

turned to look at X and me. He was stroking his penis thru his pants, maintaining erection. I nodded to him to go ahead. He moved into first stall where X began to fellate him. This took less than five minutes. He wiped penis on tissue and left. X got up, zipped pants and left.

"X" played the Passive-Insertee System throughout these encounters. "Y" followed the Active-Insertor System, with some reassurance from the observer. The total time of this encounter–from entry of "Y" until his departure–was ten minutes. Note that the glory hole has three functions (the first two of which were employed in this encounter): as a peephole for observation, as a signalling device, and as a place of entry for the penis into the insertee's stall. The latter is very rare in the tearooms observed, and I have only twice seen these openings used in such a manner.

There may be forms of contracting other than the two I have described. I once observed a contract effected by the insertor's unzipping his pants directly in front of a prospective partner in the middle of the restroom. Another time, I noticed an active insertee grope a man whose erection was showing while his pants were still zipped. The move was not rejected, and the object of this strategy then played the insertor role. In a very few instances, my observations indicate that the insertee entered a stall where the eventual insertor was seated or that the insertor took hold of the partner's exposed penis at the urinals. These exceptions, while rare, make it necessary to withhold judgment as to what roles are being played until the payoff phase itself.

## Foreplay

Although optional and quite variable, sexual foreplay may be seen as constituting a fifth phase of the tearoom encounters. Like maneuvering, it has very little communicative function and is not essential to production of the payoff. From positioning to payoff, nearly all players–and some of the waiters–engage in automanipulation. There is little need, therefore, to prepare the insertee for fellatio by any other means of stimulation.

Unlike coitus, oral-genital sex does not require rigidity of the organ for adequate penetration of the orifice. Whereas an erection is a necessary signal in the early phases of the game, interruptions and repositioning between the contract and payoff stages occasionally result in the loss of an erection by the prospective insertor. The observer has noted that it is not uncommon for a fellator to take the other man's penis in his mouth even in its flaccid state. The male sex organ is a versatile instrument. With the proper psychosocial circumstances (varying with the individual's prior conditioning), it can reach the orgasmic phase in less than a minute. The authors of *Human Sexual Response* briefly discuss the many factors that intersect in determining the length of the "sexual response cycle":

> The first or excitement phase of the human cycle of sexual response develops from any source of somatogenic or psychogenic stimulation.

The stimulative factor is of major import in establishing sufficient increment of sexual tensions to extend the cycle. If the stimulation remains adequate to individual demand, the intensity of response usually increases rapidly. In this manner the excitement phase is accelerated or shortened. If the stimulative approach is physically or psychologically objectionable, or is interrupted, the excitement phase may be prolonged greatly or even aborted. This first segment and the final segment (resolution phase) consume most of the time expended in the complete cycle of human sexual response.[4]

Foreplay may help in maintaining the level of stimulation required for advancing the response cycle. Such strategies as mutual masturbation and oral contact in the pubic area may not only add appreciably to the sensual pleasure of the players but may help to precipitate orgasm when the participants are operating under the pressure of time and threatened intrusion:

It was now raining hard. O remained standing at window, saw X leave car and enter. Y drove up as X was walking toward tearoom, waited for about three minutes in car and ran thru rain to tearoom. X went to urinal nearest window. Y went to other urinal, urinated and began to play with his penis, stroking head slowly. Couldn't see what X was doing. X then moved over by Y (they had both been looking at one another) and took hold of his penis. Y did not reciprocate or withdraw. Y then moved over to far stall, still masturbating. X went over and stood by him, taking hold of his penis again. X's pants were zipped and I could not see evidence of an erection. He unbuttoned Y's pants and slipped them down to his knees, as he did with his shorts. Playing with Y's testicles and stroking his legs, he began to fellate him. . . .

It should be noted that, due to the danger of interruption, participants in this gaming encounter seldom lower their pants to the floor or unbutton any other clothing. They generally remain ready to engage in covering action at a moment's notice. Perhaps the rain gave these men what we shall later see to be a false sense of invulnerability.

4. William H. Masters and Virginia E. Johnson, *Human Sexual Response* (Boston: Little, Brown, 1966), pp. 5–6.

## The Payoff

The action now moves into its culminating stage. As is illustrated by continuing the above narrative, intrusions may temporarily detach the payoff phase from the action that leads up to it, providing moments of incongruous suspense:

Two kids, B and C, came running toward facility with fishing poles. I coughed. Y sat down on stool and X moved over to window. B and C entered, talking loudly and laughing at the rain. They rearranged some fishing gear in a box, then ran back outside, the rain having let up slightly.

D, an older boy around fourteen, came riding up on a bicycle from the bridge. I did not see him coming, but X and Y were still separated. D entered, went to urinal, urinated, looked out window by me and said, "Sure is raining out!" I remarked that it was letting up. "Guess I'll make a dash for it," he said. He left and rode off toward street. [This is an example of the lack of "consent to copresence" in these settings. See Chapter 8.]

X and Y resumed activity with X working his head back and forth and rubbing his hands up under shirt of Y, who was again standing. I saw A coming up walk and coughed. X and Y broke–Y sat down–X moved back to window. A entered and I recognized him. I nodded to X and Y, who resumed fellating position. A peered around edge of stall to watch, then stood up and looked over partition to get a better view, masturbating as he stood. Y moaned at orgasm and pressed on back of X's head. X stood up and continued masturbating Y even after orgasm. Y withdrew in a minute and pulled up pants. X moved back to window. Y looked for paper in other stall but it had been used up. He tucked his penis in pants, zipped up and left. X came over to window by me and looked me over. I smiled and left. A remained on stool.

Among other things illustrated here, one may notice the importance of hand play in the sexual act itself. The observations indicate that body and hand movements carry the action through stages that, lacking conversation, might otherwise be awkward. Primarily by means of the hands, the structure of the encounter is well maintained, in spite of the absence of verbal encouragement. Caresses, friendly pats, relaxed salutes, support with the hands, and thrusting motions are all to be observed throughout the action. Normally, the man who takes the insertor role will sustain the action of the fellator by clasping the back of his head or neck or by placing his hands on the partner's shoulders. As a frequent insertee points out:

When you are having sex, it's not just that the sexual organ is being activated. The whole body comes into it. And you want to use your whole body, and your hands are a very important part in sex. Next to the organs themselves, I think the hands are the most important part, even more important than the mouth for kissing. I really think the hands are more important–because you can do fantastic things, if you know how to do them. You can do fantastic things with your hands to another person's body.

Without the use of scientific instruments other than the human eye, it is impossible to say what proportion of the hand play during the sexual act is voluntary or involuntary. During the orgasmic phase, undoubtedly, there is a great deal of involuntary, spasmodic movement of the extremities, such as that described by Masters and Johnson:

This involuntary spasm of the striated musculature of the hands and feet is an indication of high levels of sexual tension. Carpopedal spasm has been observed more frequently during male masturbatory episodes than during intercourse, regardless of body positioning.[5]

For physiological reasons, such spasmodic clutching of the hands is engaged in only by the insertor and confined mostly to the period surrounding orgasm.

The insertee, however, may have certain functional reasons for handling his partner. Some respondents have spoken of clutching the base of the penis with a hand, in order to ward off a thrust that may cause them to gag or choke:

If the man has a very large piece of meat–I know from experience–I will not have somebody ram that thing down my throat. I'm sorry, but that hurts! It can cause a person to vomit. [Like if you put your fingers down your throat?] Exactly, and this can be very embarrassing. So, ordinarily, I will try to hold on. I know just about how much I can take.

5. *Ibid.*, p. 173. See also pp. 296–297.

Then I am going to put my hand in a certain place, and I know it can't go any further than my hand. . . .

The same participant continues by describing another functional use of the hands during fellatio:

Then I use my hands on the balls, too—on the scrotum. This can do wild things! [You said something about the hips. Or did I imagine that?] The hips or the backs of the legs. Now, there is one value in this which some people don't realize: these muscles contract first at the point of orgasm. This is one of the first signs of orgasm. When these muscles back in here begin to contract (the legs stiffen, these muscles contract or flex, or whatever—they get hard), you can tell at this point the orgasm is about to be reached. It is very helpful to know these things, especially if you are doing somebody. Because you can tell to go faster—or keep doing what you are doing. You can at least get ready and know not to pull away all of a sudden.

I suspect that, if one were to concentrate on observing peripheral matters in a study of heterosexual intercourse, he would find the same pattern of hand involvement: exploration of the partner's body, support of the head or pressure on the back, stimulation of the erotic zones, numerous caresses. At least in the payoff phase, silence in sexual encounters is not confined to the tearooms. When body communicates directly with body, spoken language is no longer essential. Thus far in history, the action of sex is the only universal language—perhaps because the tongue is but one among many members to convey the message, and the larynx is less important than the lips.

As has been indicated, it is a lack of such physical involvement —along with the silence—that tends to make tearoom sex less personal. When hand play does occur, therefore, it tends to raise the involvement level of the sexual action. Perhaps for that reason, some people attempt to avoid it:

I saw X's hand as he motioned Y over into his stall. Y entered, stood facing X and unzipped. X ran his hands all over Y's buttocks, the back of his legs and up under his shirt while sucking. Y stood rather still with hands held out just far enough from his sides to give X freedom of movement *without touching him.*

The primary physical connection between the partners is that of the mouth, lips, and tongue of the fellator with the penis of the insertor. The friction and sucking action in the meeting of these organs is what produces the orgasm upon which the encounter focuses. A number of my respondents claim that the physical sensation of oral-genital copulation, while not unlike that of coitus, is actually more stimulating—or "exciting," as they generally word it. While some of the married men among the cooperating participants say that they actually prefer the sensations of fellatio to those of coitus, most agree that this is true only when certain other variables are held constant, when both acts take place in bed, for example. Many tend to look on tearoom sex as only a substitute for "the real thing."

> It's different—and I like both. I guess you could say I'd rather have sex with my wife. Getting a blow job isn't like having the real thing, but it has its points, too. I just don't know. I hadn't thought about it that way. I guess you really can't compare the two. Let's just say I like them both.

Some insertees retain the seminal fluid and swallow it: others clear their throats and spit it out. In one-fifth of the encounters observed, I noted that the insertee spit following the ejaculation of his partner. One respondent claimed that he only spits it out "when it tastes bad":

> The variety of tastes is unbelievable! You can almost tell what a person's diet is by what it tastes like. A person with a good, well-balanced ordinary diet, the fluid has a very mild, tangy, salty flavor. A person who has been drinking heavily—even if they aren't drunk or suffering from a hang-over, if they drink a lot—the stuff tastes like alcohol. And I mean pure, rot-gut alcohol, the vilest taste in the world!

I was unable to find any medical references to the taste of ejaculatory fluid, so I have not been able to verify this connoisseur's judgment. Other respondents will say only that they do think "some men taste different than others."

Acts of fellatio generally take place within the stall. This puts the insertee in a more comfortable position than crouching on his haunches elsewhere in the room. It also has an advantage in case of an intrusion, in that only one party to the action needs to move. There are certain tactical advantages as well. If the man who prefers the insertee position takes a stall and remains there for any length of time, he legitimizes himself, indicates the role he wishes to play, and needs only to wait for a partner to arrive.

Another twenty-nine per cent of the observed acts took place in front of the urinals. From that position, both may turn to face the fixtures in case of an intrusion. The fellator is poorly braced for his action, however, and probably quite uncomfortable. Occasionally, the act will occur in front of a window. I am informed that this is especially true when no lookout is present, because it has the advantage of enabling the insertor to double as lookout. When the oral-genital contact takes place away from the stool, the insertee will generally squat or drop to his knees to make the necessary contact.

During oral copulation, other men may come from around the room into viewing position. Many will proceed to masturbate while watching, sometimes without opening their pants for the automanipulation. Seldom does the exchange that is the focal point of this attention last more than a few minutes. In looking over my data, I found indications that I had grossly overestimated the amount of time lapsed between insertion and orgasm. What seemed to me like "a long time" (sometimes recorded as five or ten minutes) was probably a reflection only of my nervousness during the payoff stage. Since I was attempting to pass as a voyeur-lookout (both aspects of the role requiring my closest attention during these moments), it was impossible for me to use my watch in timing. No true voyeur would glance at his watch in the middle of a sex act! Actually, I suspect that the oral penetration ranged from ten seconds to five minutes, not counting interruptions.

I have twice seen couples engaging in anal intercourse. This is a form of sexual activity rare in most tearooms, probably due to the greater amount of time required and the drastic rearrangement of clothing involved, both of which tend to increase the danger of being apprehended in the act. Mutual masturbation is an occasional means of reaching orgasm, particularly by the urinals or elsewhere in a crowded room.

## Clearing the Field

Once the sexual exchange is accomplished, most insertors step into a stall to use the toilet paper. After the penis is cleansed, clothes are rearranged and flies zipped. In those rare cases in the observed facilities where a workable wash basin is provided, the participants may wash their hands before leaving.

Nearly always in the observation records, when a man took the insertor role he left for his car immediately after cleansing. The insertee may leave, too, but he frequently waits in the tearoom for someone else to enter. Sometimes he becomes the insertor in a subsequent encounter, as in the following account:

> [X is about forty-five, wearing a green banlon shirt, light blue slacks, driving a red, late model sports coupe. Y is about thirty, driving a green Ford convertible. He wears a light blue shirt, dark blue slacks, and a conservative tie. He is described as being tan, masculine, well dressed. B is about forty, balding, thin, tanned, wearing horn-rimmed glasses and a grey sport shirt. It is 2:25 on a beautiful Thursday afternoon, and there are few people in the park.]
>
> B was seated on stool when O entered. O stood at urinal a minute, noticed B watching him through glory hole. Crossed to far window, looked out and lit cigarette. Y entered and went to first urinal. X came in soon after Y and went to third urinal. They stood there for about five minutes. X kept peering over edge of stall at B and also at me. I crossed to opposite window and looked out missing pane. X was masturbating. Y went to second stall, lowered pants and sat down. I went back to window on right. Y spread his legs and began masturbating. (He had removed his coat and hung it over edge of stall.) He had slumped on the stool seat as if sitting in camp chair, legs stretched out almost straight in front of him but spread apart and was masturbating obviously. I went back to window overlooking street. X then moved to window by Y, stood there a minute, then leaned over and took hold of Y's penis and began stroking it. He then knelt on the floor to begin fellatio. B just sat in his stall and masturbated. Y moaned a bit at climax. He then wiped and X stood back by window and masturbated while watching Y. Y flushed toilet, put on his coat, zipped pants and left. X stepped into B's stall and was sucked by him. This didn't take more than a minute. X then went to urinal, cleared throat, spit and left. (I was able to see autos of both X and Y through window.)

This is what I have labeled a series encounter. Generally, in order to facilitate the eventual analysis, I have broken these up into "Encounter A," "Encounter B," etc. In the above instance and in a few others among my systematic observations, I was not able to do so because of the rapid succession of events. During the hunting season, series encounters are the most common variety. Once the action begins to "swing," a series may last throughout the day, each group of participants trading upon the legitimation process of the previous game.

Another type of action that tends to swell the volume of sexual acts in a given facility is the simultaneous encounter, in which more than one sexual act is in process at the same time. The payoff phases are seldom reached at exactly the same time in these encounters, but they are staggered as in a round.

[It is a warm, humid, Friday afternoon. A few youngsters are playing ball in the park and some heterosexual couples are parked nearby. X is about thirty-five, tough looking, tattooed, dirty working clothes, drives an old Chevrolet. Y is about forty-five, lean and tanned, wearing tan work clothes. A is about thirty-two, neatly dressed with sport shirt and tie. I describe him as "masculine looking but wore pinky ring." He drove a new, foreign economy car. B is about fifty, heavy set, grey hair, sports clothes, rather unkempt. C is about forty, with a pot belly, wearing white sports shirt, dark blue pants.]

When O entered, X and Y were seated on stools with A standing by far window facing into room. While O urinated, he noticed that X was watching him through glory hole. O lingered at urinal for about four minutes, during which time A moved into stall with X (X is a noisy sucker, much "slurping," so I could tell what was happening but could not see). O crossed to far window, lit cigarette and peered out. A left first stall and stepped into space between Y and O. He stood there, masturbating both himself and Y, who had stood up. Meanwhile, C, who was sitting on bridge watching tearoom when O entered, came into the room. O saw him approaching thru window and coughed. Y and A broke contact for the moment but, recognizing C, returned to action. C stood at urinal less than a minute, halted for another minute opposite stalls, then went into stall with X, who proceeded to fellate him. Y then stood on the toilet seat, watching X and C, while A sucked Y (A had to crouch but continued to masturbate). It was getting crowded on that side of the room, so O moved to opposite window. From this position, he could only see part of A's backside, Y's face and shoulders, and the backside of C. X kneeded C's buttocks and ran his hands up and down the backs of

C's legs. When C finished, he left without wiping. A finished with Y about this time, went to urinal number three and spit. Y wiped and left. A stepped over to window by O, peered out through broken pane. His pants were still unzipped and he proceeded to masturbate and to look at O suggestively. O, feeling uncomfortable, went back to far window. B entered and A zipped up pants. B looked around as he went to middle urinal but stayed there for a brief time. He then moved over to stall with X. No one seemed to be made uncomfortable by B and seemed to recognize him. O then left, followed closely by A, who engaged him in conversation by water fountain. . . . All of this took place in twenty-five minutes.

The reader should be able to sense, at this point, that what I have described as a rather simple, six-step game (only four of which are essential to the action) may be acted out with infinite variety and confusing modifications. Every encounter reduces, ultimately, to the basic steps of positioning, signaling, contracting, and payoff; but no two of them are quite alike.

A pat on the shoulder, a wave of the hand, an occasional whispered "thanks" concludes the action. The departure ritual is simple and brief. Once the field is cleared, some individuals go to their homes or jobs, others return to their cars and await the arrival of fresh players, and a few may venture to a different tearoom to take their positions in another encounter.

The length of these games was observed to range between five and forty minutes, with an average duration of about eighteen minutes. Tearoom encounters, then, require relatively little time—a quarter of an hour if one knows where to go and how to play the game. Many suburban housewives may think their husbands delayed by the traffic when, in reality, the spouses have paused for a tearoom encounter.

## Coping with Intrusions

Intrusion of a new person through the interaction membrane nearly always causes a break in the action. The man entering *must* be legitimized or the game will be disrupted, at least for the duration of his presence. Until the legitimation or departure of the intruder, a sort of panic reaction ensues; play becomes disorganized and the focus of strategies shifts from the payoff—first to self-protection and then to appraisal of the membrane-violator:

> Okay, they're making out or doing something in the tearoom; and, all of a sudden, the door bangs open and in comes someone. They break off right away. There is this twisting of bodies: one twists around in the stall; the other turns, stands up. . . . They change positions. The third party goes over to one of the urinals. Then they look over the top of the stall. He's looking over the tops of the stalls, too. They're thinking: "Do I know him? Have I seen him in here or not?" That's the first thing. . . . So you watch and see: "How long is he going to stay there? Is he urinating or just standing there?" All these different things come into it. So then you decide: "Alright, I'm safe." You hope he is not a cop playing games.

Other than by "cutting out," giving up on the game altogether, I find three chief means of coping with the tension generated by such intrusions into the gaming encounter. The first is the almost automatic and universal response of zipping the fly. The first reaction of a man, when threatened, is to cover his exposure. Since (in the case of deviant action such as a sexual game) the exposure is not so much physical as moral, this covering mechanism is a matter of hiding the incriminating evidence rather than "taking cover." In the game of warfare, where physical protection is paramount, the first response to the crisis of intrusion is "hitting the dirt." Because the negative consequences of a deviant game are more apt to be realized in a courtroom than in a base hospital, however, the immediate problem is one of disposing of potentially damaging evidence. Thus pot-smokers "stash the shit," thieves "ditch the loot," and tearoom players zip the fly.

Actually, I find that zipping the fly occurs not only when the players are threatened by intrusion crises but whenever there is penetration of the interaction membrane. At all points where the outer world impinges upon the inner world, zipping the fly is apt to occur.[6] (Such "involuntary" movements as checking the fly to make sure it is zipped should be included within this general cate-

6. Erving Goffman, *The Presentation of Self in Everyday Life* (Garden City, New York: Doubleday Anchor, 1959), p. 137. These points may be compared with Goffman's discussion of the dramaturgical problem of segregating audiences.

gory of protective action.) Few tearoom participants fail to engage in this action just prior to leaving the restroom scene. Likewise, hip persons generally check the "pad" to make certain the "shit" is "stashed" and all "roaches" disposed of, before venturing out into the world.

The second common coping mechanism is looking innocent, by which means participants dissociate themselves from the deviant action. One of my respondents described this as a "huge elaborate disinterest." On many occasions, when my entry into a tearoom disrupted the action, I encountered this sort of elaborate nonchalance; however, it was never maintained for long.

There is a remarkable tendency for the normal, payoff-focused action of a gaming encounter to overcome disruption and reorganize. Legitimation never seems to take long: straights seldom stay for more than two minutes; waiters tend either to begin the opening moves of the game or to commence service as lookouts: teen-agers generally cause permanent disruption of the encounter. It may be that legitimation constitutes less of a problem in the city where most observations took place because the metropolitan police no longer use decoys in the tearooms. Where decoys are a threat, the legitimation process would be longer and more elaborate.

The third observed means whereby participants in the tearoom game cope with disruptive entries involves what I would call "speculative inquiry." As illustrated in the previous quotation, every man becomes his own, self-appointed investigating committee. Speculative inquiry requires careful observation, by which the participants pick up identification clues dropped by the new arrival. Once someone decides the newcomer is safe, nods may pass around the room, the action is resumed (somewhat cautiously at first), and the crisis of intrusion passes.

Some intrusion crises are not so easily resolved, and the tearoom game may end in disaster rather than payoff. In spite of the development of patterns of collective action to maintain the noncoercive and noncommital nature of the encounters, defenses may fail and the feared consequences materialize. The most careful and elaborate structuring of rules, roles, and strategies sometimes collapses. In the next chapter, forms of the resulting exposure are discussed as risks of the game.

# *Chapter 5.* Risks of the Game

I am primarily concerned with this grieving family in my parish, with the fact that we have lost such a wonderful man, and the news media played such an important part in driving him to suicide. There is no question but that his learning that his name had been published was the direct cause of his jumping off a bridge. While I will agree with those who have told me that men who need to search for their sexual outlet in public men's rooms are sick people, I would wonder whether these same people would approve of our listing the names of people going into mental hospitals. I also would say very strongly that a society that pays its policemen to spend hours on their haunches or lying prostrate on the top of a building peering through a hole to spy on men is a very sick society.[1]

IN CHAPTER 3, I indicated that the excitement of the tearoom encounters–that which makes them games of chance–is the outgrowth of a great deal more than the mere possibility of success or failure in the payoff phase of the action. The salient risks of the

1. Excerpt from an anonymous letter in the "Correspondence" column of *Christianity and Crisis,* Vol. 26, No. 10 (June 13, 1966), p. 135.

game are the long-range contingencies, particularly those that may result in injury or stigmatization, in damage to the participant's person or his personal identity.

What the person who engages in covert deviant behavior (especially when that behavior is sexual) fears most is discovery, exposure that might do irreparable harm to the whole network of social and psychological images we call the self.

> Discovery prejudices not only the current social situation, but established relationships as well; not only the current image others present have of him, but also the one they will have in the future; not only appearances, but also reputation. The stigma and the effort to conceal it or remedy it become "fixed" as part of personal identity.[2]

As one respondent expressed himself in discussing his fear of possible disclosure:

> Sometimes, when I come out of a tearoom, I look up at the sky just to make sure some plane isn't flying around up there, writing "[JOHN JONES] IS A PERVERT"!

The type of insecurity expressed by participants is like that which causes little boys in our society to dream they are standing up before the whole classroom with their pants unzipped. For thousands of men in this country each year, however, being "caught with their pants down" in the tearooms is no mere nightmare. It is a real possibility that may destroy them as persons.

Every state in America has codes prohibiting sexual activities in public places, and arrest is an ever present possibility for the participants in tearoom encounters. The Los Angeles County Sheriff's Department, for instance, arrested seventy men in one public restroom during a recent year. [3] Where decoys are used, as they are in many jurisdictions, this is probably not an uncommon rate. What little data are available indicate that the majority of arrests in the United States on charges related to homosexual behavior are made in the tearoom purlieus. Undoubtedly, the major source of concern

2. Erving Goffman, *Stigma* (Englewood Cliffs, New Jersey: Prentice-Hall, 1963), p. 65.

3. Jon J. Gallo and others, "The Consenting Adult Homosexual and the Law: An Empirical Study of Enforcement and Administration in Los Angeles County," *UCLA Law Review,* 13 (March, 1966), p. 688.

to those who frequent these facilities is the possibility of their apprehension by the agents of social control.

Blackmail is not only a threat to all who take part in games of deviant sexuality but, when that activity takes a homosexual form, the participants gain the distinction of being the only known group who are discriminated against for being prone to blackmail. According to government policy, homosexuals may not be hired for federal or defense-related jobs—or allowed to serve in the armed forces—primarily because their lack of defense against being blackmailed makes them poor security risks. Because the role of blackmailer is scarcely distinguishable from that of the police in the tearoom game, it will be discussed as part of the police problem in the course of this chapter.

There are other threats to the reputations and bodies of men who go to tearooms for sex. One of these is the possibility of discovery by someone who knows the participant in the "outside" world. As Goffman suggests, this is a problem of information control:

> When his differentness is not immediately apparent, and is not known beforehand (or at least known by him to be known to the others), when in fact he is a discreditable, not a discredited person, then the second main possibility in his life is to be found. The issue is not that of managing tension generated during social contacts, but rather that of managing information about his failing. To display or not to display; to tell or not to tell; to let on or not to let on; to lie or not to lie; and in each case, to whom, how, when, and where.[4]

This threat will vary with the size of the community, the prominence of the individual, and the proximity of a given facility to the places where he lives and works. It is an obvious danger, and one we all share to some extent in the task of keeping our audiences segregated.

The other general categories of risk that confront tearoom participants involve the possibility of bodily, rather than social, harm. The first of these is the threat of the teen-ager or other "tough." As outlined in Chapter 3, the roles that are manifested in the course of tearoom action include four that are played primarily by teen-agers

4. Goffman, *Stigma,* p. 42.

("chicken"): straights, enlisters, hustlers, and toughs. The first two constitute threats only because their presence on the scene is apt to bring police into the action. The hustlers can be annoying at any time but become threatening only as their role distintegrates into that of the toughs. It is the latter who can, and do, become a source of real physical danger to those who meet in tearooms.

It has been postulated that tearoom sex constitutes a threat not only to the health of the individuals involved but to that of the whole society, as a means of spreading venereal disease. Two officials of a V. D. Clinic operated by the U. S. Public Health Service indicated to the interviewer that, although "there is no *one* meeting place that presents a problem, public park restrooms are probably among the sources of infection." [5] More research is needed before we may deny or confirm their suspicions in this regard.

Finally, this chapter will include discussion of whether the dangers of tearoom encounters are directed inward upon the participants or outward against society as a whole. Whatever conclusions the reader may reach, he should arrive at a realization of the strength of the element of fear in these games of chance. Like the smell of urine, fear pervades the atmosphere of the tearooms, making furtive every stage of the interaction.

## The Police

Sex statutes applicable to homosexual offenses between consenting adults in the fifty states range from those governing vagabonds and vagrants to those in condemnation of sodomy and fellatio.[6] Although variably enforced by the agents of social control, these statutes hang like a sword over the tearooms. Stories of police raids in the parks constantly make the round in gay circles, and many newspapers across the country publish the names, addresses, and sometimes occupations of men who are charged as a result of such raids.

Recently, the advancing technology of police operations has begun to invade the tearoom scene. The Mansfield, Ohio, police de-

5. These interviews were conducted by Henry Korman.
6. Gallo and others, "The Homosexual and the Law," pp. 830–832.

partment has developed a technique using a two-way mirror and a sixteen mm. camera in a public restroom for recording incriminating evidence against suspects. In the space of two weeks, they recorded sexual acts involving sixty-five different men by means of these devices. "A radio transmitter enabled the watching police to signal to colleagues waiting outside, prepared to identify and arrest the offenders as they emerged." [7] Since publication of this successful application of new techniques in the police journal *Law and Order* in 1963, the popularity of such practices has spread. (The FBI has reprinted this article for distribution to all police departments across the country.) Reportedly, such use of the camera is now made in Miami Beach, Florida, and Lake Milton, Ohio. Laguna Beach, California, is planning to install closed circuit television in order to keep watch on such activities along a two and one-half mile area; and the executive secretary of the Central YMCA of Philadelphia has prepared a "Confidential Report" entitled: "The Use of Closed Circuit TV for the Study and Elimination of Homosexual Activity in the YMCA." [8]

Until these recent developments were introduced, police detection had taken three basic forms: spying, the use of decoys, and raids. The first is the strategy of which the above techniques are merely refinements. Police have been known to observe tearoom activity through mirrors, grills, pipes installed in the ceiling–and even through glory holes. Because this necessitates long hours of duty (sometimes in cramped positions) from men who may be needed elsewhere, spying activities of this outdated variety may be on the decline.

In many areas of the country, decoys are the most popular means of apprehending men who engage in restroom sex. Officers are sent into the tearooms in the hope of being approached by participants for illegal purposes. Such procedures have been declared invalid by the courts under certain circumstances, so they, too, may be waning.[9]

7. D. J. West, *Homosexuality* (Chicago: Aldine, 1968), p. 89. This completely updated rewriting of an old classic in the field is the most complete survey of social scientific research on homosexuality.

8. Council on Religion and the Homosexual, "The Challenge and Progress of Homosexual Law Reform" (San Francisco: Council on Religion and the Homosexual, 1967), pp. 68–69.

9. Gallo and others, *op. cit.*, pp. 690–707.

Raids continue to be popular, both for reactive purposes (in response to specific complaints) and for the prevention of prohibited sexual activity (proactive measures). In the city where most of my observations were made, the policy is to engage in raids only in response to complaints or when the city's image might be damaged by the proximity of tearoom activity to some public event. A former police official has told me of a recent raid by the vice squad upon one of the parks in this study that netted so many men during one afternoon that the police facilities were overwhelmed. Reportedly, after this experience, decisions were made to book none of the violators and to engage in no more such roundups.

As a result of such police procedures as these, the tearooms in America have become the scenes of thousands of arrests each year on charges relating to homosexual activity. Because criminologists are not provided with an adequate breakdown in crime data (filtered to the public, as they are, by the FBI), it is impossible to ascertain the exact number of such arrests. In the four-year period covered by the exhaustive project of the School of Law of the University of California at Los Angeles, 274 of the 493 felony arrests on such charges and 139 of the 434 disorderly conduct arrests were made in public restrooms in Los Angeles County. Due to these and other data in their comprehensive study, the project's report concluded:

> Activity in public restrooms presents the most serious challenge to enforcement agencies in terms of frequency of the activity, gravity of the offense likely to be committed, and degree of conspicuousness.[10]

Elsewhere in California, as in other states, reports have been made of the volume of arrests in tearooms: the Berkeley, California, police report 240 such arrests in a twenty-one month period;[11] about 150 homosexual arrests are made in Chicago each month, most of them in public restrooms.[12] If sixty-five different men are caught engaging in the tearoom game in the course of two weeks in one restroom in the small city of Mansfield, Ohio, what

10. *Ibid.*, p. 689.

11. Berladt Konstantin, "Minorities–'2700 Homosexuals at Cal,'" *Daily Californian*, (Berkeley), November 29, 1965.

12. Louis Wille, "Police Watch Homosexuals' Hangouts Here," *Chicago Daily News*, June 22, 1966, p. 3.

does this suggest as to the number of men involved in such activity over a year's time in the hundreds of public facilities in metropolitan areas with populations in the millions?

## Police Lawlessness

If, as the UCLA study reports, "interviews with police departments indicate that communications from citizens complaining about solicitations by homosexuals are rare," [13] there may be some reason for objecting to any police activity in the tearooms at all. This is particularly true in the light of evidence that indicates that such enforcement procedures are ineffective in controlling the proscribed behavior.[14] The advisability and legality of such practices as spying and vice squad raids are really outside the range of this research and should be left to those who are trained in the preparation of legal briefs.

In the case of decoy activity, however, my data call for application to this aspect of the police problem. Let us look again at what the decoy does:

> The decoy's *modus operandi* at a public restroom may be to loiter inside engaging a suspect in friendly conversation, using handwashing or urinal facilities, or even occupying a commode for long periods of time. (One agency regularly operates in this manner. When a homosexual takes a seat in the adjacent commode and starts tapping his foot, the decoy will tap back.) [15]

According to the analysis presented in Chapters 3 and 4, most activities of this kind violate the role of the straight in tearoom encounters. "Loitering" and activity on the commode are signals that the straight role has melted into that of the waiter or player. The decoy approached after such signaling is no longer straight in the eyes of the participants but has already indicated his willingness to play the game. By overstaying the time limit of the straight role, such de-

13. Gallo and others, *op. cit.*, p. 698.
14. Edwin M. Schur, *Crimes Without Victims* (Englewood Cliffs, New Jersey: Prentice-Hall, 1965), p. 114.
15. Gallo and others, *op. cit.*, pp. 691–692.

coys are engaging in entrapment rather than detection. "Entrapment is activity by police officers which is designed to foster rather than to prevent and detect crime." [16]

Furthermore, my observations suggest that (barring the possibility of verbal suggestions in settings other than I have observed) physical overtures will be made to no man in the tearoom settings who has not previously given consent by manifesting an erect penis. That this may be what actually happens in such instances of reported "lewd solicitation," is suggested in the UCLA study:

> One police official told of a prosecution that had been dismissed because the decoy was standing so far away from the urinal with his penis exposed as to constitute an invitation equivalent to entrapment.[17]

Because of such evidence, the study goes on to make the following recommendation:

> Empirical data indicate that utilization of police manpower for decoy enforcement is not justified. Societal interests are infringed only when a solicitation to engage in a homosexual act creates a reasonable risk of offending public decency. The incidence of such solicitations is statistically insignificant. *The majority of homosexual solicitations are made only if the other individual appears responsive and are ordinarily accomplished by quiet conversation and the use of gestures and signals having significance only to other homosexuals.* Such unobtrusive solicitations do not involve an element of public outrage. The rare indiscriminate solicitations of the general public do not justify the commitment of police resources to suppress such behavior.[18]

To these conclusions, I should add that such utilization of police manpower is not only unjustified but illegal, tending to foster crime by adopting the role of a potential insertor in a gaming encounter that is focused on a legally proscribed payoff. Moreover, my data indicate that such decoy operations sometimes lead to related crimes of a much more serious nature, to blackmail and the corrupting of minors.

16. *Ibid.*, p. 701.
17. *Ibid.*, p. 692.
18. *Ibid.*, p. 796. Italics mine.

## Blackmail

On the basis of my interviews, three impressions take shape in regard to the blackmailing of tearoom participants: (1) most blackmailing is done by law enforcement personnel and as a result of decoy operations; (2) some blackmailing is practiced by those who pose as police officers; (3) a small amount is attempted (seldom with success) by close friends of the victims.

Because I was unable to observe any blackmail in progress, I rely upon the accounts of respondents for data on instances of extortion and payoffs to the police. Although it is always possible that those whom I interviewed may have fabricated such stories, my respondents have never given me reason to doubt their veracity. Recognizing the serious nature of this study, they provided me with detailed accounts of their encounters with police. After repeated questioning, I could discover no inconsistencies. Not only have I found no reason to doubt their truthfulness, but the reader should note that, on the whole, tearoom participants were more positive in their attitudes toward the police than were members of the control samples (see Chapter 7). These, then, are the accounts of "friendly" rather than "antagonistic" witnesses. Most deviants prefer corruptible policemen to those who make arrests. This is particularly true when the apprehended person is a man of such means that he needs only to use pocket money for payoffs.

Every respondent over the age of thirty whom I interviewed extensively had at least one story of police payoffs amounting to blackmail. With some, the police were paid by sexual services rendered. In two instances, "donations" were made to a "charity fund" in return for release. One man alone—a prosperous married salesman who travels a great deal—has provided me with detailed accounts of eight instances in which he has "bought off" decoys for amounts ranging from sixty to three hundred dollars. In each of these encounters with the law, the respondent had been "led on" by the decoy.

Without such operations on the part of the police, the stage would not be set for those who prey upon the tearoom participant by masquerading as detectives. Because most men involved for any length of time in homosexual activities have had experience with police blackmail, they are ripe for exploitation by those who take such poses.

Ultimately, of course, it is the law—not the law enforcer—that must be blamed for the crime of blackmail. The prohibition of such common behavior as occurs in tearoom encounters creates a population without recourse to the law for protection. As Schur points out in regard to police lawlessness in these cases:

> The strong public disapproval believed to attach to homosexuality, the extreme reluctance of homosexuals to report victimization (particularly at the hands of the police), and the discretion the officer may exercise in deciding when homosexual behavior is an "offense," all serve as inducements.[19]

The use of decoys by the police has helped shape the structure of the tearoom game: its concern with legitimation of the participants, its use of an erection as the vital sign, its smothering of identity in silence have all been influenced by police activity. Without these agents of social control as constant (if sometimes invisible) "participants" in the encounters, the game might be less exciting. The "other team" is important to the course of play and the maintenance of thrills in the action. The game, in turn, has had its effect on the police, providing them with the opportunity for exploitation of victims who are almost certain to remain silent.

## The Case of Tim

One respondent has not remained silent. At the time of interviewing, he was nineteen—the youngest participant in the sample. This is one of many interviews I have had with him, none of which have given me any cause to doubt his veracity and complete willingness to cooperate in the spirit of his research. Slight changes have been made in the transcript in order to hide the identity of the respondent and other persons involved, but I have attempted to remain faithful to all items that have implications for this research and its application. Tim should be pictured as a handsome, well-built

19. Schur, *Crimes Without Victims,* p. 83.

young man, with dark hair and of medium height. He speaks with a slight southern accent in an informal, slangy manner that belies his intelligence. When interviewed, he was a college student.

*Interviewer:*

You did some work in Louisiana, for a while–when you were younger–for the police department. Now, would you like to tell me how old you were then?

*Tim:*

O God, the summer before I started my sophomore year in high school. What is it?

*Interviewer:*

That would make you about fifteen.

*Tim:*

Not quite that. I guess I was fourteen and a half. Yes, it was during the summertime.

*Interviewer:*

Now, how did you get started in this? Start from the first experience that really got you going, working for the police.

*Tim:*

Well–like I got in some trouble. I guess you'd say I did a little shoplifting and got caught–right there in the store–with the stuff; and they got the things I took back. But the cops were really up tight about it all. Well, then, my folks were pretty stiff with me then, and I threw a big thing about not wanting them to know. So this one officer offered me a way out. He took me down to the vice squad–and they put me to work.

*Interviewer:*

What did you do for them?

*Tim:*

What they had me do was–I had to work alone really–was they would tell me the different places to go. And then, when I had the chance, I should call them, tell them where I was at the time, and follow the man. And if they didn't see me following him to the place of business (because downtown it was mostly just businessmen)–and if they didn't see me following him to the place of business, I should go back to the john and the police would be there. . . .

They would take me down to the station and have me sign a statement. They always prepared them, of course. . . . Then they kept making comments about how they would like to get me to tell my folks that I was going to a football game or something, and come down at night where we could get the young people and college kids that were hanging around the bus station. But that would have to wait; because, as a fourteen-year-old kid, I just couldn't get out at night. But, as it happened, I just got fed up with it and never did go to the bus station. But they were always telling me where to go and everything.

*Interviewer:*

Were there many young kids involved?

*Tim:*

No. Just the older ones: salesmen or businessmen that worked in the downtown area.

*Interviewer:*

Did you get paid for doing all of this?

*Tim:*

In that summer, I cleared about two hundred dollars from them. It was all cash and never listed in the police department or anything like this.

*Interviewer:*

Well, in all of these cases, the idea was that a man was supposed to give you a blow job?

*Tim:*

Yes, they had to go down on me, before they could do anything.

*Interviewer:*

Was there ever any suggestion that you would go down on them?

*Tim:*

No. But I was curious as hell! And then they kept making all these suggestions about the bus station . . . and they had said that they had no one there, that the bus station was in such a position that they couldn't use the mirror and they couldn't use the camera because it was set up where the mirror and wash tables were all along a solid wall that was out by the waiting room, and they had absolutely no way of setting up anything in the john. They had no men they could use as decoys. They made it completely obvious to me that it was wide open. They had nothing else they could do there. So one night I went down there, and I *did* get a blow job.

*Interviewer:*

Do you think that this experience—working for the police, and then you getting in later on with the gay crowd—do you think you would have gotten in with them anyway, eventually?

*Tim:*

No, because I thought it was just a few, individual, sick, perverted people—like the typical description is, or the little snickers in the locker room. In the mind's eye, it was all these sick people that were a menace to society. I didn't realize until after the police that there could be seemingly normal people who could cultivate a normal conversation and that I would consider as the best of friends.

## Arrested Research

"Another police practice extensively used consists of compiling lists of names of known or suspected homosexuals." [20] In connection with amassing these lists of suspects, there occurs a subtle form of police blackmail that may be quite threatening to the tearoom participants. From the beginning of my research, I had heard of the police practice of entering a tearoom—or stopping men in the vicinity of one—and demanding the name, address, place of employment, and date and place of birth of each "suspect." If the person cooperates, the officer fills out a form with the information

20. Council on Religion and the Homosexual, "Homosexual Law Reform," p. 23.

thus acquired, warns the subjects to stay away from that restroom, and no arrest takes place.

Men are frightened by such procedures. Their social identities are at stake. I know these exchanges occur frequently, because I have counselled the victims. I have also repeatedly witnessed and made notes of such pseudoarrests. Finally, I experienced this harassment myself.

On a Friday afternoon in July I was standing about ten feet outside a tearoom at the junction of two paths, talking with a potential respondent. At 2:45, a pale green Chevrolet approached at high speed from the east and turned from the road onto the path leading to the tearoom. Directly in front of the door, it came to a sudden halt; two men jumped out and ran into the tearoom, leaving both car doors ajar and the motor running. Having seen one of the men at another tearoom on Wednesday, I commented to my companion that I thought they were from the vice squad.

I could hear voices inside the tearoom. In a few minutes, an older, white-haired man emerged, replacing what appeared to be a wallet in the inside pocket of the coat he was carrying. He hurried down the walk to his car and drove off. The younger detective then emerged and walked quickly around the tearoom. A minute later, the older, taller officer, whom I had seen on Wednesday, came out of the tearoom and got into the driver's seat of the automobile. I watched them closely, without attempting to cover my interest. The younger man then sat down in the other front seat. They drove the car a few feet along the walk toward us, causing me to step onto the grass to allow their passage. As the driver came opposite me, less than a foot away, he stopped. I nodded at him, and he said, "Do you live around here?" I said, "Yes." "Where do you live?" he asked. I replied with the name of my suburb. "Do you call that close to here?" "Yes," I replied again. "Where do you live?" he asked my companion. He replied, indicating a nearby apartment building.

The older, taller officer then asked my name. "I'm sorry," I said, "that's none of your business." He turned immediately and shouted to his companion, "Put him under arrest!" The other officer jumped out of the car and ran around the front end. Grabbing hold of my arm, he pulled me back a couple of feet so the first detective could get out of the auto. Then, holding me by both arms, they put me into the back seat of the car. The younger officer got in the front seat and reached over to lock the back doors. The older man took a printed pad of forms out of his pocket and, resting it on the hood of the car, proceeded to question my companion, who gave the desired information. He then walked with the man toward the center arch dividing the two restrooms and they parted in a minute, with my acquaintance walking toward the northeast, away from the facility. The three of us then drove to the district police station. On the way, the following conversation ensued:

*Older Officer:*

Now, will you give us your name and address?

*Researcher:*

No, sir, I will not give you any information until I have talked with my attorney. [pause] I should call my wife, too, and let her know where I am.

*Younger Officer:*

You'll be allowed just one phone call at the station.

*Researcher:*

Can you tell me what the charges will be?

*Older Officer:*

You'll find out when we book you. Didn't I see you in this park the other day, driving that white Dodge?

*Researcher:*

Yes, sir, you may have. I saw you. [silence for a few blocks] I'm concerned about letting my wife know.

*Younger Officer:*

You should have thought about that before.

*Researcher:*

Before what? I'd like to know what I've done wrong.

*Younger Officer:*

Put out that cigarette!

Although it was my last, I obediently snuffed it. A little over two hours later I was released from police custody. During that time in the precinct station, I was questioned, frisked, stripped of my wallet and keys, booked on a charge of loitering, locked up in an all-metal cell, and deprived of cigarettes. In spite of much pleading on my part, I was never allowed to make a phone call. They insisted upon calling my wife for me. Suppressing her laughter, she phoned my attorney. After an extensive lecture about always giving officers my "name, rank, and serial number" and about the dangers of "hanging around those park restrooms," I was released on summons. Because I am a minister and have an astute attorney, my case never appeared in court. I am an arrest statistic, not a conviction statistic.

I suffered no harm and learned a great deal from my only experience with arrest and incarceration. I was not even forced to apprise the police of my research activities. The experience provided me with valuable data and some good conversation material. But that is because I was *who* I was, engaged in *what* I was doing. A different man, engaging in no more deviant activity than I was on that afternoon, could have been ruined. The integrity of his family, his business, and his reputation could have been destroyed in those two hours. The question remains: Is the sexual activity in public restrooms sufficiently damaging to society to warrant even the sort of degradation I endured for loitering in the park—much less the disruption of life and threat to social identity that many others suffer as a result of such vice squad activity?

The official degradation rituals of the courts and possible prison terms are not within the scope of this research. However, the data reported here do tend to confirm the conclusion of the Council on Religion and the Homosexual: "What the arrested homosexual has to fear is not the severity of his sentence, but the consequences of revelation." [21]

## When Friends Drop In

Respondents assure me that one of the more attractive aspects of the tearooms as places of sexual rendezvous is that they offer an instant alibi for one's presence. Although some park restrooms are

21. *Ibid.*, p. 18.

seldom used for rest or any other conventional purpose, all of them share a manifest function as places open to the public for elimination. A person's presence in or at such facilities is thus readily explainable. "I was driving through the park and merely dropped in to take a leak," is the common form of such excuse. There is no such instant alibi for being caught in a gay bar or in a public bath. For this reason, married men, business and professional leaders, and other highly discreditable persons tend to prefer the tearooms above any other place of homosexual exchange.

The instant alibi may fold, however, when a friend drops in on a tearoom encounter. If caught in the action, a loss of reputation might result. Even under favorable circumstances, or when the friend is also seeking sexual contact, the consequences can be embarrassing. One morning a respondent called from a pay phone in a bar and invited me to join him for a drink. When asked, "Why this early?" he replied:

> I need one! I'm still shaking from a scare I had this morning. [What happened?] I stopped to cruise that tearoom on the north side of the park. Well, I was there, cruising this good-looking young man, and one of the men from the plant walked in. . . . [What did you do?] Well, this other fellow and I both had a hard on—but I lost mine fast and got out of there! I tried to act calm but it probably didn't work. [Did you speak to him?] We said "Hello" to each other—but thank God he didn't call me by name!

Some men attempt to cover this threat by operating only in parks far removed from their homes and businesses; however, the vast majority stay close to their regular routes of travel, thus keeping the instant alibi in constant readiness.

## Teen-agers and Toughs

As has already been pointed out, teen-agers may cause police intrusion on the tearoom scene even when they are not acting the decoy role. In the city where most of my observation took place, police cruisers tend to remain parked some distance away from the active tearooms, usually at a point where the scene may be easily surveyed. The approach of a teen-ager has been seen to bring law enforcement officers into immediate action. In other parks, elderly men are hired to sit on benches in uniform (or at least with conspicuous badges), in order to see that youths stay out of the facilities. Although these may be wise precautionary strategies on the part of the police, I do not think them necessary—or even particularly effective. As some of the systematic observations quoted in previous chapters show, tearoom activity does not seem to lessen when an officer is seated outside the interaction membrane. It is doubtful that many could be persuaded to spend their working hours inside.

Penetration of the encounter's boundaries by persons who are obviously minors (both of the men under twenty-one in my sample *appear* to be in their early twenties) results in disruption of the action. The possibility of such entries' triggering police reaction is probably the least of the reasons for this panic reaction. The primary cause is the tendency of the teen-age role to melt. Straights will walk in and out again, but enlisters tend only to inhibit the progress of the game. It is too difficult to distinguish them from hustlers or toughs.

Because the tearoom expectation, in Hooker's words, is "that sex may be had without obligation or commitment," the hustler is neither desired nor appreciated in these settings. He is looked upon only as an annoyance or potential threat. Outside tearooms, throughout the parks and on city streets, these male prostitutes operate with more success.

One park, in particular, seemed to draw a large number of these young men. It is situated in a part of the city to which large numbers of lower class whites have lately migrated from southern states. This area of the city has a large teen-age population. Throughout the summer months, youths walk along the drives, hoping to hitch a ride with a "score." When someone parks near an active tearoom, two or three boys are apt to lean in the window before the driver can get out; "Got a dollar mister?," a boy about thirteen will say; "I'll let you suck my cock." Because participants lack normal recourse to the law, they fear that an abrupt refusal may bring physical attack from a group of youths. With some practice, regulars in this action will learn to play it cool, joking with the teen-agers while firmly rejecting their offers. Often they ask for cigarettes as an opener in the pick-up game. It is best to yield to their demands without prolonging the interaction. Without the exchange of cash, the teen-ager may turn tough in a short period of time.

On a Thursday in August, I experienced an encounter inside a tearoom in which mild harassment from youngsters turned to an exchange of name-calling and thence to violence. Beginning with four youths (estimated ages from fourteen to sixteen) who ran in and out of the restroom to disrupt the action, the group swelled to eleven within thirty minutes. They began to yell and make lewd gestures toward those of us inside. In the midst of the tension, an unusual phenomenon occurred: the rule of silence was relaxed. The participants began to communicate in loud voices, even with sexual activity in progress. One very masculine and well-dressed young participant began to shout through the window to the teen-agers: "Tell that one in the red pants I'll take care of him if he wants it."

In a few minutes, it was necessary for those of us serving as lookouts to brace ourselves against the door to prevent their entering. (A sexual act in a stall was in the payoff phase.) Finally, after two of the five participants had left to run for their cars, a tough ran up and wedged a stick in the hasp of the door. During the next half hour, the three remaining participants endured a barrage of stones and bottles, which broke every window in the facility, scattering glass the full width of the floor. Even had we been able to exit, I doubt that any of us would have ventured out.

Finally, the toughs tired of their game and one removed the stick from the door. We exited with only a few remarks hurled at us. Fortunately, none of us was injured. All of us were a little more convinced that the teen-ager is a source of danger.

## Venereal Disease

Another threat to be considered is the risk of infection from venereal disease. Interviews conducted with two staff members of a V. D. clinic operated by the Public Health Service produced few substantial data. Plagued by the suspicion that infected persons tend to conceal any homosexual involvement, the staff members could only provide us with estimates. The more dependable of these data follow:

Out of 102 male cases of reported syphilis in the city in 1967, thirty-three admitted having one or more male contacts. This figure is consistent with reports taken elsewhere in the United States. A physician interviewed estimated that sixty to seventy per cent of the clinic's cases resulted from homosexual contacts. But it is important that neither of the officials remembered any *oral* cases of syphilis during the previous year (both men were new at this work). They joined in guessing that ninety-five per cent of the homosexual cases were anally contracted, but they lacked data on oral infections.

Dr. William Masters, the noted authority on human sexual behavior, when interviewed on this subject, could recall having seen one oral syphilitic chancre (on the tonsils) in the course of his medical experience. Beyond this, he could state only that, for syphilis at least, evidence of oral contagion is very rare.

The only medical literature to which the venereal disease control people refer for information on the subject of infection resulting from homosexual behavior is a single paper of little assistance, at least as regards syphilis. Published in 1944, it says only that: "The man or woman with chancre of the soft palate or tonsil should be suspected of having practiced fellatio." It then lists four such cases as having been reported in all the literature on venereal disease up to the time of publication: One was reported by Krafft-Ebing in 1898, and three persons, all of whom "confessed to bestial practices," evidenced chancre of the tonsil in a report by Bulkely in 1894.[22]

A number of cases of oral infection of a gonorrheal nature have been reported, but, with the possible exceptions listed above, I have been unable to find data indicating the buccal cavity as a locale of syphilitic infection. Nearly all of the cases of syphilis reported as resulting from homosexual contact were contracted through anal intercourse.

22. Josephine Hinrichsen, "The Importance of a Knowledge of Sexual Habits in the Diagnosis and Control of Venereal Disease, with Special Reference to Homosexual Behavior," *The Urologic and Cutaneous Review*, Vol. XLVIII, No. 10, p. 3. This reprint is an encyclopedia of misinformation on homosexuality, interesting only in that it reflects the mythology of the pre-Kinsey period.

This is important in terms of tearoom sex. If anal intercourse is the sole source of syphilitic infections from homosexual contact, this disease consititutes a very minor threat to tearoom participants. I have already noted that anal intercourse occurred in only about 1 per cent of the tearoom encounters observed, the sexual contact being almost exclusively of an oral-genital nature in such facilities.

My interviews support this assessment. None of the cooperating respondents admits having had syphilis at any time in his sexual history, although four report having had gonorrheal infections. All four of these cases resulted from anal intercourse, and none of them were contracted in the tearooms.

This information is only indicative. It is to be hoped that some person with sufficient medical knowledge will undertake research in this area. First, he should attempt to test the hypothesis that fellatio is seldom, if ever, a source of syphilitic infection. Subsequently, he might try to find out why. Is there, perhaps, some ingredient in human saliva that inhibits or destroys the syphilis spirochete? Meanwhile, it must be conjectured that the sexual practices within the tearooms pose no threat of the spread of syphilis and very little threat of spreading any other venereal disease.

## Who Is in Danger?

Thus far, we have considered only the dangers to which tearoom participants are normally subject because of their encounters. At least from the police and the toughs, these threats are severe enough to provide an objective basis for the fear that maintains the excitement, the risk-taking nature of this game.

There remains the possibility that the risks of the game are incumbent upon the outside world—that even those who are ignorant of what goes on in those little buildings in the parks may be harmed by these encounters. According to the data at hand, this activity constitutes no threat to physical health through the spread of venereal disease. It is also strongly evident that, because of cautions built into the strategies of the encounters, no grown men need fear being molested in those facilities.

Within the interaction membrane itself, there seems to be only one possibility for threat to public safety or morals left to be considered: what about the youngster? Might he be seduced into sexual involvement? Is there danger of recruitment into the homosexual practices of the tearoom?

All indications of this investigation are that recruitment into homosexual activity is a rare phenomenon. When seduction (and I here use this term as synonymous with recruitment) does occur, it is usually in the privacy of the home, the automobile, the tutor's study or private garden. In these settings, a high degree of consent to availability has already been given and the social definition of the situation is such as to preclude the need for further consent.

In my interview sample of fifty tearoom participants, one man (Tim) was nineteen, another twenty. All others were adults. In the fifty systematic observations, 173 participants were seen. Of these, nine were thought to be minors: two (both estimated as being twenty) were insertors who actively sought involvement; one stood by and masturbated; two were enlisters who were attempting, without success, to be involved in the play; and four were toughs who intruded into the action. A number of other toughs and hustlers stood around outside. After one such encounter, as we walked along the path from a restroom, I asked a man about the youngster whose arrival had occasioned our departure: "What's the matter," I inquired, "Aren't you interested in that one back there?" "Shit!" he replied, "I've got enough problems as it is without getting mixed up with one of those."

Both the observations and interviews of this study indicate that the public concern with recruitment of boys by homosexual men is doubly misplaced. What seduction there is occurs in private settings. The teen-agers I have observed in tearooms are too busy enlisting to allow for recruitment.

This is not to say that many persons, including the young, might not be embarrassed by what they might stumble upon in public restrooms. Participants in the game take every precaution possible to preclude embarrassment, but there are bound to be sudden entries that will catch men with their flies unzipped. Protection against public embarrassment is governed by the structure of face-to-face interaction and should require neither severe legal sanctions nor their rigorous enforcement. It is not necessary to use atomic weapons for killing flies. As MacNamara has pointed out:

> That society has the right, and indeed the duty, to protect itself against sexual violence, and to prevent sexual aggression or seduction directed at its young, is incontestable. That society may rightly discourage or prevent sexually motivated nuisance conduct is equally defensible. That highly restrictive laws and rigorous penal sanctions contribute to the realization of these objectives is not demonstrable.[23]

The remaining possibility, then, is that sexual activity in the tearoom is socially damaging in its effect on the lives and families of the men who engage in it. In the next chapter, this question will be given careful consideration on the basis of data gained by methods other than those of participant observation.

23. Donal E. J. MacNamara, "Sex Offenses and Sex Offenders," *The Annals of The American Academy of Political and Social Science*, 376 (March, 1968), 150.

# *Chapter 6.* The People Next Door

It was hard for me to grasp that men respected in their professions and devoted to their families could also be involved in furtive, "queer" behavior. That happened in flashy novels, not to the people next door.[1]

IN PREVIOUS chapters we have looked at a special kind of organized activity that attracts a large number of participants—enough to produce the majority of arrests for homosexual offenses in the United States. Now, employing data gained from both formal and informal interviews, we shall consider what these men are like away from the scenes of impersonal sex. "For some people," says Hooker, "the seeking of sexual contacts with other males is an activity isolated from all other aspects of their lives." [2] Such segregation is apparent with most men who engage in the homosexual activity of public restrooms; but the degree and manner in which

1. From "Tragic Marriage," an article by an anonymous wife of a homosexual, in *Good Housekeeping,* Vol. 167, No. 1 (July, 1968), pp. 40, 42.
2. Evelyn Hooker, "Male Homosexuals and Their 'Worlds,'" in Judd Marmor, ed., *Sexual Inversion* (New York: Basic Books, 1965), p. 92.

"deviant" is isolated from "normal" behavior in their lives will be seen to vary along social dimensions.

For the man who lives next door, the tearoom participant is just another neighbor—and probably a very good one at that. He may make a little more money than the next man and work a little harder for it.[3] It is likely that he will drive a nicer car and maintain a neater yard than do other neighbors in the block. Maybe, like some tearoom regulars, he will work with Boy Scouts in the evenings and spend much of his weekend at the church. It may be more surprising for the outsider to discover that most of these men are married.

As I have indicated previously, the majority (54 per cent) of my research subjects are married and living with their wives. From the data at hand, there is no evidence that these unions are particularly unstable; nor does it appear that any of the wives are aware of their husbands' secret sexual activity. Indeed, the husbands choose public restrooms as sexual settings partly to avoid just such exposure. I see no reason to dispute the claim of a number of tearoom respondents that their preference for a form of concerted action that is fast and impersonal is largely predicated on a desire to protect their family relationships.

Superficial analysis of the data indicates that the maintenance of exemplary marriages—at least in appearance—is very important to the subjects of this study. In answering questions such as "When it comes to making decisions in your household, who generally makes them?," the participants indicate they are more apt to defer to their mates than are those in the control sample. They also indicate that they find it more important to "get along well" with their wives. In the open-ended questions regarding marital relationships, they tend to speak of them in more glowing terms.

Upon rereading the interview schedules, however, a pattern emerges in the marriages of participants that may best be expressed in terms of what Rainwater calls conjugal role segregation:

> Segregated conjugal role-relationship refers to relationships in which the predominant pattern of marital life involves activities of husband

3. Although the samples were matched by job classifications, the participants report an average work week of 50.5 hours, against 45 hours for those in the control sample. See also Table 6.1.

and wife that are separate and different but fitted together to form a functioning unit or that are carried out separately by husband and wife with a minimum of day-to-day articulation of the activity of each to the other.[4]

Eleven (40.7 per cent) of the twenty-seven married couples represented in the deviant sample manifest this sort of role relationship. This is true of only three couples in the control group. An example of such a segregated relationship, as rearranged from data in the interview schedule, follows:

## The Role Relationship of Tom and Myra

This handsome couple live in ranch-style suburbia with their two young children. Tom is in his early thirties—an aggressive, muscular, and virile-looking male. He works "about seventy-five hours a week" at his new job as a chemist. "I am *wild* about my job," he says. "I really love it!" Both of Tom's "really close" friends he met at work.

He is Methodist and Myra a Roman Catholic, but each goes to his or her own church. Although he claims to have broad interests in life, they boil down to "games—sports like touch football or baseball."

When I asked him to tell me something about his family, Tom replied only in terms of their "good fortune" that things are not worse:

> We've been fortunate that a religious problem has not occurred. We're fortunate in having two healthy children. We're fortunate that we decided to leave my last job. Being married has made me more stable.

They have been married for eleven years, and Myra is the older of the two. When asked who makes what kinds of decisions in his family, he said: "She makes most decisions about the family. She keeps the books. But I make the *major* decisions."

4. Lee Rainwater, *Family Design: Marital Sexuality, Family Size, and Contraception* (Chicago: Aldine, 1965), p. 30. Here, Rainwater is following the conceptual approach developed by Elizabeth Bott, *Family and Social Network* (London: Tavistock, 1957), pp. 53–55.

Myra does the household work and takes care of the children. Perceiving his main duties as those of "keeping the yard up" and "bringing home the bacon," Tom sees as his wife's only shortcoming "her lack of discipline in organization." He remarked:

> She's very attractive . . . has a fair amount of poise. The best thing is that she gets along well and is able to establish close relationships with other women.

Finally, when asked how he thinks his wife feels about him and his behavior in the family, Tom replied: "She'd like to have me around more–would like for me to have a closer relationship with her and the kids." He believes it is "very important" to have the kind of sex life he needs. Reporting that he and Myra have intercourse about twice a month, he feels that his sexual needs are "adequately met" in his relationships with his wife. I also know that, from time to time, Tom has sex in the restrooms of a public park.

As an upwardly mobile man, Tom was added to the sample at a point of transition in his career as a tearoom participant. If Tom is like others who share working class origins, he may have learned of the tearoom as an economical means of achieving orgasm during his Navy years. Of late, he has returned to the restrooms for occasional sexual "relief," since his wife, objecting to the use of birth control devices, has limited his conjugal outlets.

Tom still perceives his sexual needs in the symbolic terms of the class in which he was socialized: "about twice a month" is the frequency of intercourse generally reported by working class men; and, although they are reticent in reporting it, they do not perceive this frequency as adequate to meet their sexual needs, which they estimate are about the same as those felt by others of their age. My interviews indicate that such perceptions of sexual drive and satisfaction prevail among working class respondents, whereas they are uncommon for those of the upper-middle and upper classes. Among the latter, the reported perception is of both a much higher frequency of intercourse and needs greater in their estimation than those of "most other men."

## The Aging Crisis

Not only is Tom moving into a social position that may cause him to reinterpret his sexual drive, he is also approaching a point of major crisis in his career as a tearoom participant. At the time when I observed him in an act of fellatio, he played the insertor role. Still relatively young and handsome, Tom finds himself sought out as "trade." [5] Not only is that the role he expects to play in the tearoom encounters, it is the role others expect of him.

"I'm not toned up anymore," Tom complains. He is gaining weight around the middle and losing hair. As he moves past thirty-five, Tom will face the aging crisis of the tearooms. Less and less frequently will he find himself the one sought out in these meetings. Presuming that he has been sufficiently reinforced to continue this form of sexual operation, he will be forced to seek other men. As trade he was not expected to reciprocate, but he will soon be increasingly expected to serve as insertee for those who have first taken that role for him.

In most cases, fellatio is a service performed by an older man upon a younger. In one encounter, for example, a man appearing to be around forty was observed as insertee with a man in his twenties as insertor. A few minutes later, the man of forty was being sucked by one in his fifties. Analyzing the estimated ages of the principal partners in 53 observed acts of fellatio, I arrived at these conclusions: the insertee was judged to be older than the insertor in forty cases; they were approximately the same age in three; and the insertor was the older in ten instances. The age differences ranged from an insertee estimated to be twenty-five years older than his partner to an insertee thought to be ten years younger than his insertor.

From the interviewed respondents, for whom the ages are known rather than estimated, a like picture emerges: 78 per cent of those age twenty-four or less were observed taking the insertor role: 63 per cent of those in the twenty-five to thirty-four age range were

5. In the homosexual argot, "trade" are those men who make themselves available for acts of fellatio but who, regarding themselves as "straight," refuse to reciprocate in the sexual act.

insertors; but only 46 per cent of men in the thirty-five to forty-four range were insertors when observed, as were only 8 per cent of those forty-five and older.

Strong references to this crisis of aging are found in my interviews with cooperating respondents, one of whom had this to say:

> Well, I started off as the straight young thing. Everyone wanted to suck my cock. I wouldn't have been caught dead with one of the things in my mouth! . . . So, here I am at forty–with grown kids–and the biggest cocksucker in [the city]!

Similar experiences were expressed, in more reserved language, by another man, some fifteen years his senior:

> I suppose I was around thirty-five–or thirty-six–when I started giving out blow jobs. It just got so I couldn't operate any other way in the park johns. I'd still rather have a good blow job any day, but I've gotten so I like it the way it is now.

Perhaps by now the writings of Hooker, Hoffman, and others have dispelled the idea that men who engage in homosexual acts may be typed by any consistency of performance in one or another sexual role. Undoubtedly, there are preferences: few persons are so adaptable, their conditioning so undifferentiated, that they fail to exercise choice between various sexual roles and positions. Such preferences, however, are learned, and sexual repertories tend to expand with time and experience. This study of restroom sex indicates that sexual roles within these encounters are far from stable. They are apt to change within an encounter, from one encounter to another, with age, and with the amount of exposure to influences from a sexually deviant subculture.

It is to this last factor that I should like to direct the reader's attention. The degree of contact with a network of friends who share the actor's sexual interests takes a central position in mediating not only his preferences for sex role, but his style of adaptation to–and rationalization of–the deviant activity in which he participates. There are, however, two reasons why I have not classified research subjects in terms of their participation in the homosexual subculture. It is difficult to measure accurately the degree of such involvement; and such subcultural interaction depends upon other social variables, two of which are easily measured.

The first of these characteristics is marital status. In his study of jazz musicians, Becker pointed out that "the musician's family (both the one he is born into and the one he creates by marrying) has a major effect on his career." [6] Family status has a definitive effect on the deviant careers of those whose concern is with controlling information about their sexual behavior. The married man who engages in homosexual activity must be much more cautious about his involvement in the subculture than his single counterpart. As a determinant of life style and sexual activity, marital status is also a determinant of the patterns of deviant adaptation and rationalization. Only those in my sample who were divorced or separated from their wives were difficult to categorize as either married or single. Those who had been married, however, showed a tendency to remain in friendship networks with married men. Three of the four were still limited in freedom by responsibilities for their children. For these reasons, I have included all men who were once married in the "married" categories.

The second determining variable is the relative autonomy of the respondent's occupation. A man is "independently" employed when his job allows him freedom of movement and security from being fired; the most obvious example is self-employment. Occupational "dependence" leaves a man little freedom for engaging in disreputable activity. The sales manager or other executive of a business firm has greater freedom than the salesman or attorney who is employed in the lower echelons of a large industry or by the federal government. The sales representative whose territory is far removed from the home office has greater independence, in terms of information control, than the minister of a local congregation. The majority of those placed in both the married and unmarried categories with *dependent* occupations were employed by large industries or the government.

Median education levels and annual family incomes displayed in Table 6.1 indicate that those with dependent occupations rank lower on the socioeconomic scale. Only in the case of married men, however, is this correlation between social class and occupational

6. Howard S. Becker, *Outsiders* (New York: The Free Press, 1963), p. 103.

autonomy strongly supported by the ratings of these respondents on Warner's Index of Status Characteristics (see Chapter 2). Nearly all the married men with dependent occupations are of the upper-lower or lower-middle classes, whereas those with independent occupations are of the upper-middle or upper classes. For single men, the social class variable is neither so easily identifiable nor so clearly divided. Nearly all single men in the sample can be classified only as "vaguely middle class."

As occupational autonomy and marital status remain the most important dimensions along which participants may be ranked, we shall consider four general types of tearoom customers: (1) married men with dependent occupations, (2) married men with independent occupations, (3) unmarried men with independent occupations, and (4) unmarried men with dependent occupations. As will become evident with the discussion of each type, I have employed labels from the homosexual argot, along with pseudonyms, to designate each class of participants. This is done not only to facilitate reading but to emphasize that we are describing persons rather than merely "typical" constructs. In the following table, the defining variables are to be found in the second and third rows ("Marital Status" and "Occupations"), the first row presenting the labels for each class and the names I have chosen for each typical representative.

## Type I: Trade

The first classification, which includes nineteen of the participants (38 per cent), may be called "trade," since most would earn that appellation from the gay subculture. All of these men are, or have been, married—one was separated from his wife at the time of interviewing and another was divorced.

Most work as truck drivers, machine operators, or clerical workers (see Table 6.1). There is a member of the armed forces, a carpenter, and the minister of a pentecostal church. Most of their wives work, at least part-time, to help raise their median annual family income to $8,000. One in six of these men is black. All are normally masculine in appearance and mannerism. Although four-

*Table 6.1: Characteristics of Tearoom Participants by Type, Compared with Control Sample*

| *Type:* <br> *[Number]* | *Type I* <br> *"Trade"* <br> *(George)* <br> *[19]* | *Type II* <br> *"Ambisexual"* <br> *(Dwight)* <br> *[12]* | *Type III* <br> *"Gay"* <br> *(Ricky)* <br> *[7]* | *Type IV* <br> *"Closet Queens"* <br> *(Arnold)* <br> *[12]* | *Total* <br> *Participants* <br> [50] | *Total* <br> *Controls* <br> *"Straights"* <br> [50] |
|---|---|---|---|---|---|---|
| | *Married* | | *Single* | | | |
| Marital Status | 1 div. <br> 1 sep. <br> 17 m. | 2 div. <br> 10 m. | 7 s. | 12 s. | 3 div. <br> 1 sep. <br> 19 s. <br> 27 m. | 3 div. <br> 0 sep. <br> 20 s. <br> 27 m. |
| | *Dependent* | *Independent* | | *Dependent* | | |
| Occupations | semiskilled, truck drivers, army; 11 large industry, 3 government | executives, decorators, sales; 1 large industry | students, artist, beautician | clerical workers, teachers, sales; 6 large ind; 2 gov't. | Matched on I.S.C. job classification. Lacking in lower-lower class representation. | |

| | | | | | | |
|---|---|---|---|---|---|---|
| Median Education Level | 12 grades | 16 grades | 16 grades | 14 grades | 14 grades | 15 grades |
| Median Annual Family Income | $8,000 | $16,000 | $3,000 | $6,000 | $9,000 | $7,000 |
| Mean No. Children for Those Wed | 2.2 | 1.6 | ——— | ——— | 1.9 | 2.6 |
| Mean No. Friends | 4.3 | 5.6 | 7.1 | 4.6 | 4.9 | 4.9 |
| Sex Role: | 1 no data | | | 1 no data | 2 no data | 50 no data |
| Insertees | 6 | 9 | 4 | 5 | 24 | ——— |
| Insertors | 12 | 3 | 3 | 6 | 24 | ——— |
| Median Age | 38 | 43 | 24 | 32 | 34 | 39 |
| Present Religion | 12 RC | 5 Episc.<br>3 Prot. | 3 Unit.<br>2 RC | 6 RC | 20 RC<br>6 Episc.<br>8 None | 12 RC<br>2 Episc.<br>12 None |

teen have completed high school, there are only three college graduates among them, and five have had less than twelve years of schooling.

George is representative of this largest group of respondents. Born of second-generation German parentage in an ethnic enclave of the midwestern city where he still resides, he was raised as a Lutheran. He feels that his father (like George a truck driver) was quite warm in his relationship with him as a child. His mother he describes as a very nervous, asthmatic woman and thinks that an older sister suffered a nervous breakdown some years ago, although she was never treated for it. Another sister and a brother have evidenced no emotional problems.

At the age of twenty he married a Roman Catholic girl and has since joined her church, although he classifies himself as "lapsed." In the fourteen years of their marriage, they have had seven children, one of whom is less than a year old. George doesn't think they should have more children, but his wife objects to using any type of birth control other than the rhythm method. With his wife working part-time as a waitress, they have an income of about $5,000.

"How often do you have intercourse with your wife?" I asked. "Not very much the last few years," he replied. "It's up to when she feels like giving it to me—which ain't very often. I never suggest it."

George was cooking hamburgers on an outdoor grill and enjoying a beer as I interviewed him. "Me, I like to come home," he asserted. "I love to take care of the outside of the house. . . . Like to go places with the children—my wife, she doesn't."

With their mother at work, the children were running in and out of the door, revealing a household interior in gross disarray. George stopped to call one of the smaller youngsters out of the street in front of his modest, suburban home. When he resumed his remarks about his wife, there was more feeling in his description:

> My wife doesn't have much outside interest. She doesn't like to go out or take the kids places. But she's an A-1 mother, I'll say that! I guess you'd say she's very nice to get along with—but don't cross her! She gets aggravated with me—I don't know why. . . . Well, you'd have to know my wife. We fight all the time. Anymore, it seems we just don't

get along—except when we're apart. Mostly, we argue about the kids. She's afraid of having more. . . . She's afraid to have sex but doesn't believe in birth control. I'd just rather not be around her! I won't suggest having sex anyway—and she just doesn't want it anymore.

While more open than most in his acknowledgement of marital tension, George's appraisal of sexual relations in the marriage is typical of those respondents classified as trade. In 63 per cent of these marriages, the wife, husband, or both are Roman Catholic. When answering questions about their sexual lives, a story much like George's emerged: at least since the birth of the last child, conjugal relations have been very rare.

These data suggest that, along with providing an excuse for diminishing intercourse with their wives, the religious teachings to which most of these families adhere may cause the husbands to search for sex in the tearooms. Whatever the causes that turn them unsatisfied from the marriage bed, however, the alternative outlet must be quick, inexpensive, and impersonal. Any personal, ongoing affair—any outlet requiring money or hours away from home—would threaten a marriage that is already shaky and jeopardize the most important thing these men possess, their standing as father of their children.

Around the turn of the century, before the vice squads moved in (in their never ending process of narrowing the behavioral options of those in the lower classes), the Georges of this study would probably have made regular visits to the two-bit bordellos. With a madam watching a clock to limit the time, these cheap whorehouses provided the same sort of fast, impersonal service as today's public restrooms. I find no indication that these men seek homosexual contact as such; rather, they want a form of orgasm-producing action that is less lonely than masturbation and less involving than a love relationship. As the forces of social control deprive them of one outlet, they provide another. The newer form, it should be noted, is more stigmatizing than the previous one—thus giving "proof" to the adage that "the sinful are drawn ever deeper into perversity."

George was quite affable when interviewed on his home territory. A year before, when I first observed him in the tearoom of a park about three miles from his home, he was a far more cautious man. Situated at the window of the restroom, I saw him leave his old station wagon and, looking up and down the street, walk to the facility at a very fast pace. Once inside, he paced nervously from door to window until satisfied that I would serve as an adequate lookout. After playing the insertor role with a man who had waited in the stall farthest from the door, he left quickly, without wiping or washing his hands, and drove away toward the nearest exit from the park. In the tearoom he was a frightened man, engaging in furtive sex. In his own back yard, talking with an observer whom he failed to recognize, he was warm, open, and apparently at ease.

Weighing two hundred pounds or more, George has a protruding gut and tattoos on both forearms. Although muscular and in his mid-thirties, he would not be described as a handsome person. For him, no doubt, the aging crisis is also an identity crisis. Only with reluctance—and perhaps never—will he turn to the insertee role. The threat of such a role to his masculine self-image is too great. Like others of his class with whom I have had more extensive interviews, George may have learned this sexual game as a teen-age hustler, or else when serving in the army during the Korean war. In either case, his socialization into homosexual experience took place in a masculine world where it is permissible to accept money from a "queer" in return for carefully limited sexual favors. But to use one's own mouth as a substitute for the female organ, or even to express enjoyment of the action, is taboo in the trade code.[7]

Moreover, for men of George's occupational and marital status, there is no network of friends engaged in tearoom activity to help them adapt to the changes aging will bring. I found no evidence of friendship networks among respondents of this type, who enter and leave the restrooms alone, avoiding conversation while within. Marginal to both the heterosexual and homosexual worlds, these men shun involvement in any form of gay subculture. Type I participants report fewer friends of any sort than do those of other classes. When asked how many close friends he has, George answered: "None. I haven't got time for that."

It is difficult to interview the trade without becoming depressed over the hopelessness of their situation. They are almost uniformly

7. Albert J. Reiss, Jr., "The Social Integration of Queers and Peers," *Social Problems,* Vol. 9, No. 2 (Fall, 1961), p. 114.

lonely and isolated: lacking success in either marriage bed or work, unable to discuss their three best friends (because they don't have three), en route from the din of factories to the clamor of children, they slip off the freeways for a few moments of impersonal sex in a toilet stall.

Such unrewarded existence is reflected in the portrait of another marginal man. A jobless Negro, he earns only contempt and sexual rejection from his working wife in return for baby-sitting duties. The paperback books and magazines scattered about his living room supported his comment that he reads a great deal to relieve boredom. (George seldom reads even the newspaper and has no hobbies to report.) No wonder that he urged me to stay for supper when my interview schedule was finished. "I really wish you'd stay awhile," he said. "I haven't talked to anyone about myself in a hell of a long time!"

## Type II: The Ambisexuals

A very different picture emerges in the case of Dwight. As sales manager for a small manufacturing concern, he is in a position to hire men who share his sexual and other interests. Not only does he have a business associate or two who share his predilection for tearoom sex, he has been able to stretch chance meetings in the tearoom purlieu into long-lasting friendships. Once, after I had gained his confidence through repeated interviews, I asked him to name all the participants he knew. The names of five other Type II men in my sample were found in the list of nearly two dozen names he gave me.

Dwight, then, has social advantages in the public restrooms as well as in society at large. His annual income of $16,000 helps in the achievement of these benefits, as does his marriage into a large and distinguished family and his education at a prestigious local college. From his restroom friends Dwight learns which tearooms in the city are popular and where the police are clamping down. He even knows which officers are looking for payoffs and how much they expect to be paid. It is of even greater importance that his attitudes toward—and perceptions of—the tearoom encounters are shaped and reinforced by the friendship network in which he participates.

It has thus been easier for Dwight to meet the changing demands of the aging crisis. He knows others who lost no self-respect when they began "going down" on their sexual partners, and they have helped him learn to enjoy the involvement of oral membranes in impersonal sex. As Tom, too, moves into this class of participants, he can be expected to learn how to rationalize the switch in sexual roles necessitated by the loss of youthful good looks. He will cease thinking of the insertee role as threatening to his masculinity. His socialization into the ambisexuals will make the orgasm but one of a number of kicks to be found in such sexual encounters.

Three-fourths of the married participants with independent occupations were observed, at one time or another, participating as insertees in fellatio, compared to only one-third of the trade. Not only do the Type II participants tend to switch roles with greater facility, they seem inclined to search beyond the tearooms for more exotic forms of sexual experience. Dwight, along with others in his class, expresses a liking for anal intercourse (both as insertee and insertor), for group activity, and even for mild forms of sadomasochistic sex. A friend of his once invited me to an "orgy" he had planned in an apartment he maintains for sexual purposes. Another friend, a social and commercial leader of the community, told me that he enjoys having men urinate in his mouth between acts of fellatio.

Dwight is in his early forties and has two sons in high school. The school-bound offspring provide him with an excuse to leave his wife at home during frequent business trips across the country. Maintaining a list of gay contacts, Dwight is able to engage wholeheartedly in the life of the homosexual subculture in other cities—the sort of involvement he is careful to avoid at home. In the parks or over cocktails, he amuses his friends with lengthy accounts of these adventures.

Dwight recounts his first sexual relationship with another boy at the age of "nine or ten":

My parents always sent me off to camp in the summer, and it was there that I had my sexual initiation. This sort of thing usually took the form of rolling around in a bunk together and ended in our jacking each other off. . . . I suppose I started pretty early. God, I was almost in college before I had my first woman! I always had some other guy on the string in prep school–some real romances there! But I made up for lost time with the girls during my college years. . . . During that time, I only slipped back into my old habits a couple of times–and then it was a once-only occurrence with a roommate after we had been drinking.

Culminating an active heterosexual life at the university, Dwight married the girl he had impregnated. He reports having intercourse three or four times a week with her throughout their eighteen married years but also admits to supplementing that activity on occasion: "I had the seven-year-itch and stepped out on her quite a bit then." Dwight also visits the tearooms almost daily:

> I guess you might say I'm pretty highly sexed [he chuckled a little], but I really don't think that's why I go to tearooms. That's really not sex. Sex is something I have with my wife in bed. It's not as if I were committing adultery by getting my rocks off–or going down on some guy–in a tearoom. I get a kick out of it. Some of my friends go out for handball. I'd rather cruise the park. Does that sound perverse to you?

Dwight's openness in dealing with the more sensitive areas of his biography was typical of upper-middle and upper class respondents of both the participant and control samples. As was mentioned in Chapter 2, actual refusals of interviews came almost entirely from lower class participants; more of the cooperating respondents were of the upper socioeconomic ranks. In the same vein, working class respondents were most cautious about answering questions pertaining to their income and their social and political views.

Other researchers have encountered a similar response differential along class lines, and I realize that my educational and social characteristics encourage rapport with Dwight more than with George. It may also be assumed that sympathy with survey research increases with education. Two-thirds of the married participants with occupational independence are college graduates.

It has been suggested, however, that another factor may be operative in this instance: although the upper class deviants may have more to lose from exposure (in the sense that the mighty have farther to fall), they also have more means at their disposal with which to protect their moral histories.[8] As noted in Chapter 5, some need only tap their spending money to pay off a member of the vice squad. In other instances, social contacts with police commissioners or newpaper publishers make it possible to squelch either record or publicity of an arrest. One respondent has made substantial contributions to a police charity fund, while another hired private detectives to track down a blackmailer. Not least in their capacity to cover for errors in judgment is the fact that their word has the backing of economic and social influence. Evidence must be strong to prosecute a man who can hire the best attorneys. Lower class men are rightfully more suspicious, for they have fewer resources with which to defend themselves if exposed.

This does not mean that Type II participants are immune to the risks of the game but simply that they are bidding from strength. To them, the risks of arrest, exposure, blackmail, or physical assault contribute to the excitement quotient. It is not unusual for them to speak of cruising as an adventure, in contrast with the trade, who engage in a furtive search for sexual relief. On the whole, then, the action of Type II respondents is apt to be somewhat bolder and their search for "kicks" less inhibited than that of most other types of participants.

Dwight is not fleeing from an unhappy home life or sexless marriage to the encounters in the parks. He expresses great devotion to his wife and children: "They're my whole life," he exclaims. All evidence indicates that, as father, citizen, businessman, and church member, Dwight's behavior patterns–as viewed by his peers–are exemplary.

Five of the twelve participants in Dwight's class are members of the Episcopal church. Dwight is one of two who were raised in that church, although he is not as active a churchman as some who became Episcopalians later in life. In spite of his infrequent attendance at worship, he feels his church is "just right" for him and needs no changing. Its tradition and ceremony are intellectually and esthetically pleasing to him. Its liberal outlook on questions of morality round out a religious orientation that he finds generally supportive.

8. The author is indebted to John I. Kitsuse for this valuable suggestion, giving rise to the analysis of types in terms of their resources for information control.

In an interview witnessed by a friend he had brought to meet me, Dwight discussed his relationship with his parents: "Father ignored me. He just never said anything to me. I don't think he ever knew I existed." [His father was an attorney, esteemed beyond the city of Dwight's birth, who died while his only son was yet in his teens.] "I hope I'm a better father to my boys than he was to me," Dwight added.

"But his mother is a remarkable woman," the friend interjected, "really one of the most fabulous women I've met! Dwight took me back to meet her—years ago, when we were lovers of a sort. I still look forward to her visits."

"She's remarkable just to have put up with me," Dwight added:

> Just to give you an idea, one vacation I brought another boy home from school with me. She walked into the bedroom one morning and caught us bare-assed in a 69 position. She just excused herself and backed out of the room. Later, when we were alone, she just looked at me—over the edge of her glasses—and said: "I'm not going to lecture you, dear, but I do hope you don't swallow that stuff!"

Although he has never had a nervous breakdown, Dwight takes "an occasional antidepressant" because of his "moodiness." "I'm really quite moody, and I go to the tearooms more often when my spirits are low." While his periods of depression may result in increased tearoom activity, this deviant behavior does not seem to produce much tension in his life:

> I don't feel guilty about my little sexual games in the park. I'm not some sort of sick queer. . . . You might think I live two lives; but, if I do, I don't feel split in two by them.

Unlike the trade, Type II participants recognize their homosexual activity as indicative of their own psychosexual orientations. They think of themselves as bisexual or ambisexual and have intellectualized their deviant tendencies in terms of the pseudopsychology of the popular press. They speak often of the great men of history, as well as of certain movie stars and others of contemporary fame, who are also "AC/DC."[9] Goffman has remarked

9. Because these men label themselves as Ambisexual, I call them that; however, most of those in other categories may also engage in heterosexual as well as homosexual behavior.

that stigmatized Americans "tend to live in a literarily-defined world." [10] This is nowhere truer than of the subculturally oriented participants of this study. Not only do they read a great deal about homosexuality, they discuss it within their network of friends. For the Dwights there is subcultural support that enables them to integrate their deviance with the remainder of their lives, while maintaining control over the information that could discredit their whole being. For these reasons they look upon the gaming encounters in the parks as enjoyable experiences.

A physician (not included in my sample) whom I visited repeatedly outside the tearooms says that his day is not complete without a visit to the public johns. His children are raised; he loves his wife "dearly"; he enjoys stature in his profession; normally masculine in appearance, he has never been publicly labeled as deviant. His sexual aberrance is a routinized part of his life, isolated from the rest chiefly by means of information control, much as a surreptitious gambling habit might be hidden from his family and neighbors. As long as knowledge of his ventures in public sex is kept from his mate (whom he believes to be sexually inadequate), it is possible that the sexual activity in his favorite tearoom may actually be functional for the maintenance of his marital stability.

## Type III: The Gay

Like the ambisexuals, unmarried respondents with independent occupations are locked into a strong subculture, a community that provides them with knowledge about the tearooms and reinforcement in their particular brand of deviant activity. This open participation in the gay community distinguishes these single men from the larger group of unmarrieds with dependent occupations. These men take the homosexual role of our society, and are thus the most truly "gay" of all participant types.[11] Except for Tim, who was introduced to the tearooms by the decoy squad of a police depart-

10. Erving Goffman, *Stigma* (Englewood Cliffs, New Jersey: Prentice-Hall, 1963), p. 25.

11. For the importance of speaking of the homosexual role rather than of some vague condition called homosexuality, see Mary McIntosh, "The Homosexual Role," *Social Problems,* Vol. 16, No. 2 (Fall, 1968), pp. 182–192.

ment (see Chapter 5), Type III participants learned the strategies of the tearooms through friends already experienced in this branch of the sexual market.

Typical of this group is Ricky, a twenty-four-year-old university student whose older male lover supports him. Ricky stands at the median age of his type, who range from nineteen to fifty years. Half of them are college graduates and all but one other are at least part-time students, a characteristic that explains their low median income of $3,000. Because Ricky's lover is a good provider, he is comfortably situated in a midtown apartment, a more pleasant residence than most of his friends enjoy.

Ricky is a thin, good-looking young man with certain movements and manners of speech that might be termed effeminate. He is careful of his appearance, dresses well, and keeps an immaculate apartment, furnished with an expensive stereo and some tasteful antique pieces. Seated on a sofa in the midst of the things his lover has provided for their mutual comfort, Ricky is impressively self-assured. He is proud to say that he has found, at least for the time being, what all those participants in his category claim to seek: a "permanent" love relationship.

Having met his lover in a park, Ricky returns there only when his mate is on a business trip or their relationship is strained. Then Ricky becomes, as he puts it, "horny," and he goes to the park to study, cruise, and engage in tearoom sex:

> The bars are o.k.—but a little too public for a "married" man like me. . . . Tearooms are just another kind of action, and they do quite well when nothing better is available.

Like other Type III respondents, he shows little preference in sexual roles. "It depends on the other guy," Ricky says, "and whether I like his looks or not. Some men I'd crawl across the street on my knees for—others I wouldn't piss on!" His aging crisis will be shared with all others in the gay world. It will take the nightmarish form of waning attractiveness and the search for a permanent lover to fill his later years, but it will have no direct relationship with the tearoom roles. Because of his socialization in the homosexual society, taking the insertee role is neither traumatic for him nor related to aging.

Ricky's life revolves around his sexual deviance in a way that is not true of George or even of Dwight. Most of his friends and social contacts are connected with the homosexual subculture. His attitudes toward and rationalization of his sexual behavior are largely gained from this wide circle of friends. The gay men claim to have more close friends than do any other type of control or participant respondents. As frequency of orgasm is reported, this class also has more sex than any other group sampled, averaging 2.5 acts per week. They seem relatively satisfied with this aspect of their lives and regard their sexual drive as normal—although Ricky perceives his sexual needs as less than most.

One of his tearoom friends has recently married a woman, but Ricky has no intention of following his example. When asked if he had any intention of marrying in the future, his reply was:

> If you mean marry a woman, the answer is no—definitely not! I have a lover as it is, and I'm a good lover for this man.

Another of his type, in response to the same question, said: "I prefer men, but I would make a good *wife* for the right *man*."

The vocabulary of heterosexual marriage is commonly used by those of Ricky's type. They speak of "marrying" the men they love and want to "settle down in a nice home." In a surprising number of cases, they take their lovers "home to meet mother." This act, like the exchange of "pinky rings," is intended to provide social strength to the lovers' union.

Three of the seven persons of this type were adopted—Ricky at the age of six months. Ricky told me that his adoptive father, who died three years before our interview, was "very warm and loving. He worked hard for a living, and we moved a lot." He is still close to his adoptive mother, who knows of his sexual deviance and treats his lover "like an older son."

Ricky hopes to be a writer, an occupation that would "allow me the freedom to be myself. I have a religion [Unitarian] which allows me freedom, and I want a career which will do the same." This, again, is typical: all three of the Unitarians in the sample are Type III men, although none was raised in that faith; and their jobs are uniformly of the sort to which their sexual activity, if exposed, would present little threat.

Although these men correspond most closely to society's homosexual stereotype, they are least representative of the tearoom population, constituting only 14 per cent of the participant sample. More than any other type, the Rickys seem at ease with their behavior in the sexual market, and their scarcity in the tearooms is indicative of this. They want personal sex—more permanent relationships—and the public restrooms are not where this is to be found.

That any of them patronize the tearooms at all is the result of incidental factors: they fear that open cruising in the more common homosexual market places of the baths and bars might disrupt a current love affair; or they drop in at a tearoom while waiting for a friend at one of the "watering places" where homosexuals congregate in the parks. They find the anonymity of the tearooms suitable for their purposes, but not inviting enough to provide the primary setting for sexual activity.

## Type IV: Closet Queens

Another dozen of the fifty participants interviewed may be classified as single deviants with dependent occupations, "closet queens" in homosexual slang. Again, the label may be applied to others who keep their deviance hidden, whether married or single, but the covert, unmarried men are most apt to earn this appellation. With them, we have moved full circle in our classifications, for they parallel the trade in a number of ways:

1. They have few friends, only a minority of whom are involved in tearoom activity.
2. They tend to play the insertor role, at least until they confront the crisis of aging.
3. Half of them are Roman Catholic in religion.
4. Their median annual income is $6,000; and they work as teachers, postmen, salesmen, clerks—usually for large corporations or agencies.
5. Most of them have completed only high school, although there are a few exceptionally well-educated men in this group.
6. One in six is black.

7. Not only are they afraid of becoming involved in other forms of the sexual market, they share with the trade a relatively cautious and furtive involvement in the tearoom encounters.

In the next chapter, Marvin, Karl, and John—all of whom are closet queens—will be discussed. For purposes of illustration at this point, however, Arnold will be used as the typical case. Only twenty-two, Arnold is well below the median age of this group; but in most other aspects he is quite representative, particularly in regard to the psychological problems common to men of Type IV.

A routine interview with Arnold stretched to nearly three hours in the suburban apartment he shares with another single man. Currently employed as a hospital attendant, he has had trouble with job stability, usually because he finds the job unsatisfactory. He frequently finds himself unoccupied:

*Arnold:*

> I hang around the park a lot when I don't have anything else to do. I guess I've always known about the tearooms . . . so I just started going in there to get my rocks off. But I haven't gone since I caught my lover there in September. You get in the habit of going; but I don't think I'll start in again—unless I get too desperate.

*Interviewer:*

> Do you make the bar scene?

*Arnold:*

> Very seldom. My roommate and I go out together once in a while, but everybody there seems to think we're lovers. So I don't really operate in the bars. I really don't like gay people. They can be so damned bitchy! I really like women better than men—except for sex. There's a lot of the female in me, and I feel more comfortable with women than with men. I understand women and like to be with them. I'm really very close to my mother. The only reason I don't live at home now is because there are too many brothers and sisters living there. . . .

*Interviewer:*

> Is she still a devout Roman Catholic?

*Arnold:*

Well, yes and no. She still goes to mass some, but she and I go to seances together with a friend. I am studying astrology and talk it over with her quite a bit. I also analyze handwriting and read a lot about numerology. Mother knows I am gay and doesn't seem to mind. I don't think she really believes it, though.

Arnold has a health problem: "heart attacks," which the doctor says are psychological and which take the form of "palpitations, dizziness, chest pain, shortness of breath, and extreme weakness." These attacks, which began soon after his father's death from a coronary two years ago, make him feel as if he were "dying and turning cold." Tranquilizers were prescribed for him, "but I threw them out, because I don't like to become dependent on such things." He quoted a book on mental control of health as stating that such drugs are "unnecessary, if you have proper control."

He also connects these health problems with his resentment of his father, who was mentally ill:

*Arnold:*

I don't understand his mental illness and have always blamed him for it. You might say that I have a father complex and, along with that, a security complex. Guess that's why I always run around with older men.

*Interviewer:*

Were any of your brothers gay?

*Arnold:*

Not that I know of. I used to have sex with the brother closest to my age when we were little kids. But he's married now, and I don't think he is gay at all. It's just that most of the kids I ran around with always jacked each other off or screwed each other in the ass. I just seemed to grow up with it. I can't remember a time when I didn't find men attractive. . . . I used to have terrible crushes on my gym teachers, but nothing sexual ever came of it. I just worshipped them, and wanted to be around them all the time. I had coitus with a woman when I was sixteen–she was twenty-two. After it was over, she asked me what I thought

> of it. I told her I would rather masturbate. Boy, was she pissed off!
>
> I've always liked older men. If they are under thirty, I just couldn't be less interested. . . . Nearly all my lovers have been between thirty and fifty. The trouble is that *they* always want sex–and sex isn't really what I want. I just want to be with them–to have them for friends. I guess it's part of my father complex. I just want to be loved by an older man.

Few of the Type IV participants share Arnold's preference for older men, although they report poorer childhood relationships with their fathers than do those of any other group. As is the case with Arnold's roommate, many closet queens seem to prefer teen-age boys as sexual objects. This is one of the features that distinguishes them from all other participant types. Although scarce in tearooms, teen-agers make themselves available for sexual activity in other places frequented by closet queens. A number of these men regularly cruise the streets where boys thumb rides each afternoon when school is over. One closet queen from my sample has been arrested for luring boys in their early teens to his home.

Interaction between these men and the youths they seek frequently results in the sort of scandal feared by the gay community. Newspaper reports of molestations usually contain clues of the closet queen style of adaptation on the part of such offenders. Those respondents whose lives had been threatened by teen-age toughs were generally of this type. One of the standard rules governing one-night-stand operations cautions against becoming involved with such "chicken" (see Chapter 3). The frequent violation of this rule by closet queens may contribute to their general disrepute among the bar set of the homosexual subculture, where "closet queen" is a pejorative term.

One Type IV respondent, an alcoholic whose intense self-hatred seemed always about to overflow, told me one night over coffee of his loneliness and his endless search for someone to love:

> I don't find it in the tearooms–although I go there because it's handy to my work. But I suppose the [hustler's hangout] is really my meat. I just want to love every one of those kids!

Later, this man was murdered by a teen-ager he had picked up.

Arnold, too, expressed loneliness and the need for someone to talk with. "When I can really sit down and talk to someone else," he said, "I begin to feel real again. I lose that constant fear of mine—that sensation that I'm dying."

Social isolation is characteristic of Type IV participants. Generally, it is more severe even than that encountered among the trade, most of whom enjoy at least a vestigial family life. Although painfully aware of their homosexual orientations, these men find little solace in association with others who share their deviant interests. Fearing exposure, arrest, the stigmatization that might result from participation in the homosexual subculture, they are driven to a desperate, lone-wolf sort of activity that may prove most dangerous to themselves and the rest of society. Although it is tempting to look for psychological explanations of their apparent preference for chicken, the sociological ones are evident. They resort to the more dangerous game because of a lack of both the normative restraints and adult markets that prevail in the more overt subculture. To them, the costs (financial and otherwise) of operating among street corner youths are more acceptable than those of active participation in the gay subculture. Only the tearooms provide a less expensive alternative for the closet queens.

## Styles of Deviant Adaptation

I have tried to make it impossible for any close associate to recognize the real people behind the disguised composites portrayed in this chapter. But I have worked equally hard to enable a number of tearoom players to see themselves in the portrait of George, and others to find their own stories in those of Dwight, Ricky, or Arnold. If I am accurate, the real Tom will wonder whether he is trade or ambisexual; and a few others will be able to identify only partly with Arnold or Ricky.

My one certainty is that there is no single composite with whom all may identify. It should now be evident that, like other next door neighbors, the participants in tearoom sex are of no one type. They vary along a number of possible continua of social characteristics.

They differ widely in terms of sexual career and activity, and even in terms of what that behavior means to them or what sort of needs it may fulfill. Acting in response to a variety of pressures toward deviance (some of which we may never ascertain), their adaptations follow a number of lines of least resistance.

In delineating styles of adaptation, I do not intend to imply that these men are faced with an array of styles from which they may pick one or even a combination. No man's freedom is that great. They have been able to choose only among the limited options offered them by society. As Lindesmith and Gagnon have asserted in a discussion of drug addiction:

> The pressures toward deviance originating in the social structure tend to manifest themselves, it may be postulated, in accordance with what may be called the "allocation of stigma" within a given social system. The individual who feels the pressure selects his mode of adaptation to it, not from a set of specific and fixed forms of behavior with immutable and universal significance, but from the particular set of alternatives with which his society confronts him and which it defines.[12]

These sets of alternatives, which determine the modes of adaptation to deviant pressures, are defined and allocated in accordance with major sociological variables: occupation, marital status, age, race, amount of education. That is one meaning of social probability. What this chapter has described is a number of such probabilities. When the combined factor of education-occupation-social class (another way of expressing occupational independence) is added to that of marital status, one may predict the styles of adaptation for various men who are pressed toward sexual deviance.

Such prediction is possible because these variables determine the resources each man has for information control. In the next chapter, we shall see how these resources vary from trade to ambisexual to gay and closet queen—and then observe how covert deviants, lacking the resources to control information about their stigmatized behavior, tend to compensate for them.

12. Alfred R. Lindesmith and John H. Gagnon, "Anomie and Drug Addiction," in Marshall B. Clinard, ed., *Anomie and Deviant Behavior* (New York: Free Press, 1964), p. 187.

# *Chapter 7.* The Breastplate of Righteousness

FROM ONE viewpoint, tearoom encounters may be analyzed as structured interaction that evolves from the need for information control: signals and strategies are developed to exclude the potentially threatening and uninitiated intruder, while informing potential partners of one's willingness to engage in sex; silence serves to protect participants from biographical disclosure; and locales are chosen for an ease of access that keeps wives, employers, and others from discovering the deviant activity. Scott has made just this sort of analysis of horse racing as an "information game." [1]

In considering the types of participants in these encounters, information control has again appeared as a crucial variable for those who engage in sexually deviant activity. Married men with dependent occupations have more to fear—and less to enjoy—from their clandestine behavior because they are deficient in means of countering exposure when compared with men of greater auton-

1. Marvin B. Scott, *The Racing Game* (Chicago: Aldine, 1968), p. 159. "In *information games,* the participants seek to conceal and uncover certain kinds of knowledge."

omy. The ambisexuals, along with single men in unthreatened occupations, have access to information sources that facilitates their activity in the restroom settings.

The unmarried man who is able to cross over into the world of overt homosexuality is not obsessed with guarding data. His moral history is, in most cases, already public—at least in the sense that his parents, customers, and close friends have been made aware of it. This gives him greater resistance to being discredited. Even arrest and publicity (if not accompanied by severe penalties) on a morals charge would not be disastrous. The degree of resistance, then, refers to the relative ability of a person to withstand the shock of exposure.

The overt single man also has better reception than other types of participants. He is in a better position to receive information that may be of use to him in locating, performing, and safeguarding his chosen brand of deviant action. Thievery, pot-smoking, or homosexual activity—almost any sort of deviance—is made both easier and safer by the communication networks that are built into deviant subcultures. Participants in the homosexual subculture do not have to depend, as does the researcher, on repeated excursions or the observation of physical traces to discover where the action is. They learn of the popular spots in any season at all sorts of homosexual gatherings. By the same channels, they will be informed of hidden cameras or decoys in the public restrooms that might result in arrest.

Of all tearoom participants, those who might be labeled homosexuals in the secondary or subcultural sense are least susceptible to arrest. The professional, experienced, well-informed criminal is in far less danger of being a "loser" than the man who dabbles in deviance. This irony is illustrated in an interview with Tim, the former police decoy:

*Interviewer:*

Was there publicity about people being arrested?

*Tim:*

No, they really kept it quiet. There was so much bullshit!

*Interviewer:*

Don't things usually get around in the gay circles?

*Tim:*

Well, see, the gay circles were the younger people.

*Interviewer:*

The men [in the tearooms] weren't organized in groups or anything like that? The men were just individuals?

*Tim:*

Yes, the men who were arrested in the tearooms were just individuals who hadn't gotten into a group–or who were businessmen who couldn't get into a group.

*Interviewer:*

Because they were married or something like that?

*Tim:*

Yes, most of them were married.

Once learned, the rules and strategies of the game, like other means of avoiding entrapment and exposure, become part of the skills an actor has on tap. Socialization in the deviant subculture thus adds to the reservoir of defense and adaptation that is essential in transforming drudgery into adventure. Such resources include both capital and skill. What the gay men lack in capital they make up in skill. The ambisexuals are apt to have a good deal of both: a learned ability to manipulate the game to their advantage, accompanied by the means to buy and bluff their way out of danger.

As both occupation and marital status combine to lower resistance, restrict reception, and limit skill and capital, the deviant actor is increasingly frightened and desperate. His stigmatized behavior becomes more furtive and less enjoyable. Lacking control of information, threatened with exposure, the Georges and Arnolds are moved from tearoom to tearoom by a double nightmare of flight from fear and pursuit of satisfaction.

Under these adverse conditions, with such high costs, the trade and closet queens might be expected to withdraw altogether from the sexual market of public restrooms. The data indicate, however, that this is seldom the case–tearoom behavior is not easily extinguished. At least two methods of minimizing costs tend to preserve a margin of profit sufficient to sustain such activity for years. The first of these methods is discussed in Chapter 4 as the structuring of interaction so as to minimize revelation. The second is a process whereby the threatened deviant supplements his resistance. As socioeconomic factors and poor reception limit resources—and resistance is decreased—the covert participant engages in a strategy of information control that is designed to increase resistance by detracting from his deviance.

Ball, in his discussion of the management of respectable appearances, refers to this phenomenon as "misdirection," a substrategy of "concealment":

> The basic technique here is to present information or activity of a sufficiently engrossing nature that the performer is able to carry on other affairs unnoticed.[2]

Whether one interprets such misdirection as a method of achieving concealment or of building up resistance depends largely on his view of the intentions of the actor. "Concealment" has certain negative connotations, implying a degree of dishonest or deceptive intent, which I should like to avoid.

The emphasis of psychoanalytic theory on unconscious motivation (always a convenient evasion of the question of intent) has resulted in the development of the theory of reaction formation, which may also provide a suitable conceptualization for description of this strategy. I am no more convinced of the unconscious or nonrational nature of this method of information control, however, than I am of its deceptive intent. I propose, therefore, to direct our thinking toward a fresh vocabulary and conceptualization.

## Refulgent Respectability

What is needed here is a term that implies the taking on of a protective covering, the assumption of a defensive shield to ward off social disapproval. There is also a positive aspect to the phenomenon

2. Donald W. Ball, "The Problematics of Respectability," to appear in Jack D. Douglas, ed., *Deviance and Respectability: The Social Construction of Moral Meanings* (New York: Basic Books, forthcoming), p. 50 of the unpublished manuscript.

observed. These men are not only concerned with avoiding trouble but are involved, as well, in the creation of a social image, in presenting themselves as respectable members of society.

In the process of getting to know the secret deviant, the researcher soon realizes that he must first penetrate a thick nimbus of propriety. The person who is easily discredited because of an occasional hidden act seldom appears so apart from that act. He zips his pants and straightens his tie before leaving the tearoom and, in a short period of time, has resumed life as the respectable next door neighbor, homemaker, and businessman.

For lack of more appropriate conceptualization, I suggest the use of a biblical phrase which, having suffered from misleading translation in the King James version and a subsequent history of theological misuse, might be put to more constructive use in the sociology of deviant behavior. I refer to a portion of "the armour of God" that the author of the letter to the Ephesians would have us put on: "the breastplate of righteousness" (*Ephesians* 6:14).

In donning the breastplate of righteousness, the covert deviant assumes a protective shield of superpropriety. His armor has a particularly shiny quality, a refulgence, which tends to blind the audience to certain of his practices. To others in his everyday world, he is not only normal but righteous—an exemplar of good behavior and right thinking. However much the covert participant may be reacting to guilt in erecting this defensive barrier, he is also engaging in a performance that is part and parcel of his being. Goffman remarks that "there is often no reason for claiming that the facts discrepant with the fostered impression are any more the real reality than is the fostered reality they embarrass." [3] The secret offender may well believe he is more righteous than the next man—hence his shock and outrage, his disbelieving indignation, when he is discovered and discredited.

Motivated largely by his own awareness of the discreditable nature of his secret behavior, the covert deviant develops a presentation of self that is respectable to a fault. His whole life style becomes an incarnation of what is proper and orthodox. In manners

3. Erving Goffman, *The Presentation of Self in Everyday Life* (Garden City, New York: Doubleday Anchor, 1959), p.65.

and taste, religion and art, he strives to compensate for an otherwise low resistance to the shock of exposure.[4]

The breastplate of righteousness is most evident—and most easily measured—in the respondents' views on social and political issues. Early in the analysis of data from the interview schedules, indices of liberal opinion were constructed for each of four sets of social issues on which the views of research subjects were sought: measures of economic reform, police practices, the civil rights movement, and the Vietnamese war. From these indicators, a composite liberalism index was constructed, which facilitated ranking the subjects in terms of their scores on these questions and their classification as conservatives, moderates, or liberals.

Answers to 11 questions on social and economic issues revealed the sharpest differences observed between the control and participant samples. As shown in Table 7.1, the orientations on these

*Table 7.1. Mean scores on liberalism indices by type of tearoom participants, compared with control sample scores (in parentheses).*

| | *Type I "Trade"* | *Type II "Ambi-Sexual"* | *Type III "Gay"* | *Type IV "Closet Queens"* | *Total Partici-pants* | *Total Controls "Straights"* |
|---|---|---|---|---|---|---|
| Economic | 4.4 | 2.3 | 6.3 | 4.2 | 4.2 | (6.2) |
| Police | 2.0 | 4.0 | 6.6 | 3.3 | 3.4 | (4.3) |
| Civil Rights | 2.0 | 1.9 | 5.3 | 1.7 | 2.4 | (3.3) |
| Vietnam | 3.7 | 6.2 | 8.3 | 5.3 | 5.3 | (6.7) |
| Totals | 12.1 | 14.4 | 26.5 | 14.5 | 15.3 | (20.5) |
| (Controls) | (18.3) | (18.2) | (28.0) | (22.3) | | |

issues differ markedly between the two samples, the participants in homosexual acts being more conservative in each of the areas. Among the participants, 16 were ranked as conservatives, 26 as moderates, and only 7 as liberals. In the control sample, only 4 might be called conservatives, 31 moderates, and 15 liberals. For the total scores on the composite liberalism index, the median for the participants was 14; that of the nondeviants was 20.

4. My thanks to Irving Horowitz, who suggested that this phenomenon might best be expressed in terms of compensation.

By comparing the mean scores on the liberalism indices for each of the participant types with those of their matched partners from the control sample, it is possible to discern the degree to which the various participant types supplement their resistance by putting on the breastplate of righteousness. Such compensation, along with other resources for information control, is illustrated in Table 7.2. The ambisexual and gay men have little or no need for the breastplate of righteousness and are thus only slightly more conservative than those in the control sample with whom they are matched.

In order to check for social factors that might explain differences on these indices between the groups because of disproportionate representation in the samples, a number of cross-tabulations were run. Variables of socioeconomic status, race, age, education, type of military service, and religion were all tabulated against the scores of the composite liberalism index for both samples. As was expected from care taken in matching the samples, few differences were found for the statistics of these variables between the two groups. The only major differences were evident in regard to the variables of age, education and religious affiliation. There was a higher proportion of men in their thirties in the participant sample, twice as many persons with graduate education in the control sample, and a disproportionately high representation of Roman Catholics and Episcopalians in the participant sample.

Analysis of the data casts doubt on the possibility that differences in these social characteristics explain away the disparity in social outlooks. If, for instance, the relatively small number of men with graduate education among the participants had evidenced a degree of liberalism consonant with those in the control sample, this might have explained some of the between-sample difference. But persons with this degree of education in the participant sample included *no* liberals.

On the other hand, had the proportion of conservatives among Roman Catholics or men in their thirties in the control sample been consistent with those in the deviant group, it might have been possible to attribute the differences in social views to the variation in age and religion representation between samples. Again, this does not hold. There are no conservatives among the men in their thirties in the straight sample (as contrasted with eight conservatives in

*Table 7.2. Relative resources for information control by participant types.*

| | *MARRIED* | *UNMARRIED* |
|---|---|---|
| *INDEPENDENT OCCUPATION* | *Type II*<br>*"Ambisexual"*<br>*(Dwight)*<br><br>Moderate Reception<br>High Skills<br>High Capital<br>Moderate Resistance<br>(Some Need for Breastplate)<br>Mean Liberalism Score:<br>Observed 14.4<br>Expected 18.2*<br>–3.8 | *Type III*<br>*"Gay"*<br>*(Ricky)*<br><br>High Reception<br>High Skills<br>Low Capital<br>High Resistance<br>(No Need for Breastplate)<br>Mean Liberalism Score:<br>Observed 26.5<br>Expected 28.0*<br>–1.5 |
| *DEPENDENT OCCUPATION* | *Type I*<br>*"Trade"*<br>*(George)*<br><br>Low Reception<br>Low Skills<br>Low Capital<br>Low Resistance<br>(Breastplate Essential)<br>Mean Liberalism Score:<br>Observed 12.1<br>Expected 18.3*<br>–6.2 | *Type IV*<br>*"Closet Queens"*<br>*(Arnold)*<br><br>Some Reception<br>Some Skills<br>Low Capital<br>Low Resistance<br>(Breastplate Needed)<br>Mean Liberalism Score:<br>Observed 14.5<br>Expected 22.3*<br>–7.8 |

* "Expected" scores are the mean scores on the Composite Liberalism Index for members of the control sample matched with these types.

that age range among the participants) and only one who took a comparable position among the Roman Catholics in the control group.

Such specification, then, does not enable us to discern any causal factors among the social variables considered. This is not to say that age, race, education, and religion are unimportant in determining the outlook of these respondents on social issues; rather, what is indicated here is that at least one other intervening variable serves to distort and intensify the effects of characteristics which would normally be expected to influence social and political views.

## Afraid of Being Liberal

Turning directly to the interviews, it becomes apparent that the fear of exposure and stigmatization serves as an intervening lens through which the effects of other social characteristics are filtered and distorted. Social conservatism is revealed as a product of the illegal roles these men play in the hidden moments of their lives. An example is found in the case of Marvin, a young Negro in his mid-twenties:

*Interviewer:*

> Have you ever participated in a civil rights march, picket line or other such demonstration?

*Marvin:*

> Look, I'm black and I'm gay! Isn't that asking for enough trouble without getting mixed up in this civil rights stuff, too?

This man shares a very neat, if modest, apartment with another unmarried man of the same race. He drives a late-model economy car–not flashy but well cared for. He works forty-eight hours each week as a salesman of men's clothing. In reply to questions about his activities and interests, he says: "I just work, go to church, come home, go out to a movie occasionally."

Marvin's concern with projecting a nonstigmatizing image crops up throughout the interview. When asked about his good points, he says: "I try to respect other people's feelings and stay by myself to keep out of trouble." Most of his social activities center around his church, a fundamentalist congregation, which he serves as organist on a part-time basis. He rates himself at ten on a ten-point scale of participation in church activities. "I go to church whenever the doors are open."

Marvin does not know who his father was. His mother, who later married a laborer, raised him in a city ghetto. She always suffered from bad health, and both of her other children died at childbirth. Marvin left high school in the eleventh grade. He doesn't like living in his declining neighborhood and feels that it is not safe there.

Although many of those with whom he was raised may be prime candidates for riot participation, Marvin comes closer to qualifying for membership in the John Birch Society. Concerning the "civil rights movement, as a whole," he believes it has "stirred up people to commit criminal acts." He replied, "Definitely not!" when asked if citizens should participate in demonstrations against the war.

On the composite liberalism index, with a range from three to thirty-seven points, Marvin scored thirteen—two points below the median for his sample of fifty men. For purposes of analysis, he was thus ranked with the moderates. His liberalism on economic questions kept him from joining the ranks of conservatives in the study.

The black man matched with him in the control sample was rated as a liberal by his score of twenty-eight. Although this non-deviant is nearly thirty years older than Marvin (controls for age not being permitted by the sampling technique), there is little difference in socioeconomic background between the two men. The liberal also ranked himself at ten in terms of his religious activity.

A white, upper class participant who, like Marvin, scored below the median of his sample on the composite liberalism index reflected the same concern with exposure. In one of the lengthy, open-ended interviews with this man, I asked why he wasn't active in politics like another member of his family. "With my clandestine activities," he replied, "who wants to get involved in politics? The last thing I need is to get my picture in the papers or on television!"

One of the trade, when questioned about his attitude toward war protestors, says: "We ought to send the bastards over there! They'd see what it's like!" Another Type I participant, a minister, thinks "we should give our wholehearted support to those who fight godless Communism." This same man believes the civil rights movement has "made people dissatisfied with what the Lord has given them. . . . God made the races separate–we shouldn't interfere!"

Knowing of the constant threat to the trade from members of the vice squad, I expected these participants to evidence some anti-police sentiment in that portion of the interviews. Quite the opposite was true. The minister quoted above felt that the police should not give as much regard as they do to the rights of citizens. Vice squad activity, he insisted, should be increased: "This moral corruption must be stopped!" One young closet queen had this to say about vice squad activity: "They should be more strict. I can think of a lot of places they ought to raid."

So consistent were the replies of trade and closet queens (the participants most apt to be arrested in tearooms) in encouraging more vice squad activity that a portrait emerges of these men as moral crusaders. This at least suggests the ironic possibility of a type of moral entrepreneur who contributes to his own stigmatization.[5] Homosexual folklore insists that "there is a witch behind every witch hunt." These data suggest not only the truth underlying that perception but that deviant behavior may be plagued by a sort of moral arms race, in which the deviant is caught in the cycle of establishing new strategic defenses to protect himself from the fall-out of his own defensive weapons. It is not necessary to adopt a psychoanalytic viewpoint in order to discern the self-hatred behind such a punishment process.

Karl, a closet queen whom I have interviewed repeatedly, is a member of the John Birch Society. His parents are prosperous and well-educated people who "never really accepted" him as an equal with his brother. "They have always thrown him at me as an example and deeply resent my remaining unmarried. Father has also criticized me for not being a famous athlete. . . . I've never seemed to be good enough for them." Although slight of build, this respondent showed the greatest interest in athletics of any person in his sample.

5. For a discussion of moral enterpreneurship, see Howard S. Becker, *Outsiders* (New York: The Free Press, 1963), pp. 147–163.

In his search for acceptance and masculinity on his parents' terms, Karl has driven himself in work and play, study and religious orthodoxy, at a determined and nervous pitch. It was his idea to spend his adolescent years in a military prep school and to join the Marines at the time of the Korean war. Like Mack in *The Authoritarian Personality,* this man reveals a tendency to displace his hostility onto outgroups:

> The frustrating, punishing, persecutory features which had to be denied in the father were seen as originating in outgroups who could then be hated in safety, because they were not strong in actuality, and in good conscience, because the traits ascribed to them were those which the ingroup authorities would condemn.[6]

Karl speaks of Negroes as "those damned Ethiopians" and claims that they are "taking over the church and the country."

It is possible that this respondent's conservatism and his tearoom activities both arise from a common, psychological source. He rates his father at one (very cold) on a six-point scale of warmth of relationship with him as a child. His mother was rated at six. Both parents received a one for strictness. He looks back on his childhood as "not too happy." On the other hand, there is much evidence of feedback from his deviant sexual activity into the motivational network behind Karl's intense concern with social respectability, orthodoxy, and masculine image. Highly critical of most others in the homosexual "fraternity," he speaks disparagingly of those who patronize the bars and coffeehouses of the gay community. For the sake of his job and social position, he fears being identified with the more obvious of his kind.

This man, like another closet queen whom I shall call John, will not turn to psychiatric help, although both expressed a belief that they were on the verge of a "nervous breakdown" at the time of the interviews. Karl's response to nervousness and depression is to "throw myself into activity." John, who doesn't want to see a physician or psychiatrist "because they can't change me," finds solace with his friends. The important point is that these men are both

6. R. Nevitt Sanford, "Genetic Aspects of the Authoritarian Personality: Case Studies of Two Contrasting Individuals," in Adorno and others, *The Authoritarian Personality* (New York: Harper, 1950), pp. 805–806.

strong conservatives: highly moralistic, supportive of stronger police activity and intensification of the war in Vietnam, and derogatory in speaking of Negroes. They are defensive and uneasy about their own sexual tendencies and highly motivated toward the maintenance of their images of occupational and political respectability.

## Gay Liberals

It is interesting to note that five of the eight liberals in the participant sample are classified as Type III, gay participants. In talking of their homosexual activity, these men seemed more accepting of their own sexual natures and more intent upon establishing love relationships with others. One high-scoring liberal insists that he is looking for a "permanent lover" among those whom he fellates in the tearooms. Frenkel-Brunswick found that those men scoring low on the Fascism Scale manifest a "fusion of sex and affect, a tendency to more personalized sex relations."[7] My interviews give strong support to these findings by the Adorno group.

An interesting parallel between changing social views and sexual adjustment was traced in an interview with David:

*David:*

> When I was first in college, the thing that stands out in my mind most was my attitude towards Negroes. Oh, I believed in civil rights, but civil rights meaning separate but equal. On the war, I just wanted to get it over with—drop a couple of atomic bombs! And then, I was much more religiously orthodox than now.
>
> I first started coming out of this whole morass of conservatism shortly after I came here. I had had a series of very bad love affairs. Then my priest demanded I quit being gay or be denied the sacraments. I quit going to church altogether for the entire summer. . . . and began to come to terms with myself as a sexual person.
>
> At this point, I met [Rodger]. It had been a bad week—

7. Else Frenkel-Brunswick, "Sex, People, and Self as Seen Through the Interviews," in Adorno and others, *The Authoritarian Personality*, p. 397.

a number of very sordid one-night-stands, tearooms and bar hopping. Through him, I started on a course of changing churches and working out a meaningful pattern of life. I had been experimenting with a semi-Bohemian type of life–but scared to death of drugs of any sort. Was carrying on a respectable daytime job and playing the Bohemian part at night, but didn't accept the philosophy behind the life. It was more a way of having some sort of sex without any obligations attached.

*Interviewer:*

What sort of attitudes did you have then toward your own sexual orientation?

*David:*

Strictly a "numbers" attitude.[8] I was a typical tearoom type. Used to stand on the street until three or four in the morning looking for a trick. But I was playing it straight in the daytime. I was working with straights down at the office. Doing my best to pass with them, I strictly played the masculine bit, telling dirty jokes, trying to date girls. I kept a pretty conventional apartment–regular bed, sofa, hi-fi, chairs, and such.

My ideas on politics were completely nil in those days. I was so busy trying *not* to do something that I could never develop a valid spiritual life or social consciousness. It wasn't until I met [Roddy] that I really turned on to who I was or what was going on in the world.

The three highest scorers among participants–the three most liberal deviants–were the men of this sample whom I would consider the best adjusted of the tearoom clientele. In this connection, it should be noted that the average score on the index for the five men from the combined samples who admit to having undergone psychiatric therapy was twenty-three–a score well above the mean for even the control group. The highest scoring liberals in each sample were men who have had psychiatric help. This finding calls to mind Bay's hypothesis that "the better the individual has been able to

8. Here the respondent is referring to John Rechy, *Numbers* (New York: Grove Press, 1967). In this novel, a former hustler engages in a compulsive search for impersonal sexual contacts.

resolve his own anxieties, the more likely that he will empathize with others less fortunate than himself."[9]

## The Covert Life Style

The secret offender's breastplate of righteousness is not limited to right-wing social and political attitudes. His performance of duties as husband, father, neighbor, and friend is likewise bent in a direction that might give credence to his life of respectability. It has already been pointed out in Chapter 6 that he is apt to earn more money than his straight counterpart and to spend more hours each week at his work. From the standpoint of surface appearance, at least, the participant marriages are "smoother" than those of the control sample.

One of the early impressions formed from research among these men was the remarkable neatness and propriety of their style of life. The automobiles that cluster around the tearooms are almost uniformly clean and well polished and generally of a late-model vintage. Moreover, the personal attire and grooming of the participants was noteworthy for its neatness. "Impeccable" was a word frequently used in description: well-tailored suits, conservative ties, clean work clothes appear to be almost mandatory for tearoom activity.

The condition of their residences was striking. In 50 per cent of the cases, my descriptions included such comments as "very neat," "well kept," "nicest house (or apartment building) in the neighborhood." New awnings, a recent coat of paint, or an exceptionally well-trimmed yard became trademarks that often enabled me to single out the home of a respondent from others down the block. More of these men listed devoting time to their families and homes as their chief interest in life than did those in the control sample. Twice as many expressed an interest in arts and crafts (excluding the fine arts) and in improving the appearance of their homes.

Whereas eight of those in the nondeviant group manifested a Bohemian (or hip) life-style, as seen in furnishings or personal

9. Christian Bay, "Political and Apolitical Students: Facts in Search of Theory," *Journal of Social Issues,* Vol. 23, No. 3, (July, 1967), p. 90.

attire, this was true of only four of the participants. The general antipathy of covert deviants toward hippies is illustrated by negative reactions in the "Letters" column of a San Francisco-based homophile magazine, following the publication of a "hippie" issue. The following letter is representative:

> To identify the homosexual community with any adjunct of the hippie mentality is as gross a distortion as identifying all Birchers as anti-Semites. There may be a few "gays" in the Haight Street scene, and there may be a few "kooks" in the Birch Society, but, for the main, the bulk of responsible adults in both are ashamed of the harmful image created by an irresponsible few. I speak first hand being both a homosexual and a Bircher, and I for one am speaking out against any equation which your July issue might have created as between the "homo" and the "hip".[10]

For those participants with less autonomy, the trade and closet queens, the breastplate of righteousness is thick and almost blinding with the polish of frequent use. It might be said of the covert deviant that he takes on "the whole armour of God." This is true in an almost literal sense, his religious orientation tending to the more authoritarian bodies. Eighteen of these men are Roman Catholics, most of whom express some resentment over changes taking place in the Church. Another is a fundamentalist minister, some of whose views have already been quoted. Most other trade and closet queens belong to no organized religion but are quick to add that they have "strong religious convictions." These men indicate bitterness at "the direction in which the churches are moving."

Two covert participants informed me that they are members of the John Birch Society, although there were no questions aimed at acquiring such data on the interview schedule. After interviews with them, the researcher gains the impression that "the Bible on the table and the flag upon the wall" may be signs of secret deviance more than of "right thinking."

There appear to be two variables that interact with other social characteristics to determine the life style and sociopolitical position of any type of deviant actor: first, the intensity of anticipated sanctions against the particular deviant behavior; second, the degree of autonomy governing the control of information. As anticipated sanctions increase and autonomy decreases, the more elaborate

10. From a letter to the editor, published in the August 1967 issue of *Vector*.

and encompassing will be the breastplate of righteousness the deviant assumes for his overt performances in life. This hypothesis should be seen as cognate to that of Bay: "To the extent that a person is deeply worried about his popularity, his career prospects, his financial future, his reputation, etc., he will utilize his political opinions not for achieving realistic insight but for impressing his reference groups and his reference persons favorably."[11]

In this light, I would suggest that another factor be added to a recent hypothesis of Horowitz and Liebowitz.[12] Because I regard as important their argument that "the line between the social deviant and the political marginal is fading," I would suggest they qualify this theory by adding the word overt in order to make the thesis supportable. Not only for homosexuals but for other deviants as well there is a growing body of evidence that the more overt (autonomous) social deviants are becoming political deviants. However, for the vast majority, the unseen deviants, the breastplate of righteousness replaces the offensive weapons of all but the most conservative political action.

Because I have not engaged in research with other types of marginal people in our society, I am thrown back upon the literature and ten years of experience in the pastoral ministry in order to extend the applicability of my hypothesis to other than participants in homosexual encounters. I recall years of puzzlement over the striking respectability of the visible lives of so many of those who came to my pastoral attention: the countless alcoholics with exceptionally neat apartments and tidy houses; the highly respected businessmen arrested in tearooms; the hyperorthodox clergymen with extracurricular sex lives. In one pastorate, three of my laymen were active in the John Birch Society. One of these was a secret alcoholic who beat his wife, another was a tearoom habitue, and the third stole from his employer with regularity. I use these illustrations (which, as isolated cases, can prove nothing) to underline my point that the secret alcoholic, the embezzler, the tearoom customer, may appear to his neighbors as the paradigm of propriety,

11. Bay, "Political and Apolitical Students," p. 87.

12. Irving Louis Horowitz and Martin Liebowitz, "Social Deviance and Political Marginality: Toward a Redefinition of the Relation between Sociology and Politics," *Social Problems*, Vol. 15, No. 3 (Winter 1968), p. 285.

the finest of citizens. It is not at all unlikely that he will be a moral entrepreneur, serving on the vice squad or heading the local League for Decent Literature.

At home, a Mafia leader "is the soul of respectability–an affectionate husband, a kind father, usually temperate and a faithful worshipper at his church."[13] Centuries of experience as a population of covert deviants has taught the Mafia to incorporate the breastplate of righteousness into its code of behavior. Only when deviants achieve relative autonomy, when information control becomes less problematic, can they afford to be different.

13. Frederic Sondern, Jr., *Brotherhood of Evil: The Mafia* (New York: Farrar, Straus and Cudahy, 1959), p. 55.

# *Chapter 8.* Kicks, Commitment, and Social Control

Call me what you like–adventurer, pervert, or slob–some of my best tricks and thrills have come from public episodes. The excitement that [*sic*] the danger of being caught in the act makes it all the more exciting for me to pursue it further. I'm not interested in having a ridiculous "love affair" with some hair burner and taking up "housekeeping"–I'd much rather solicit the momentary services of some stud in the bushes and finish it right there; this is more thrilling to me, and the more dangerous the better I like it. The more I can get, the happier I am, whether it happens in a head, through a glory-hole–or dilly-dallying around in the bushes with four or five guys at a throw.[1]

As WE approach the conclusion of this examination of the men who meet in tearooms, we must attempt to develop some theory of causation–some explanation of why men with families and prestige risk the destruction of their social identity for a furtive orgasm in a toilet stall. Although the action described may seem unrewarding to most readers, it is apparently sufficiently rewarding for a

1. Letter in "Sex in Public Places," *Vector*, May, 1967, p. 15.

large number of men in our society to cause them to brave the risks of engagement in these encounters.

There is no single explanation of "the call" to tearoom action—not for any one participant, much less for all the diverse personalities who congregate there. Throughout this writing, I have suggested a number of causes—various ways in which this game is reinforcing to different people. It is only as these reasons add up to the promise of profit that any individual will trade in the tearoom market.

It is most helpful at this point to consider the public restooms as sexual market places. They are certainly among the more popular ones for those who prefer the commodity in its homosexual form. As has been indicated in Chapter 6, there is a demand for these services from a population that has been conditioned by certain configurations of family and social structure to search for sex that may be had without obligation or commitment. The disinterested or threatening father may be sufficient to confound the normal process of developing sexual identity, thus shaping one for later reinforcement in deviant behavior. Later the sexual isolation of a prep school or deprivation of heterosexual contact in the armed forces may mark the individual as a prospective customer for the tearoom market. [2]

Discussions of etiology in regard to homosexual preferences have been so clouded by the results of samples gathered from the couches of therapy that in my opinion it is useless to search for an ultimate cause of such a widespread and diverse phenomenon. What is important, and verifiable on the basis of this research, is that the tearoom market offers certain advantages to many men. As in any other market research, my concern in this study has been to identify and examine the social factors that make this particular form of commerce attractive to some and not to others.

Let us consider the advantages of restroom encounters for the

2. Sixty per cent of those in the deviant sample were veterans of the armed forces, compared with 52 per cent of the nondeviants. The distribution was approximately the same, with the exception that there were more Navy veterans in the sample of tearoom participants and more ex-Marines among the nondeviants. An interesting note is that all of the ex-Navy men in the deviant sample were observed in the insertee role, whereas the ex-Marines were all insertors.

men who, drawn to sexual deviance by any number of pressures, choose the covert action of this sex market.

## Kicks as a Come-On

The widespread use in our time of games of chance as come-ons for potential customers in filling stations and supermarkets illustrates the drawing power of such devices. If interested in a particular give-away gimmick or contest, some persons will overlook other advantages or disadvantages of trading in a particular market, simply because of the attraction of playing the game. The kicks of the tearoom game provide just this sort of reinforcement for whatever other attraction these sexual encounters may provide. The risk-taking nature of sexual action in public restrooms is one of the more important attractions they offer, at least to those participants with independent occupations.

My interviews indicate that much of the effective value of the sexual release found in tearooms would be lost without the consequentiality that lies beyond the payoff phase of the game. Some of the older men said they were no longer able to reach orgasm outside the excitement of tearoom encounters. During the attack on the restroom by teen-age toughs that was recounted in Chapter 5, I observed three acts of fellatio within our besieged shelter. I find it impossible to understand how sexual acts could have occurred under those circumstances without recognizing the aphrodisiacal effect of danger.

This, I suspect, is one factor that differentiates the sexual experience of tearoom action from that of masturbation. Autoerotic stimulation provides another common sort of sexual outlet free from personal involvement, but it is not an encounter, a game, a risk-taking adventure. Solitary masturbation involves neither conquest nor submission. One does not leave it with the feeling of having played the game well or of having participated in a new experience. For those respondents with whom I have discussed the matter, masturbation is not considered a satisfactory alternative to tearoom contacts. They desire something more exciting, more stimulating—and that is available in the tearoom market place.

Kicks are but one type of attraction to this form of sexual action, however. Four other factors should be reintroduced at this point in order to gather together all of the motivating forces that draw the participants. They are the *availability, invisibility, variety,* and *impersonality* of tearoom encounters.

The first two of these marketing advantages are particularly attractive to the less autonomous, more covert participants. As discussed in Chapter 1, the more popular tearooms are all located near major commuter routes through the city. They are easily accessible to men on their way to and from work and during the lunch hour. Popular facilities not in the parks are always located in shopping centers or other commercial areas. Many of these are easily reached on foot by those who stop over at the major hotels. The action is liveliest, then, in those places and during those times of the day that are most convenient for men who adapt to their deviance in covert patterns: the young white-collar bachelor or the working class husband in transit to his home.

Bars, baths, and coffeehouses lack similar availability. They are often open only at night and may be located in out-of-the-way parts of the city. All of these are market places for one-night-stand operations, but the emphasis is often on "night." The conditions of these games being what they are, pick-ups from most other homosexual service centers also take much more time than the fifteen or twenty minutes of the tearooms. It is easy to fit the latter encounters into a busy man's schedule, and as we have seen, tearoom customers tend to be busy men. Public restrooms, as the places best suited for instant sex, are especially functional for the covert deviant in urban society.

Invisibility is also important for these men. The easily discredited individual will seek a locale for his deviant behavior that provides him with an instant alibi, an automatic explanation for his presence. As my sampling methods attest, the park drives are not always the best places for maintaining anonymity. There are, however, reasons for being in those places other than for engaging in sexual encounters. Such excuses are weaker if one is seen in a gay bar or a steam bath.

For the "oncer," the man who finds variety in sexual partners particularly appealing, the tearoom encounters are ideal. The rate of turnover in these facilities is high enough, during busy seasons, to provide a wide range of prospective sexual partners. Again, it should be noted that diversity in sexual partners may be valued by some as a sexual stimulant, rather than solely as the result of some sort of "compulsion to promiscuity." As Liebow has written:

> Variety is not only the spice of sex life, it is an aphrodisiac which elevates the man's sexual performance.[3]

## Sex without Commitment

Socialized as we Americans are into a James Bond world of cops and robbers, the idea of "disposable sex"–particularly when coupled with a risk-taking encounter–might be expected to attract a wide following. I found it necessary to stay away from James Bond movies during the course of the research in order to avoid running into the many respondents with whom these shows are popular. Not only do many of the participants find the actor who plays Agent 007 "attractive," his treatment of women as sexual objects to be enjoyed and discarded meets with the approval of homosexually oriented men.

A large part of the cost of the more "normal" sexual games of our society–those that are more heterosexual, along with courtship activity in the gay world–is the emotional involvement and personal commitment that may be demanded of the players. Some men have reasons to avoid such sexual action. Apart from any psychological theories that may be applied to explain preferences for impersonal sex, I believe there are situational and social factors of a relatively simple nature that may cause one to prefer sex without commitment.

Although the data of this study include no references to female prostitution, I have conjectured that some of the trade might have been satisfied customers in the old "twenty-minute" whorehouses:

> A large number of men want to avoid obligations, are afraid of impregnating a girl, or want to avoid emotional entanglements. . . . A

3. Elliot Liebow, *Tally's Corner* (Boston: Little, Brown, 1967), p. 123.

visit to a prostitute may be, for all of them, simpler, safer, and even cheaper.[4]

With the disappearance of such bordellos from the American scene, public restrooms have become the major setting for impersonal sex. Men with heavy emotional commitments to families and jobs, for example, may not be able to afford investment in other than the most transient and impersonal types of extramarital sex. One married respondent expressed it in this way, when asked if there weren't times when he would like to get to "know" some of his tearoom partners:

> I'm emotionally involved with my wife and children. I haven't time or energy or money to invest in anyone else. I don't want to know those men in there. I'm here for sex—not friendship.

The silent detachment evident throughout these games of chance is functional for the covert deviant, not only in maintaining secrecy about his behavior and shielding his social biography from stigma, but in avoiding commitment. The breastplate of righteousness is removed when he steps into the tearoom—but it will be waiting at the door when he leaves. He lives two lives, and emotional involvement in the deviant one could shatter the other.

What the covert deviant needs is a sexual machine—collapsible to hip-pocket size, silent in operation—plus the excitement of a risk-taking encounter. In tearoom sex he has the closest thing to such a device. This encounter functions, for the sex market, as does the automat for the culinary, providing a low-cost, impersonal, democratic means of commodity distribution.

## What's Wrong with Public Sex?[5]

As America creeps slowly out of its Puritan cocoon, there is evidence of perceptible change in attitudes toward sexual deviation.

4. Harry Benjamin and R. E. L. Masters, *Prostitution and Morality* (New York: Julian Press, 1964), p. 195.

5. This section was presented as a paper at the meetings of the American Sociological Association, San Francisco, California, September 4, 1969. My thanks to Delbert S. Elliott, chairman of the criminology section, for his recommended improvements.

Even the churches are undergoing a change of conscience regarding homosexuals and their behavior, as indicated by the growth of the Council on Religion and the Homosexual, the recent appointment of a study commission on this subject by the Episcopal church, and the statements of a number of major theologians.[6] In line with recommendations by the American Bar Association, the State of Illinois is the first in the United States to bring its penal code on homosexual activity into accord with the statutes of European nations that operate under the Napoleonic Code.

Such statutory reforms, however, condone homosexual acts only when engaged in by consenting adults in private, and the consensus still condemns such behavior in public settings. The majority of students in one of my criminology classes were inclined to censure those who chose a park restroom for homosexual liaisons. Having been instructed in an examination to act as if each were the judge in the trial of two men who had been apprehended by a plain clothes detective in such an act, 52 per cent of the students replied that they would reprimand thc guilty parties or refer them to psychiatric treatment, not because there was anything wrong with what the men had done but because they had chosen an inappropriate place to do it. One student answered, in part:

> If [police] do come upon such activity they should reprimand the parties and tell them to "move on" to more private quarters, even though arrest and degradation rituals of the courts are of no value in dealing with these matters.

Another student, a member of the vice squad of the metropolitan police department, replied as follows:

> This sexual liaison was criminal due to the fact that it was in a public place even though there was no one else present except the detective. The participants disregarded the proper moral standards of society by using such a place.

Since they were writing an examination for an instructor who made his bias on this subject known, their answers may not be

6. For examples of such positions see The Council on Religion and the Homosexual, "Churchmen Speak Out on Homosexual Law Reform," (San Francisco: The Council on Religion and the Homosexual, 1967).

taken as representative of even a university-level population; nonetheless, it is noteworthy that the public place of the offense bore such great weight in their judgments. Not the nature of the act, but the attendant circumstances, were thought to be worthy of censure.

Reiss has noted this same phenomenon:

> The more public the circumstances in which any sexual behavior takes place, the stronger the taboo and the sanctions against violators. By way of illustration, masturbation is generally permitted in private, but it is strongly tabooed in public as a form of exhibition.[7]

Granted that there is no qualitative difference between masturbation in private and in public, between acts of fellatio performed in a public john and the same acts taking place in bedrooms, what is there about public sex that evokes the taboo? Our first sociological task is to isolate the attendant conditions that result in condemnation of public sex. How does society define what is public and what is private for the purpose of imposing its sanctions?

Reiss uses the term social visibility in discussing public offenses, but without distinguishing between social and physical visibility. The physical visibility of an offense is the obvious, common-sense answer to how the public situation should be socially defined. Tiffany, McIntyre, and Rotenberg comment that police enforcement is directed against the homosexual who solicits in public, "for he, like the streetwalking prostitute, is visible to the public,"[8] but again they fail to define the nature, degree, or extent of visibility necessary for invoking sanctions. Can there be auditory or tactual "visibility," or is a blind man immune to such public offense? Can a prostitute escape apprehension by wearing a Scarlet *A* on her forehead that is visible only to those equipped with special colored glasses? By failing to draw her drapes, a woman in a high-rise apartment may strip before thousands of viewers, yet she is less apt to be prosecuted than are her "voyeuristic" viewers. A popular form of contemporary prostitution is engaged in by women who fellate their customers in autos that line the drives of urban

7. Albert J. Reiss, Jr., "Sex Offenses: The Marginal Status of the Adolescent," *Law and Contemporary Problems,* Vol. 25, No. 2 (1960), p. 319.

8. Lawrence P. Tiffany, Donald M. McIntyre, Jr., and Daniel L. Rotenberg, *Detection of Crime* (Boston: Little, Brown, 1967), p. 239.

parks, with little concealment from knowing viewers driving by. Men who engage in fellatio behind the closed doors of a toilet stall, however, are far more subject to arrest.

Sanctions against homosexual behavior in these places do not vary with their degree of physical visibility. Except where hidden cameras are employed by the police, it is very rare that tearoom sex is viewed by anyone other than the participants, or by a third person serving, as I did, in the role of lookout. On the other hand, my respondents consider homosexual behavior in certain public baths as much safer in spite of its greater visibility. This suggests that the question involves ownership, that public sex occurs on public property in contrast with private sex on private property. If the issue were simply one of public domain, however, the sanctions directed against fellatio in a department store toilet should be more lenient than those adverse to fellatio in the tearoom of a public park. In the United States, at least, this is not true.

Perhaps the most thorough discussion of public order in the literature of sociology is found in Goffman's *Behavior in Public Places,* and it is to this work that I turn for leads in formulating a viable theory of the social control of public sex. In discussing face-to-face interaction, he says:

> Copresence renders persons uniquely accessible, available, and subject to one another. Public order, in its face-to-face aspects, has to do with the normative regulation of this accessibility.[9]

If public order, in the sociological sense, is concerned with regulating the accessibility of persons to one another, then the specific concern of criminologists should be to isolate any social norm that, when violated in regard to copresence, activates the legal process.

Copresence, this mutual availability, occurs in a multitude of stituations, under a number of conditions that determine the social status of the relationship. It may exist between partners of a marriage, between lovers, among guests at a party, between strangers or blood brothers; it may occur in a bedroom or garden, in an auto at a drive-in movie, in a restroom, or on the street; it may be preceded by an elaborate ceremony, a passing introduction, a struc-

9. Erving Goffman, *Behavior in Public Places,* (New York: Free Press, 1963), p. 22.

tured game, or no warning at all. When such accessibility leads to a sexual act, these attendant conditions often determine the legal status of the act and, what is of greater importance, the manner and degree of involvement (if any) of the forces of social control.

In a matter such as deviant sexual behavior where the social norms are of sufficient strength to be reflected in written law, what evidence is there of factors tangential to the central action that may move or still the machinery of criminal justice? The hint of an answer is to be found in a number of criminal statutes pertaining to sexual deviance. The majority of western nations (the United States serving as the sole exception) provide no legal sanctions against sexually deviant acts as such unless certain attendant conditions are violated: (1) such acts must not take place "in public"; (2) physical force must not be used to obtain consent: (3) parental or other legal force may not be employed; (4) none of the participants may be below what each society considers the "age of consent."

Note that the last three conditions are specifically directed to the question of whether participation is voluntary. Whatever sociopsychological motives may lie behind the restriction that only adults may be considered as sex objects, legal emphasis is clearly placed on "the age of consent or discretion." The same may be said of sanctions against the sexual involvement of parents, foster parents, legal guardians, or institutional staff personnel with their wards. A case in point is the Danish legislation summarized in *The Wolfenden Report:*

> Homosexual acts committed with children under fifteen are punishable. . . . Similarly punishable are homosexual acts procured by the use of force, fear, fraud or drugs, and offenses against inmates of certain institutions (e.g., orphanages and mental hospitals) when they are committed by persons employed in or supervising such institutions. . . . Homosexual acts with a person under twenty-one are punishable if they are committed by abuse of superior age or experience. . . . Indecent behavior against any person of the same sex is an offense when the offender by his behavior violates the other person's decency or gives public offense.[10]

10. A compendium of European laws regarding homosexual activity is found in *The Wolfenden Report* (New York: Lancer Books, 1964), Appendix III.

In many of these legal codes, prohibition of sexual acts *in public* appears to be an afterthought, tacked on to a series of guarantees of free consent. If, however, the regulation of age yields to an interpretation as "that level of maturation when free consent is possible," could it be that the regulation of place speaks also to the safeguarding of consent? The "public" nature of the offense may become crucial because it violates a norm that western societies, at least, demand in the case of all sexual (and many other interpersonal) acts: The principle of free consent. The criminological concern, then, is not merely with the regulation of copresence but with measures taken to insure *the freedom of consent* to copresence.

The physical setting of sexual acts has little to do with the consent of participants unless we consider that physical settings–like physical visibility–are socially defined. That, I believe, is what Reiss means when he writes of "social visibility." Building on the basis of his theory, thus defined, we should be able to propose a series of integrated and testable hypotheses:

First, the settings for sex are socially visible in the degree to which they preclude the initial consent to copresence of those who may be involved as witnesses or participants in the act.

Second (to restate Reiss's hypothesis), the more socially visible the circumstances in which any sexual behavior takes place, the stronger the sanctions against violators.

And, in combined form, the more the social setting of a sexual act precludes the initial consent to copresence of those who may be involved as witnesses or participants, the stronger the sanctions against violators.

A definition may also be deduced from these hypotheses: "Public sex," when perceived as a threat to society, refers to sexual acts so situated as to result in the *involuntary* accessibility of others as sex objects or witnesses.

This theoretical approach should help to clarify a number of problems confronting the student of sexual deviance. For example, why is a public bath, in spite of occasional raids by the police, thought to be a safer locale for homosexual activity than a public restroom? The answer, provided by my research subjects, is that the bath is less *public*. But the bath is certainly no less *visible* than the tearoom; gay bathhouses advertise and sport neon signs, they are presumably open to use by any male, and sexual activity is frequently more obvious there than in any tearoom. Excluding private clubs and suburban health and sauna centers, however, urban baths in America have a sordid reputation. The man who enters knows what he is getting into and part of the entrance fee is surrender of his consent to copresence. There is even a ritual to symbolize this act of will: first, the customer hands over his wallet and watch in return for a locker key and then he is conducted to the locker room, where he must undress under the gaze of others. Thus dispossessed of his identity kit and other defenses, he receives a towel (always too small) and a pair of shower clogs. Of course, he may yet deny his accessibility and refuse to engage in sexual acts, but only by creating a "scene," in which he will be labeled as the offending party.

In public restrooms, however, there is no such act of will upon entering. Unless he is wise to the situation, a man may enter a tearoom where he finds himself embarrassed by his accessibility for involvement in acts to which he would not normally consent. Sexual activity in accommodations as socially visible as public restrooms thus violates a strong cultural norm against the abrogation of the individual's right of consent to copresence. At this point, another problem arises: in the course of observing some two hundred homosexual encounters in public restrooms, it became obvious that an unwilling participant may withdraw at any time from a tearoom encounter without creating a scene or losing his purity or his composure. Because of cautions built into the strategies of these encounters, no man need fear being molested in such facilities; he must first demonstrate by showing an erection that he wants to get in on the action. No one who plays the straight role properly will be shocked or offended by the sexual games that are played in tearooms.

Social creatures are always engaged in structuring interaction to provide maximum self-protection. The sexual deviant does not deviate from this rule. At a coffeehouse where male hustlers ply their trade, a young man sells drink tickets at the door and asks if the customer knows "what kind of a place this is." Consent to copresence must thus be given before entering because immediately afterward one is confronted with a scene of male couples dancing and necking. Before long, the visitor can expect a clean-cut youngster to offer to sell himself for twenty dollars. An embarrassed visitor can depart from this setting only to the accompaniment of stares and remarks.

Professional and semiprofessional male prostitutes often operate in the automobile of a "score" or customer, and any knowledgeable young hitchhiker soon learns the price, in terms of consent, that he must pay for a ride. By accepting a lift, the thumber agrees to become subject to his benefactor. If the rider stops the action short of sexual involvement, he will do so apologetically, and his denial of consent may incur the self-righteous indignation of the driver. Since hitchhikers are themselves engaging in activity of questionable legality, they are generally hesitant to report sexual advances to the police, even if they have been ordered out of the car by a disappointed driver.

Because part of our socialization consists in learning such common understandings of the social construction of reality as "what you should expect" in a particular place, the price of admission to settings of low social visibility is generally well communicated. In these settings, a high degree of consent to copresence is given upon entrance; a certain amount of accessibility may be taken for granted because it *has* been granted. In the public market place, however, such liberties may not be taken. When the consensual cover charge is low or nonexistent, the prices within the doors must remain relatively high. In tearooms, explicit signs of accessibility must be exacted *before* one may become involved in the action.

In order to facilitate testing our hypotheses of the social visibility of sexual settings, it is necessary, finally, to suggest a continuum along which a number of public situations involving sex may be placed.

At the end of the continuum, where there is the lowest level of consent to copresence granted upon entrance, I would place such localities as a church during a Sunday service. Immediately below would be shopping malls or public thoroughfares. In such public settings, the sanctions are so high as to effectively preclude all but the most daring sexual actors.

Farther down the continuum, requiring little consent at entering but an explicit expression of willingness to participate at later stages of the interaction, the tearooms should be placed. Because of their high degree of social visibility, these facilities are the scenes of much activity on the part of social control forces. Here, too, might be placed open places in the parks and public beaches.

At the next stage, more initial consent to copresence is demanded but some consent is still required later in the interaction. Here we might find automobiles on the streets and parked at drive-in movies, along with the balconies of downtown movie houses. The threat of social sanctions now diminishes rapidly.

Near the bottom of the continuum, I would place public baths and gay coffeehouses. Here, the consent to be granted at entrance is so high as to leave little doubt of the customer's intention to participate. Because the public's right to consent is guarded at the door by common knowledge, proactive police action in these settings is very rare.

A recent study of sexual activity in Philadelphia prisons suggests a final category at the very bottom of this scale of social visibility.[11] Only prisons, jails, and institutions for the "mentally defective" belong at this level. Here society has taken away entirely the right of consent to copresence. Social sanctions are almost nonexistent, even against homosexual rape. Persons in these settings are thought to be either incapable or unworthy of any act of will, thus any consent to copresence is denied them. They are accessible to anyone, because the world is inaccessible to them.

Beyond this lies the infrarealm of private sex. In the absence of social visibility and vice squad activity, strong cultural norms protect the sanctity of consent to copresence in bedrooms and parlors. Here, however, most rapes and acts of incest are committed, most child molestation is found, most seduction of teen-agers occurs.

This continuum suggests a final hypothesis: As both social visibility and sanctions decrease, due to apparent protection of the right of consent to copresence, the danger to society of sexual activity in these settings increases. It is the safeguarded, walled-in, socially invisible variety of sex we have to fear, not that which takes place in public.

11. Alan J. Davis, "Sexual Assaults in the Philadelphia Prison System and Sheriff's Vans," *Trans-action*, December, 1968, pp. 8–13.

## Suggestions for Social Policy

As indicated in Chapter 5, if there is any threat to society from tearoom action, my data do not indicate it. The only harmful effects of these encounters, either direct or indirect, result from police activity. Blackmail, payoffs, the destruction of reputations and families, all result from police intervention in the tearoom scene.

Some social scientists who study the homosexual scene apparently think these secondary crimes resulting from law enforcement are less serious than the possible embarrassment of those who might happen upon tearoom encounters. Hoffman, for instance, acknowledges the existence of transgressions by the police but follows with these statements:

> There is no question that there are many homosexuals who engage in overt sexual behavior in public places. As a matter of fact, some of them will admit that they do so *because* the fact that they might be arrested is itself sexually exciting to them. There is simply no way of preventing these individuals from engaging in activity that would, under any circumstances conceivable at the present time, outrage passers-by. Hence it seems to me that the police cannot be blamed when an individual who has been caught sucking the penis of another man in a park or public lavatory finds himself in court. I have interviewed a sufficient number of adult male homosexuals who are highly intelligent and occupy respectable and even prestigious occupational positions to assert that a substantial portion of these men–though not the majority–cruise johns and parks and engage in sexual acts in the johns and parks. Thus, some kind of police surveillance of these public places would appear to be necessary.[12]

Because I consider Hoffman one of the more astute analysts of homosexual behavior, I shall treat his argument in detail. He seems to recognize two factors as justifying police action (and arrests) in the tearooms: first, the possibility that such encounters may "outrage passers-by," and second, that a "substantial portion" of adult male homosexuals engage in such behavior. In fact, tearoom interac-

12. Martin Hoffman, *The Gay World* (New York: Basic Books, 1968), p. 89. Italics his.

tion (as described in Chapter 4) is so structured as to minimize the possibility of offending straight people; moreover, I do not believe that behavior should be proscribed merely because it has the potential of causing embarrassment or even outrage. Spectators may be outraged by others simply because they dress or act differently in public. I have been spit upon by outraged Protestants while walking down the streets of small Oklahoma towns in a clerical collar. Should clerical or hippie attire be outlawed solely on the basis that some passer-by may take offense to them?

Neither do I think that police surveillance is required by the participation of large numbers of people. Large numbers watch baseball in public, and many men participate in Masonic parades, an activity that may be highly offensive to some spectators. Until Hoffman and others can prove that tearoom encounters provide some sort of threat to the public welfare, they should not recommend proactive police operations–particularly since we do know that such law enforcement activity in itself gives rise to a number of secondary crimes.

My concern as a criminologist is to recommend that law enforcement manpower be deployed where there is the greatest need, where the welfare of individuals and society as a whole is at stake. On the basis of this study, I believe public restrooms should be given very low priority on the list. On the weekend that two well-trained detectives arrested this researcher for "loitering" in a public park, three major bank robberies took place in the metropolitan area under study. The police should intrude upon the tearoom scene only in response to specific complaints.

It is easy to make the police scapegoats for many complaints one may have with society as a whole. It is not my intention to criticize these men unduly or to add in any way to the burdens they carry for society. Quite the reverse: I should like to see some of their unnecessary duties removed, and the cessation of vice squad activity in the tearooms would be an excellent beginning.

The police are not the only agents of social control, and much of the blame for the tension and self-hatred that afflict the sexual deviant belongs elsewhere. Physicians, psychiatrists, social scientists, ministers, and officials of other social control agencies need to become informed about the dangers of condemning covert deviants. As social control agents impress upon members of a deviant group that they are "sick," so will they become.[13] Any words or activity that deepens the self-hatred of the covertly deviant population tends to be visited back on society in terms of the very behavior feared in the first place.

Suppressed in this covert role and deprived of subcultural support, the secret offender tends to act out his deviance in ways that are least socially acceptable. If homosexual, he may press his intentions upon boys hitching a ride home from school or in the balcony of a movie theater.

The less autonomous deviant, held in his role of adaptation by social pressure, tends to turn upon himself or to displace his anger onto the more obvious persons of his own group. As Goffman indicates, he then takes up "in regard to those who are more evidently stigmatized than himself the attitudes the normals take to him."[14] Worse yet, he may justify himself by degrading others, displacing his hostility onto outgroups in the manner of the authoritarian personality.

Such extremists, fortunately, are rare—only the occasional black Bircher, gay witch hunter, or hippie who "cops out to the narcs." There are other ways, however, in which covert roles are damaging to society. First among these is the manner in which the covert deviant relates to his own subculture. His contacts tend to be furtive and almost desperate in nature. Afraid and ashamed to be open even with his fellows, he is driven to impersonal encounters or intense forays under the cover of alcohol or an out-of-town trip.

Sociologists who concentrate upon the processes that reinforce deviance in the subculture often fail to grasp the healthy potential of such associations. The hip, soul, or gay subcultures provide self-

13. "I sincerely hope that as the public comes to understand homosexuality better, the afflicted will be regarded as sick persons in need of help. With a change in public attitude, I hope that the homosexual himself will recognize the true nature of his condition and instead of trying to have society accept it as a desirable way of life, he will seek treatment and cooperate in community efforts to develop more effective treatment facilities and to work toward the prevention of this distressing state." Samuel B. Hadden, "A Way Out for Homosexuals," *Harpers,* March, 1967, p. 120.

14. Erving Goffman, *Stigma* (Englewood Cliffs, N. J.: Prentice-Hall, 1963), p. 107.

esteem, relief from torment, and important training on how to avoid conflict with the law. Without normal contacts in the drug subculture, the user of even nonaddictive drugs may resort to theft or false prescriptions for his supply. Lacking guidance on what to expect from or how to use hallucinogens, the lone experimenter may suffer a "bad trip" or "freak out."[15] In discussing the influence of the subculture in helping the homosexual mediate his relationship with the larger society, Gagnon and Simon say:

> To some extent the ultimate social and psychological adjustment of the homosexual will be conditioned by the structure of role opportunities provided by the homosexual community.[16]

Those who are forced into covert adaptation by the derogation of society are denied this help from the subculture.

My own recommendations for social policy may be simply summarized: In order to alleviate the damaging side effects of covert homosexual activity in tearooms, ease up on it. Every means by which these men are helped to think better of themselves and to relate to others in the homosexual subculture will lessen any threat they may constitute for the society at large.

Sociologists engage in the study of deviant behavior because man reveals himself best in his back alleys. It is there that we may see the raw undergirding of the social structure—and, perhaps, observe our own weaknesses reflected in the behavior we fear and berate the most. As Kai Erikson has said:

> Men who fear witches soon find themselves surrounded by them; men who become jealous of private property soon encounter eager thieves. And if it is not always easy to know whether fear creates the deviance or deviance the fear, the affinity of the two has been a continuing course of wonder in human affairs.[17]

15. Howard S. Becker, "History, Culture and Subjective Experience: An Exploration of the Social Bases of Drug-Induced Experiences," *Journal of Health and Social Behavior*, Vol. 8, No. 3 (September, 1967), pp. 168–169.

16. John H. Gagnon and William Simon, eds., *Sexual Deviance* (New York: Harper and Row, 1967), p. 10.

17. Kai T. Erikson, *Wayward Puritans* (New York: John Wiley, 1966), p. 22.

# *Postscript*: A Question of Ethics

So long as we suspect that a method we use has at least *some* potential for harming others, we are in the extremely awkward position of having to weigh the scientific and social benefits of that procedure against its possible costs in human discomfort.[1]

IN THE article from which I have quoted, Erikson develops an argument against the use of disguises in gaining entrance to social situations to which the researcher would otherwise be denied admission. My research in tearooms required such a disguise. Does it, then, constitute a violation of professional ethics?

Antecedent to Erikson's focus on *methods*, there is a larger question: Are there, perhaps, some areas of human behavior that are not fit for social scientific study at all? Should sex, religion, suicide, or other socially sensitive concerns be omitted from the catalogue of possible fields of sociological research? At first glance, few

1. Kai T. Erikson, "A Comment on Disguised Observation in Sociology," *Social Problems*, Vol. 14, No. 4 (Spring, 1967), p. 368.

would answer yes to this question. Nevertheless, several have suggested to me that I should have avoided this research subject altogether. Their contention has been that in an area of such sensitivity it would be best to "let sleeping dogs lie."

I doubt that there are any "sleeping dogs" in the realm of human interaction, and certainly none so dormant as to merit avoidance by those whose commitment should be to the enhancement of man's self-knowledge. Even if there are, sexual behavior in public places is not among them. The police, the press, and many other agents of social control *make* that behavior their concern:

> In one toilet, which had no partitions between johns, we caught a guy sitting on one john reaching over for the genitals of a boy sitting on another. It wasn't very nice work, believe me.[2]

This may not have been "very nice work" for the investigator quoted; however, the crackdown on homosexuals in Boise, Idaho, of which his work was a part, produced results. Before the scandal ended in 1956, more than 1,400 persons were questioned and twenty arrested; a city of 50,000 was caught up in panic; one of the boys involved murdered his father; the chief of police was fired, as was the local probation officer; and the son of a city councilman was discharged from West Point. Most tragic of all, nine men were convicted of homosexual offenses and sentenced to the state penitentiary, their sentences ranging from five years to life, and some of these men left families behind them.

The wonder to me is not that some sociologist might endanger his ethical integrity and that of his profession by standing around in public lavatories making mental notes on the art of fellatio, but rather that a group of law students and their advisors would be the *first* to risk involvement in such a study.[3] Concern about "professional integrity," it seems to me, is symptomatic of a dying discipline. Let the clergy worry about keeping their cassocks clean; the scientist has too great a responsibility for such compulsions!

This is not to say that I am unconcerned about the inquirer's

2. John Gerassi, *The Boys of Boise* (New York: Macmillan, 1966), p. 44.

3. Jon J. Gallo and others, "The Consenting Adult Homosexual and the Law: An Empirical Study of Enforcement and Administration in Los Angeles County," *UCLA Law Review,* 13 (March, 1966).

ethics in regard to the protection of his research subjects. Quite to the contrary; as I indicate in Chapter 2, I believe that preventing harm to his respondents should be the *primary* interest of the scientist. We are not, however, protecting a harrassed population of deviants by refusing to look at them. At this very moment, my writing has been interrupted by a long-distance call, telling me of a man who has been discharged from his position and whose career has been destroyed because he was "caught" in a public restroom. This man, who protests his innocence, has suffered a nervous breakdown since his arrest. Even if acquitted, his personal identity has been damaged, perhaps irreparably, by the professional spy who apprehended him. The greatest harm a social scientist could do to this man would be to ignore him. Our concern about possible research consequences for our fellow "professionals" should take a secondary place to concern for those who may benefit from our research.

## Situation Ethics

If it be granted, then, that the sociologist may commit a grave ethical violation by ignoring a problem area, we may consider the methods that should be used in such studies. Let it be noted that any conceivable method employable in the study of human behavior has at least some potential for harming others. Even the antiseptic strategies involved in studying public archives may harm others if they distort, rather than contribute to, the understanding of social behavior. Criminologists may study arrest statistics, as filtered to us through the FBI, without stirring from the safety of their study chairs, but such research methods may result in the creation of a fictitious "crime wave," a tide of public reaction, and the eventual production of a police state–all because the methods may distort reality.

As I learned during the time I administered examinations in Christian Ethics to candidates for the priesthood, questions that arise in regard to means are always relative. There are no "good" or "bad" methods–only "better" or "worse" ones. Neither interview schedules nor laboratory experiments nor participant observation can be neatly classified as involving either "open" or "disguised" approaches. I have never known an interviewer to be completely honest with his respondents; were this so, the whole concern with constructing an "effective" questionnaire could be dropped. Neither does any researcher ever have adequate insight for a perfect representation of his identity; it is always a matter of greater or lesser misrepresentation.

The problems facing researchers, then, are of which methods may result in more or less misrepresentation of purposes and identity, more or less betrayal of confidence, and more or less positive or negative consequences for the subjects. Those who engage in the study of deviant behavior—or any behavior, for that matter—must become accustomed to the process of weighing possible social benefits against possible cost in human discomfort. Erikson describes this process as "awkward," and I shall call it "awful" in the sense of being awe-inspiring. The researcher must also keep in mind that no method can ever be completely safe for himself or his respondents, and thus must weigh it in relation to others that may be applied in any instance. The ethics of social science are situation ethics.

## Problems of Misrepresentation

At the conclusion of his article, Erikson proposes two rules regarding misrepresentation of the researcher's identity and purposes:

> It is unethical for a sociologist to *deliberately misrepresent* his identity for the purpose of entering a private domain *to which he is not otherwise eligible*.
>
> It is unethical for a sociologist to *deliberately misrepresent* the character of the research in which he is engaged.[4]

Since one's identity within the interaction membrane of the tearoom is represented only in terms of the participant role he assumes, there was no misrepresentation of my part as an observer: I was indeed a "voyeur," though in the sociological and not the sex-

4. Erikson, "Disguised Observation in Sociology," p. 373. Italics mine.

ual sense. My role was primarily that of watchqueen, and that role I played well and faithfully. In that setting, then, I misrepresented my identity no more than anyone else. Furthermore, my activities were intended to gain entrance not to "a private domain" but to a public restroom. The only sign on its door said "Men," which makes me quite eligible for entering. It should be clear, then, that I have not violated Erikson's first canon. Although passing as deviant to avoid disrupting the behavior I wished to observe, I did not do so to achieve copresence in a private domain.

The second rule may be applied to the reactive part of my research, when I interviewed persons I had observed in the tearooms under the pretext of a social health survey. Here it should be noted that all interviews were in fact made as part of a larger social health survey, and abstracted data from my interviews are already in use in that study. The problem then may be viewed in two ways: First, I gave less than full representation of what I was doing, though without giving false representation. I wore only one of two possible hats, rather than going in disguise. Second, I made multiple use of my data. Is it unethical to use data that someone has gathered for purposes one of which is unknown to the respondent? With the employment of proper security precautions, I think such multiple use is quite ethical; it is frequently employed by anyone using such data banks as the records of the Bureau of Census.

## Problems of Confidentiality

It should be apparent to readers of this treatise that I have taken every possible precaution to protect the identities of my respondents and the confidential nature of their communication with me. As outlined in Chapter 2, I have guarded the names and addresses in my sample and used only strategies that would safeguard all identities. I even allowed myself to be jailed rather than alert the police to the nature of my research, thus avoiding the incrimination of respondents through their possible association with a man under surveillance.

In writing this report, I have exercised great care to conceal all identifying tags. This is not always an easy task when one is also concerned with avoiding distortion of his data, but it is an essential one. The question I have always asked in this connection is: Could the respondent still recognize himself without having any others recognize him? I may have failed in a few cases to meet the first part of this standard, but I am confident that I have not failed to meet the second.

## Problems of Consequentiality

Finally, I must weigh the possible results of this research. It is not enough to plead that I am no seer, for I am a sociologist and should have some ability for prediction. If I have been honest enough in my analyses and convincing enough in their presentation, there should be no negative reaction from the forces of social control. I should hope they would have learned something. Perhaps some will move to construct and situate restrooms in such a way as to discourage the tearoom trade. Except where such activity constitutes an obvious public nuisance, I hope there will be no change in the tearoom scene. There is no need to drive this harmless activity underground. Those who deal in the sex market are resourceful, however, and I doubt that anything short of a total police state could erase the search for sex without commitment.

Others have suggested that I have produced an "operation manual for tearoom queens." If it is a good manual, perhaps I should be flattered, but that is not my purpose or concern. Those who know the game do not need a manual. As for the possibility of its use by potential deviants, I can only say that the world is filled with operation manuals, and people are selective as to which ones they use. I have little interest in manuals that would guide me in building a sailboat, and those who are not interested in engaging in homoerotic activity will not use this manual as a rule book.

I doubt that this work will have any effect in either increasing or decreasing the volume of homosexual activity in park restrooms. I do hope it will give readers a better understanding of the activity that is already there. I have no moral or intellectual objection to what goes on in the tearooms, and only a mild aesthetic one. I do have a moral objection to the way in which society reacts to those who take part in that action. As a scientist, I must believe that any addition to knowledge, which has suffered as little distortion as possible from the methods used, will help correct the superstition and cruelty that have marked such reaction in the past.

# Retrospect: Ethical Issues in Social Research

IT SHOULD BE evident to the reader that an author who devotes twenty percent of a monograph to exposition of his research methods and their ethical implications anticipates that some controversy will be raised about them. In 1969, however, I did not foresee the degree of both positive and negative reaction this study would inspire or that interest in its ethical implications would continue well into the following decade. The printing of excerpts from the book in *Trans-Action* magazine in January, 1970, and Nicholas von Hoffman's prompt reaction brought the issue to public attention as the first copies of the work came off the press. Rainwater and Horowitz responded with an editorial that was all the more timely because at just that time the professional associations of anthropologists, psychologists, and sociologists were debating new codes of ethics for their members. Glazer's book on field research methods appeared while "plumbers" were being dispatched from the White House as part of the most extensive program of domestic surveillance the American public has ever endured; and Warwick's paper was published while the nation was becoming increasingly sensitive to the dual dangers of snooping and secrecy. The essays I have included in this retrospect are those I judge to be the best written and most widely-read commentaries on the ethical issues elicited by my research. I hope that they, along with my own concluding essay, will provide useful material for discussion as social scientists attempt to clarify their research posture in a post-Watergate society.

# Sociological Snoopers and Journalistic Moralizers

## Part I
Nicholas von Hoffman

WE'RE so preoccupied with defending our privacy against insurance investigators, dope sleuths, counterespionage men, divorce detectives and credit checkers, that we overlook the social scientists behind the hunting blinds who're also peeping into what we thought were our most private and secret lives. But they are there, studying us, taking notes, getting to know us, as indifferent as everybody else to the feeling that to be a complete human involves having an aspect of ourselves that's unknown.

If there was any doubt about there being somebody who wants to know about anything any other human being might be doing it is cancelled out in the latest issue of *Trans-Action,* a popular but respected sociological monthly. The lead article, entitled "Impersonal Sex in Public Places," is a resume of a study done about the

"The Sociological Snoopers" reprinted by permission from the *Washington Post,* January 30, 1970. "On Journalistic Moralizers" is published by permission of Trans-Action, Inc., from *Trans-Action,* Vol. 7, May, 1970, copyright © by Trans-Action, Inc.

nature and pattern of homosexual activities in men's rooms. Laud Humphreys, the author, is an Episcopal priest, a duly pee-aich-deed sociologist, holding the rank of assistant professor at Southern Illinois University. The article is taken from *Tearoom Trade: Impersonal Sex in Public Places*.

Tearoom is the homosexual slang for men's rooms that are used for purposes other than those for which they were designed. However, if a straight male were to hang around a tearoom he wouldn't see anything out of the ordinary so that if you're going to find out what's happening you must give the impression that you're one of the gang.

"I had to become a participant observer of the furtive felonious acts," Humphreys writes in explaining his methodology, "Fortunately, the very fear or suspicion of tearoom participants produces a mechanism that makes such observation possible; a third man—generally one who obtains voyeuristic pleasure from his duties—serves as a lookout, moving back and forth from door to windows. Such a 'watchqueen,' as he is labeled in the homosexual argot, coughs when a police car stops nearby or when a stranger approaches. He nods affirmatively when he recognizes a man entering as being a 'regular.' Having been taught the watchqueen role by a cooperating respondent, I played that part faithfully while observing hundreds of acts of fellatio."

Most of the people Humphreys observed and took notes on had no idea what he was doing or that they, in disguised form, would be showing up in print at some time in the future. Of all the men he studied only a dozen were ever told what his real purpose was, yet as a sociologist he had to learn about the backgrounds and vital facts of the other tearoom visitors he'd seen. To do this Humphreys noted their license numbers and by tracing their cars learned their identities. He then allowed time to pass, disguised himself and visited these men under the color of doing a different, more innocuous door-to-door survey.

He describes what he did this way: "By passing as a deviant, I had observed their sexual behavior without disturbing it. Now I was faced with interviewing these men—often in the presence of their wives—without destroying them. . . . To overcome the danger of having a subject recognize me as a watchqueen, I changed my hair style, attire and automobile. At the risk of losing the more transient respondents, I waited a year between the sample gathering (in the tearoom) and the interviews, during which time I took notes on their homes and neighborhoods and acquired data on them from the city and county directories."

Humphreys said that he did everything possible to make sure the names of the men whose secrets he knew would never get out: "I kept only one copy of the master list of names and that was in a safe deposit box. I did all the transcribing of taped interviews myself and changed all identifying marks and signs. In one instance, I allowed myself to be arrested rather than let the police know what I was doing and the kind of information I had."

Even so, it remains true that he collected information that could be used for blackmail, extortion, and the worst kind of mischief without the knowledge of the people involved. *Trans-Action* defends the ethics of Humphreys' methodology on the basis of purity of motive and the argument that he was doing it for a good cause, that is getting needed, reliable information about a difficult and painful social problem.

Everybody who goes snooping around and spying on people can be said to have good motives. The people whom Sen. Sam Ervin is fighting, the ones who want to give the police the right to smash down your door without announcing who they are if they think you have pot in your house, believe they are well-motivated. They think they are preventing young people from destroying themselves. J. Edgar Hoover unquestionably believes he's protecting the country against subversion when he orders your telephone tapped. Those who may want to overthrow the government are just as well motivated by their lights. Since everybody can be said to be equally well motivated, it's impossible to form a judgment on what people do by assessing their intentions.

To this Laud Humphreys replies that his methods were less objectionable than getting his data by working through the police: "You do walk a really perilous tightrope in regard to ethical matters in studies like this, but, unless someone will walk it, the only source of information will be the police department, and that's dangerous for a society. The methods I used were the least intrusive possible. Oh, I could have hidden in the ceiling as the police do, but then I would have been an accomplice in what they were doing."

Humphreys believes that the police in many cities extort bribes from homosexuals they catch in tearooms. He also thinks that "what's more common is putting an investigation report on file. Often when they catch somebody, they don't arrest him but they get his name, address and employer. There's no defense against this and no way of knowing when the information will be used in the future. I agree there may be a dangerous precedent in studying deviant behavior this way but in some places vice squads use closed circuit TV to look into tearooms and in many cities they use decoys. To my mind *these* are the people who're the dangerous observers."

Some people may answer that by saying a study on such a topic constitutes deviant sociological behavior, a giving-in to the discipline's sometimes peculiar taste for nosing around oddballs. But in the study of man anything men do should be permissible to observe and try to understand. Furthermore, Humphreys has evidence and arguments to show that, far from being a rare and nutty aberration, tearoom activity is quite common.

He cites a UCLA law review study showing that in a four-year period in Los Angeles 274 of a total of 493 men arrested for homosexual activities were picked up in tearooms. He has another study in Mansfield, Ohio, that rural fleshpot, saying that police operating with a camera behind a one-way mirror caught 65 men in the course of only two weeks. FBI national crime figures don't have a special category for tearoom arrests, but Humphreys has enough indicative evidence to allow him to say it's a big problem. Even if it weren't, so many parents are worried about their sons being approached by homosexuals that we believe it's a big problem.

Humphreys' study suggests that tearoom habitues stay clear of teen-agers. "I never saw an instance of a teen-ager being approached. The men in the tearoom are scared to death of teen-agers. When a teen-ager comes in the action breaks off and everybody gets out. You have to give a definite sign before you'll be approached (in his book he goes into detail) so they never approach anyone who hasn't done so. Anyway, there's no problem of recruiting teen-agers because teen-agers are too busy trying to join."

Incontestably such information is useful to parents, teen-agers themselves, to policemen, legislators and many others, but it was done by invading some people's privacy. This newspaper could probably learn a lot of things that the public has a right and need to know if its reporters were to use disguises and the gimmickry of modern, transistorized, domestic espionage, but there is a policy against it. No information is valuable enough to obtain by nipping away at personal liberty, and that is true no matter who's doing the gnawing, John Mitchell and the conservatives over at the Justice Department or Laud Humphreys and the liberals over at the Sociology Department.

# Part II
# Irving Louis Horowitz and Lee Rainwater

COLUMNIST Nicholas von Hoffman's quarrel with Laud Humphreys' "Impersonal Sex in Public Places" starkly raises an issue that has grown almost imperceptibly over the last few years, and now threatens to create in the next decade a tame sociology to replace the fairly robust one that developed during the sixties. For most of their history, the disciplines of sociology and social psychology were considered a kind of joke, an oddball activity pursued by academic types who cultivated an arcane jargon that either concealed ivory tower views about human reality, or simply said things that everyone knew already.

Somehow, during the 1960s, that image began to shift quite dramatically. People suddenly began to look to sociologists and social psychologists for explanations of what was going on, of why the society was plagued with so many problems. Sociological jargon, perspectives and findings began to enter people's conversation and thinking in a way that no one would have imagined a few years before. All during the sixties enrollment in sociology classes in colleges and universities increased at an accelerating rate. What sociologists had to say about international relations, or race problems, or deviant behavior, or health care, or the crisis of the city became standard parts of the ways Americans explained themselves to themselves.

But as the sociological enterprise grew, there also grew up a reaction against it, especially among those who are also in the business of interpreting the society to itself. For, as sociologists know (even if they sometimes forget it), any statement, even of "fact," about a society is also a political assertion in that, whatever the motivation of the speaker, his views can have an impact on the political processes of the society. But there are other kinds of occupations that have traditionally had the right to make these kinds of statements. Foremost among them have been journalists, clergymen, politicians and intellectuals generally. When his perspectives and findings began to gain wider currency, the sociologist became willy-nilly a competitor in the effort to establish an interpretation of what we are all about. And so, these past few years, sociologists have been getting their lumps from those various groups.

With increasing stridency, traditional politicians have railed against university social scientists who exercise undue influence on the way public issues are defined. Right and left militants have sought to dry up their ability to influence public definitions through derision and systematic efforts to deny them access to sources of data. Beginning in the fifties, right wing groups launched successive campaigns against behavioral scientists, as both practitioners and teachers, culminating most recently in the John Birch Society campaign against sex education. All this has had a quiet influence on the research work of social scientists. Slowly but perceptibly over the last couple of years, and with no sign of abatement, sociologists and social psychologists are being told by a varied chorus that they talk too much, or if not too much, at least that too many of the things they say had better be left unsaid, or the saying of them ought to be left to the traditional spokesmen. What has proved particularly galling about the sociologist, as these other spokesmen view him, is his claim to the mantle of science. For all the tentativeness and roughness of sociological science, it makes at least that claim, and so represents a very powerful threat to the more traditional interpreters of reality.

Perhaps the closest competitors of all are journalists. The intertwinings of journalistic and sociological enterprise are complex indeed and have been from the early days of empirical American sociology. After all, Robert Park was a working journalist, and saw sociology simply as a better journalism because it got at the "big picture." Predictably, then, journalists often feel a deep ambivalence about empirical sociology. On the one hand, it represents a resource that can be quite useful in doing journalistic work. On the other hand, for the ambitious practitioner of personal journalism, there is always the threat to his authority, his potential punditry, by a group of fellow interpreters of the world who lay claim to science as the basis of what they say.

It is perhaps for this reason that von Hoffman so readily applies to sociologists a standard of investigative conduct that few journalists could measure up to, and why he is so unwilling to accept the relevance of the socially constructive purpose to which sociological activities are directed.

Sociologists have tended to assume that well-intentioned people fully accept the desirability of demystification of human life and culture. In the age of Aquarius, however, perhaps such a view will be recognized as naive.

"They are there, studying us, taking notes, getting to know us, as indifferent as everybody else to the feeling that to be a complete human involves having an aspect of ourselves that's unknown." Von Hoffman seems to mean this to be a statement about the right to privacy in a legal sense, but it really represents a denial of the ability of people to understand themselves and each other in an existential sense. This denial masks a fear, not that intimate details of our lives will be revealed to *others,* but rather that we may get to know *ourselves* better and have to confront what up to now we did not know about ourselves. Just as psychoanalysis was a scientific revolution as threatening to traditional conceptions as those of Galileo and Kepler had been, it may well be that the sociologist's budding ability to say something about the how's and why's of men's relationships to each other is deeply threatening not only to the established institutions in society, but also in a more personal way to all members of society.

Von Hoffman says he is talking about the invasion of privacy, but his celebration of the "aspect of ourselves that's unknown" shows a deeper worry about making rational and open what he conceives to be properly closed and dark in human reality. Von Hoffman concentrates his outrage on the methods Humphreys used to learn what he did, but we believe that at bottom he is not much different from other critics of behavioral science who make exactly the same points that von Hoffman makes with respect to research, even when it involves people who freely give their opinions, attitudes and autobiographical data to interviewers. This, too, is regarded as a threat because eventually it will remove some of the mystery from human life.

But von Hoffman recognizes that his most appealing charge has to do with privacy, and so he makes much of the fact that Humphreys collected information that could be used for "blackmail, extortion, and the worst kind of mischief without the knowledge of the people involved."

Here his double standard is most glaringly apparent. Journalists routinely, day in, day out, collect information that could be used for "blackmail, extortion, and the worst kind of mischief without the knowledge of the people involved." But von Hoffman knows that the purpose of their work is none of those things, and so long as their information is collected from public sources, I assume he wouldn't attack them. Yet he nowhere compares the things sociologists do with the things his fellow journalists do. Instead, he couples Humphreys' "snooping around," "spying on people" with similarly "well-motivated" invaders of privacy as J. Edgar Hoover and John Mitchell.

To say the least, the comparison is invidious; the two kinds of enterprises are fundamentally different. No police group seeks to acquire information about people with any other goal than that of, in some way, prosecuting them. Policemen collect data, openly or under cover, in order to put someone in jail. Whatever it is, the sociological enterprise is not that. Sociologists are not interested in directly affecting the lives of the particular people they study. They are interested in those individuals only as representatives of some larger aggregate—in Humphreys' case, all participants in the tea-room action. Therefore, in almost all sociological research, the necessity to preserve the anonymity of the respondent is not an onerous one, because no purpose at all would be served by identifying the respondents.

In this respect, journalists are in fact much closer to policemen than sociologists are. Journalists often feel that their function is to point the finger at particular malefactors. Indeed their effort to acquire information about individuals is somewhat like that of the police, in the sense that both seek to affect importantly the lives of the particular individuals who are the object of their attention. Perhaps this kind of misconception of what the sociologist is about, and the total absence of any comment on the role of the journalist, leads von Hoffman to persistently misinterpret Humphreys' research as "invading some people's privacy." Yet everything Humphreys knew about the deviant behavior of the people he studied was acquired in a public context (indeed, on public land).

We believe in the work Humphreys has done, in its principled humaneness, in its courage to learn the truth and in the constructive contribution that it makes toward our understanding of all the issues, including the moral, raised by deviant behavior in our society. *Trans-Action* has always been supportive of and open to the sort of enterprise he has so ably performed; we only wish there were more of it. Furthermore, a vigorous defense of Laud Humphreys' research (and that of others before and after him) is eminently possible and glaringly needed.

Sociologists uphold the right to know in a context of the surest protection for the integrity of the subject matter and the private rights of the people studied. Other groups in society may turn on different pivots: the right of law, the protection of individuals against invasion of privacy and so forth. But whoever is "right" in the abstract, there is a shared obligation for all parties to a controversy to step forth with fullness and fairness to present their cases before the interested public—and to permit that public to enter discussions which affect them so directly. Without this, a right higher than public disclosure or private self will be denied—the right to full public discourse.

Von Hoffman's points are: that in studying the sexual behavior of men in restrooms, Humphreys violated their rights to intimacy and privacy; that the homosexuals were and remain unaware of the true purpose of Humphreys' presence as a lookout; and that in the follow-up questionnaire the researcher further disguised himself and the true nature of his inquiry. For von Hoffman the point of principle is this: that although Humphreys' intent may have been above reproach and that in point of fact his purposes are antithetical to those of the police and other public officials, he nonetheless in his own way chipped away at the essential rights of individuals in conducting his investigations. Therefore, the ends, the goals, however noble and favorable to the plight of sexual deviants, do not justify the use of any means that further undermine personal liberties. Let us respond to these propositions as directly as possible.

## Cops and Knowledge

First, the question of the invasion of privacy has several dimensions. We have already noted the public rather than the private nature of park restrooms. It further has to be appreciated that all participants in sexual activities in restrooms run the constant risk that they have among them people who have ulterior purposes. The vocabulary of motives is surely not limited or circumscribed by one man doing research but is as rich and as varied as the number of participants themselves. The fact that in this instance there was a scientific rather than a sexual or criminal "ulterior motive" does not necessarily make it more hideous or more subject to criticism, but perhaps less so.

Second, the question of disguising "the true nature" and purpose of this piece of research has to be put into some perspective. To begin with, let us assume that the research was worth doing in the first place. We know almost nothing about impersonal sex in public places, and the fact that we know so little has in no small way contributed to the fact that the cops feel that *they* know all that needs to be known about the matter. Who, then, is going to gather this countervailing knowledge? Von Hoffman implies that the research enterprise would be ethically pure if Humphreys were himself a full participant, like John Rechy. But to be able to conduct investigations of the type Humphreys performed requires a sociological imagination rare enough among his professional peers, much less homosexuals in public places. Moreover, to assume that the investigator must share all of his knowledge with those being investigated also assumes a common universe of discourse very rarely found in any kind of research, much less the kind involving sexual deviance. Furthermore, the conduct of Humphreys' follow-up inquiries had to be performed with tact and with skill precisely because he discovered that so many of the people in his survey were married men and family men. Indeed, one of the great merits of Humphreys' research is that it reveals clearly etched class, ethnic, political and occupational characteristics of sexual participants never before properly understood. Had he not conducted the follow-up interviews, we would once again be thrown back on simple-minded, psychological explanations that are truly more voyeuristic than analytic, or on the policeman's kind of knowledge. It is the sociological dimensions of sexuality in public places that make this a truly scientific breakthrough.

To take on the ethic of full disclosure at the point of follow-up interviews was impossible given the purposes of the research. If Humphreys had told his respondents that he knew they were tea-room participants, most of them would have cooperated. But in gaining their cooperation in this way he would have had to reveal that he knew of their behavior. This he could not responsibly do, because he could not control the potentially destructive impact of that knowledge. Folding the participants into a larger sample for a different survey allowed for the collection of the data without posing such a threat. And the purpose of the research was not, after all, destruction, as von Hoffman concedes. Therefore, the posture of Humphreys toward those interviewed must be viewed as humane and considerate.

But what von Hoffman is arguing is that this research ought not to have been done, that Humphreys should have laid aside his obligation to society as a sociologist and taken more seriously his obligation to society as a citizen. Von Hoffman maintains that the researcher's intentions—the pursuit of truth, the creation of countervailing knowledge, the demystification of shadowy areas of human experience—are immaterial. "Everybody who goes snooping around and spying on people can be said to have good motives," von Hoffman writes, going on to compare Humphreys' work with policemen armed with a "no-knock" statute.

This is offensive, but it is also stupid. We have called von Hoffman a moralizer, and his moralizing consists precisely in his imputing a moral equivalence to police action, under probably unconstitutional law, and the work of a scholar. Of course the road to hell is paved with good intentions, but good intentions sometimes lead to other places as well. The great achievement of Humphreys' research has been in laying bare the conditions of the tearoom trade, the social classes who engage in such activities and the appalling idiocy and brutality of society's (police) efforts to cope with the situation. Moreover, he has, relative to some of his professional colleagues, answered the question Which side are you on? with uncharacteristic candor, while at the same time he has conducted himself in the best tradition of professional sociology.

The only interesting issue raised by von Hoffman is one that he cannot, being a moralizer, do justice to. It is whether the work one does is good, and whether the good it does outweighs the bad. "No information," he writes, "is valuable enough to obtain by nipping away at personal liberty. . . ." It remains to be proven that Humphreys did in fact nip away at anyone's liberty; so far we have only von Hoffman's assertion that he did and Humphreys' assurance that he did not. But no amount of self-righteous dogmatizing can still the uneasy and troublesome thought that what we have here is not a conflict between nasty snoopers and the right to privacy, but a conflict between two goods: the right to privacy and the right to know.

What is required is a distinction between the responsibilities of social scientists to seek and to obtain greater knowledge and the responsibilities of the legal system to seek and obtain maximum security for the private rights of private citizens. Nothing is more insidious or dangerous than the overprofessionalization of a trade. But for social scientists to play at being lawyers, at settling what the law is only now beginning to give attention to, is clearly not a sound way of solving the problems raised.

## Liberal Contradictions

It is certainly not that sociologists should deliberately violate any laws of the land, only that they should leave to the courtrooms and to the legislatures just what interpretation of these laws governing the protection of private citizens is to be made. Would the refusal of a family to disclose information to the Census Bureau on the grounds of the right to privacy take precedence over the United States government's right to knowledge in order to make budgetary allocations and legislation concerning these people? The really tough moral problem is that the idea of an inviolable right of privacy may move counter to the belief that society is obligated to secure the other rights and welfare of its citizenry. Indeed one might say that this is a key contradiction in the contemporary position of the liberal: he wants to protect the rights of private citizens, but at the same time he wants to develop a welfare system that could hardly function without at least some knowledge about these citizens. Von Hoffman's strident defense of the right to privacy is laudable; we are all behind him. What is inexcusable in someone of his intelligence is that he will not see that the issues he raises pose a moral dilemma that cannot be resolved in the abstract, only in the particular case. He may think that Humphreys' research is the moral equivalent of John Mitchell's FBI. We don't, and we have tried to explain why.

Several other minor points in the von Hoffman article require at least brief recollection. First, *Trans-Action* has made no statement until this time on the ethics of the kind of research conducted by Laud Humphreys. Indeed, our editorial statements have always emphasized the right to privacy of the researcher over and against the wishes of established authority. To say that *Trans-Action* has defended this piece in terms of "priority of motive" is an error of fact. The intent of *Trans-Action* is to present the best available social science research, and we believe Humphreys' work admirably fits that description.

## Public Rights and Private Agony

Finally, von Hoffman's gratuitous linkage of the "conservatives over at the Justice Department" and the "liberals over at the sociology department" makes for a pleasant balance of syntax, but it makes no sense in real life terms. The political ideology of Laud Humphreys is first of all not an issue. At no point in the article or outside the article is the question of the political preference of the researcher raised.

We would suggest that von Hoffman is the real "liberal" in this argument, for it is he who is assuming the correctness of the classical liberal argument for the supremacy of the private person over and against the public commonweal. This assumption makes it appear that he is willing to suffer the consequences of the abuse of homosexuals by blackmailers, policemen or would-be participants, but that he is not willing to suffer the consequences of a research design or to try to change the situation by a factual understanding of the social sources of these problems.

Laud Humphreys has gone beyond the existing literature in sexual behavior and has proven once again, if indeed proof were ever needed, that ethnographic research is a powerful tool for social understanding and policymaking. And these are the criteria by which the research should finally be evaluated professionally. If the nonprofessional has other measurements of this type of research, let him present these objections in legal brief and do so explicitly. No such attempt to intimidate Humphreys for wrongdoing in any legal sense has been made, and none is forthcoming. The only indictment seems to be among those who are less concerned with the right to know than they are with the sublime desire to remain in ignorance. In other words, the issue is not liberalism vs. conservatism or privacy vs. publicity, but much more simply and to the point, the right of scientists to conduct their work as against the right of journalists to defend social mystery and private agony.

# Tearoom Trade: Means and Ends in Social Research

Donald P. Warwick

We're so preoccupied with defending our privacy against insurance investigators, dope sleuths, counterespionage men, divorce detectives and credit checkers, that we overlook the social scientists behind the hunting blinds who're also peeping into what we thought were our most private and secret lives. But there they are, studying us, taking notes, getting to know us, as indifferent as everybody else to the feeling that to be a complete human being involves having an aspect of ourselves that's unknown.

Nicholas von Hoffman,
*The Washington Post.*

Any man who remains in a public restroom for more than five minutes is apt to be either a member of the vice squad or someone on the make. As yet, he is not suspected of being a social scientist.

Laud Humphreys, *Tearoom Trade: Impersonal Sex in Public Places, p. 26.*

Reprinted from *The Hastings Center Studies,* Institute of Society, Ethics and the Life Sciences, Vol. 1, No. 1 (1973), pp. 27-38. Reprinted with permission of the Institute of Society, Ethics and the Life Sciences, Hastings-on-Hudson, New York.

IN THE mid-1960s Laud Humphreys undertook an intensive sociological study of male homosexual activities in public restrooms. The results were published two years ago in *Tearoom Trade.* (A "tearoom" is a location in which homosexual encounters are reputed to take place.) Humphreys' methods were varied and painstaking, ranging from direct observation of homosexual acts in restrooms to a follow-up survey with men who were observed in these acts. That they were also controversial is made evident by the statement of Nicholas von Hoffman attacking the scope and methods of Humphreys' study and the growing intrusiveness of social research.

Humphreys' research provides a case study in the impact of social research on human freedom. I have chosen *Tearoom Trade* as an example partly because it is recent and controversial, partly because of its varied methodology, and partly because the author and his defenders comment explicitly on its research ethics. It is admittedly an extreme example in many respects, and it is far from typical of social scientific research. Most social scientists and social research institutes go to great lengths to avoid deception, misrepresentation, possible harm to respondents, and other problems arising in Humphreys' study of homosexuals. Because their continuing success depends precisely on maintaining the confidence and good will of the participating public, large survey research institutes are particularly scrupulous in this regard. Nevertheless, though *Tearoom Trade* is not typical, it is instructive in pointing up issues of ethics which arise in lesser degree in many other studies.[1]

## The Sociologist as Watchqueen

To grasp the implications of Humphreys' research one must have a clear picture of his strategy and tactics. Once he chose to train his

1. This paper has profited from the suggestions and criticisms of numerous colleagues and friends, including Robert Michels of Columbia University; Michael Horowitz, New York City; Herbert Kelman, Ann Orlov, Bruce Smith, and Mary Thomas, Harvard University; Paul Rosencrantz, College of the Holy Cross; C. Michael Lanphier of York University, Toronto; Leon Kass and Daniel Callahan. Lee Rainwater of Harvard University was especially helpful in commenting on the factual accuracy of my interpretations of the research in question. The manuscript was also sent to Laud Humphreys of the State University of New York for his comments.

sights on the problem of impersonal sex, he had to gain entry to the society of male homosexuals. Social deviants inside restrooms and elsewhere develop careful defenses against outsiders, including special gestures and extreme caution with strangers. After spending some time exploring various public restrooms, Humphreys discovered a relatively simple and convenient *entree* to observation: the role of "watchqueen."

Fortunately, the very fear and suspicion of tearoom participants produces a mechanism that makes such observation possible: a third man (generally one who obtains voyeuristic pleasures from his duties) serves as a lookout. Such a "watchqueen," as he is labeled in the homosexual argot, coughs when a police car stops nearby or when a stranger approaches. He nods affirmatively when he recognizes a man entering as being a "regular." Having been taught the watchqueen role by a cooperating respondent, I played that part faithfully while observing hundreds of acts of fellatio.[2]

To record the full details of his observations Humphreys made use of a "Systematic Observation Sheet." Space was provided for the time and place; the weather; the age, dress, general appearance, and automobile of the participants; their specific role in the activities; and a floor plan of the restroom. To be sure that the information was fresh, Humphreys took field notes *in situ* with the aid of a portable tape recorder hidden under a carton in the front seat of his car.

Through patient time-and-place sampling of selected sites he came up with a list of 134 active participants in fellatio. He also identified each participant (except two walkers) with an automobile and duly recorded its state and license number. He then sought to learn more about these men by finding their names, addresses, and the year and make of their cars in state license registers. "Fortunately, friendly policemen gave me access to the license registers, without asking to see the numbers or becoming too inquisitive about the type of 'market research' in which I was engaged."[3] With various kinds of attrition the final sample of identifiable tearoom participants dwindled to 100.

2. Laud Humphreys, "The Sociologist as Voyeur," *Trans-Action* 7:15, May, 1970.
3. Humphreys, *Tearoom Trade,* p. 38.

From the beginning Humphreys felt it important to do more than observe the minutiae of male homosexuality in tearooms. He also wanted to explore the social origins and present circumstances of the participants. The sample of 100 names and addresses provided an excellent opportunity to collect this information—if he could gain access to the individuals involved. Before moving to a full-scale household survey he spent a Christmas vacation recording a description of each individual's residence and neighborhood. But some questions could be answered only by personal interviews.

The author admits that this last stage of his data-collection efforts raised serious ethical problems. "I already knew that many of my respondents were married and that all were in a highly discreditable position and fearful of discovery. How could I approach these covert deviants for interviews?"[4]

The solution was again ingenious. While conducting his own research Humphreys also held another position in which he was responsible for developing an interview schedule to be used in a "social health survey" of a random sample of males in the community. "With permission from the survey's directors, I could add my sample to the larger group (thus enhancing their anonymity) and interview them as part of the social health survey."[5] The resulting "random sample" consisted of addresses of 50 homosexual and 50 control respondents.

For various reasons Humphreys was anxious to interview the homosexual group himself, but he was also concerned that he might be recognized. To minimize this possibility he waited at least one year from the date of the original contacts, and changed his hair style, dress, and car. He claims that none of the respondents recognized him or seemed unduly suspicious about the "health survey," despite the fact that it contained questions about marital sexuality. It is possible, however, that a few respondents were better at disguising their emotions than the investigator was in detecting them.

The findings of the study were reported in two forms: statistical tables with the usual controls for occupation, marital status, age,

4. Humphreys, "The Sociologist as Voyeur," p. 15.
5. *Ibid.*

etc.; and vignettes serving as case studies. The author claims that he went to unusual lengths to protect the confidentiality of the results without distorting them in the process. "The question I have always asked myself in this connection is: Could the respondent still recognize himself without having any others recognize him? I may have failed in a few cases to meet the first part of this standard, but I am confident that I have not failed to meet the second."[6]

How, then, should we evaluate the overall ethics of Humphreys' study or, for that matter, any piece of social scientific research? The task would be easier if we could dismiss the study as worthless sociology or incompetent research, but it is neither. The problem is that there are no well-developed and generally acceptable ethical standards for judging serious research. It is not just that social scientists disagree among themselves on ethics but that the conceptualization of ethical problems in research remains at a very low level, with some notable exceptions.[7] As a step toward improving the state of the art I suggest the concept of human freedom as one yardstick for assessing research. How would it apply to the Humphreys' study?

## Human Freedom

The notion of human freedom offers a useful vantage point for judging the impact of social research on both individuals and the larger society. It suggests a broader range of ethical criteria than the commonly-used yardsticks of "privacy" and "dignity," while it seems more manageable from a conceptual standpoint than the idea of "rights."

Human freedom may be defined for present purposes as *the capacity, opportunity and incentive to make reflective choices and to act on these choices.* This definition includes two elements on which there is substantial agreement among writers on freedom: (1) the individual's ability to choose among alternatives and to originate action; and (2) circumstances in the environment which are favor-

6. Humphreys, *Tearoom Trade,* p. 172.

7. Cf. Herbert C. Kelman, *A Time to Speak: On Human Values and Social Research* (San Francisco: Jossey-Bass, 1968).

able to the suggestion of alternatives and the execution of action. To be free a man must have certain qualities within himself which permit him to choose and act, and also live in an environment which aids choice and does not impede his actions. Hence we may distinguish between *personal freedom* and *environmental freedom.*[8]

*Personal freedom,* which might also be termed psychological or dispositional freedom, is built on personality tendencies which help the individual to make reflective choices and to act on these choices. Viewed positively, it consists of the ability and will to choose and act within the matrix of the opportunities provided by the society within which one lives. Viewed negatively, it is the absence of fear, anxiety, defense mechanisms and other psychic qualities which impair rationality or impede action. *Environmental freedom,* in turn, comes close to the concept of liberty in Anglo-American philosophy and law. It includes both the absence of external impediments to individual action and the presence of conditions, such as information, aiding reflection and choice.

To be fair to social research it is important to conceptualize freedom in a manner that permits improvements as well as impairment. Too often discussions of ethics and the social sciences view research as a process which can only *limit* human freedom through such means as deception or invasions of privacy. What we need now is a kind of benefit/cost matrix permitting estimates of the net gains or losses for freedom involved in a given study.

## Freedom for Whom?

Whose freedom should be considered, and with what weight, in judging the ethics of social research? In the case of research involving human subjects at least four parties are involved: the individual participant (subject, respondent), the researcher, the larger society, and the researcher's profession. Many of the ethical problems in research spring from conflicts between the freedoms of these four parties. The researcher will usually place strong emphasis on the freedom of scientific inquiry. Social scientists typically justify in-

8. Cf. Donald P. Warwick, "Human Freedom and National Development," *Cross Currents* 18:495-517, 1968.

cursions into the private life of participants on the grounds that free men have the right to know, that scientific knowledge is the basis of social progress, or that the specific knowledge generated by their research will contribute to the alleviation of some pressing social problem. But these claims may conflict with the individual citizen's desire for a sense of dignity and a private sphere of existence. Similarly, the investigator's research procedures may enhance his freedom of inquiry at the expense of other members of his own and perhaps related professions. If Humphreys' study contributes to public suspicion about the trustworthiness of social scientists, as I think it does, then my freedom and that of my professional colleagues to do our kinds of research will suffer accordingly. Hence one of the most difficult problems facing the social sciences is how to assign priorities when the freedoms of various parties are incompatible. As T. R. Vaughan writes:

> There is no natural law to which the scientist can appeal. Like others, he bases his decisions on personal predilections and particular values. But one person's predilections—be he scientist or saint—are not perforce more natural than another's. The proclivity among scientists to minimize, if not ignore, competing social ethics, and to define science in some independent sense, is quite widespread. In short, the scientist typically subscribes to the notion that the end of knowledge justifies the scientific means.[9]

The debate stirred up by *Tearoom Trade* aptly illustrates the conflict between the freedom of the researcher and that of other parties. Especially instructive in this regard was the exchange between Nicholas von Hoffman of the *Washington Post* and the editors of *Trans-Action,* Irving Louis Horowitz and Lee Rainwater. Von Hoffman's argument is well-stated in his final sentence: "No information is valuable enough to obtain by nipping away at personal liberty, and that is true no matter who is doing the gnawing, John Mitchell and the conservatives over at the Justice Department or Laud Humphreys and the liberals over at the Sociology Depart-

9. Ted R. Vaughan, "Governmental Intervention in Social Research: Political and Ethical Dimensions in the Wichita Jury Recordings," *Ethics, Politics and Social Research,* ed. Gideon Sjoberg (Cambridge, Mass.: Schenkman Publishing Co., 1967), p. 71.

ment." Horowitz and Rainwater (who were listed by Humphreys as advisors to his research) responded in an editorial entitled "Sociological Snoopers and Journalistic Moralizers." Von Hoffman is portrayed there as a journalistic poacher who had invaded the sacred preserves of sociology. His main intent is not to question the ethics of social research, but to give sociology a few knocks to keep it in place. He is thus linked to "clergymen, politicians, and intellectuals generally" who are envious of sociology's rising power because it is a threat to their own.

## Social Research and the Individual Participant

Some of the most critical questions of ethics in social research deal with its impact on the individual participant, such as the respondents in Humphreys' study. Following the approach to freedom suggested earlier, we can point to positive as well as negative effects of the research process on such individuals.

### Benefits

What are some of the ways in which social research might enhance the personal freedom of the participant? Let us take survey research as an example. Critics of this method commonly emphasize the inconvenience and intrusions associated with surveys, but they overlook a number of satisfactions which it can provide.

First, individuals who know something about surveys may find in them an opportunity for self-expression. People often derive satisfaction from providing information or expressing an opinion on subjects in which they are interested. Often this satisfaction is enhanced when the resulting information may have some effect on the policies of a nation, community or employer. Another positive effect may stem from interpersonal response—the satisfaction found in sharing important events in one's life with a sympathetic listener. In Humphreys' study twelve of the men observed in public restrooms agree to be interviewed in some detail about their background and experiences. The author's account suggests that these men, who were told the purposes of the study, may have found it helpful to discuss their lives and problems with an outsider. A third positive quality is the sheer intellectual challenge of some studies. Respondents will often agree to be interviewed to satisfy their curiosity about what goes on in surveys and polls or to reduce loneliness and boredom. Fourth, the interview may lead to insights which are helpful and rewarding. There is some evidence, for example, that interviews following upon personal or social disasters, such as suicides among family members or deaths caused by tornadoes, help the respondent to make sense of highly confusing experiences. These four conditions can be considered positive contributors to individual freedom to the extent that they provide the individual with opportunities for self-expression or contribute to a reduction of fear and anxiety.

## Costs

Every method of social research using live human subjects entails certain potential risks or hazards to the freedom of the individuals involved. Foremost among these are deception, invasions of privacy, and harmful uses of the research findings.

*Deception.* Humphreys' research provides a unique case study of deception. The concatenation of misrepresentations and disguises in this effort must surely hold the world record for field research. Consider the following:

1. In the initial stages the author spent several months passing as a deviant ("another gay guy") in private gatherings, gay bars, an annual ball, a local bathhouse, movie theaters, and tearooms. "On one occasion, for instance, tickets to an after-hours party were sold to the man next to me at a bar. When I asked to buy one, I was told that they were 'full up.' Following the tip of another customer, I showed up anyway and walked right in."[10] All of this was to tool up for passing in closer quarters.

10. Humphreys, *Tearoom Trade,* p. 25.

2. Humphreys misrepresented his identity while serving as "watchqueen" in the public restrooms. While carrying out his duties in this role he gave no indication to the lead actors about his real reasons for being there. He defends his actions on the following grounds:

Since one's identity within the interaction membrane of the tearoom is represented only in terms of the participant role he assumes, there was no misrepresentation on my part as an observer: I was indeed a "voyeur," though in the sociological and not the sexual sense. My role was primarily that of watchqueen, and that role I played well and faithfully. In that setting, then, I misrepresented my identity no more than anyone else.[11]

Humphreys gives himself away with his comments on being a "voyeur." It is clear that he represented himself to the participants as a voyeur in the *sexual* sense, and made himself credible in that role by acting as the good and faithful watchqueen. Also, it is plain that he did misrepresent his identity more than others, save visiting policemen or blackmailers. The men who came to the tearooms saw each other accurately—as individuals seeking a certain type of satisfaction with anonymity and little commitment. Humphreys came there *primarily* as a sociologist carrying out research on deviance.

3. Humphreys disguised the fact that he was making an oral record of his observations by hiding a tape recorder in the front seat of his car. The point of this procedure was to avoid the possibility that those frequenting nearby tearooms would discover his true identity.

4. He deceived the police about the nature of his study ("market research") in order to gain access to automobile license registers.

5. In carrying out the household survey he allowed a year to lapse from the time of the original contacts and changed his appearance, attire, and automobile to avoid being recognized as the watchqueen. Is this deception? The author denies any false representation in this procedure, resorting again to the "two hats" argument. "I

11. *Ibid.*, pp. 170-171.

wore only one of two possible hats, rather than going in disguise."[12] The only problem is that while changing hats he also changed the hair styles, looks, and clothes beneath them and switched cars.

6. Presumably when he introduced the study he told the respondents that they were part of a random cross-section sample chosen to represent the whole metropolitan area, that this was a "social health survey of men in the community," and that they were anonymous. If so, the first point is a grave misrepresentation of the actual sampling procedures, the second is at best misleading and incomplete, while the third is simply untrue (he knew their names). There would be fewer problems, on the other hand, if the respondents were told that the information was confidential, rather than anonymous. Though Humphreys does not go into detail about his procedures, he implies that the participants were promised anonymity.

7. In a larger sense, both Humphreys and the project director of the "social health survey" may have distorted that study by allowing a sub-sample of 50 homosexuals to be blended into the total cross-section. Random (probability) sampling is generally understood to include only those processes of selection in which the units of the sample are chosen by "chance" methods. Though Humphreys tried to adhere to this canon in choosing his own sample, it is hard to see how these individuals could be treated in one moment as persecuted social deviants and in the next as representative males in the metropolitan area.

Humphreys justifies his research tactics on the grounds of "situation ethics."

> As I learned during the time I administered examinations in Christian Ethics to candidates for the priesthood, questions that arise in regard to means are always relative. There are no "good" or "bad" methods—only "better" or "worse" ones. Neither interview schedules nor laboratory experiments nor participant observation can be neatly classified as involving either "open" or "disguised" approaches. I have never known an interviewer to be completely honest with his respondents; were this so, the whole concern with constructing an "effective" questionnaire

12. *Ibid.*, p. 171.

could be dropped. Neither does any researcher ever have adequate insight for a perfect representation of his identity; it is always a matter of greater or lesser misrepresentation.[13]

This statement invites several comments. First, it is grossly misleading to imply that Christian ethics as a whole has embraced the absolute relativism of extreme situation ethics. Even a casual reading of recent work on the ethics of research should lay this notion to rest.[14] Second, and more serious, by the author's logic there is no *intrinsic* evil in any research procedure, including the medical experimentation carried out in Nazi Germany, the use of torture to determine the character of human behavior under extreme stress, or the injection of live cancer cells into healthy subjects without their knowledge or consent. None of these methods is *bad*—only *worse* in comparison with others. Admittedly the situation and circumstances are important considerations in evaluating the ethics of research, but Humphreys seems to rule out any notion of inviolable rights for the individual. This position seems curious in view of his absolute moral outrage at the situation of homosexuals in contemporary society. Third, the author is guilty of ethical sleight-of-hand in equating the seriousness of outright deception with situations in which researchers are not "completely honest" with their subjects or try to construct an "effective" questionnaire. Here we are very much in the realm of the relative, but important distinctions can still be drawn. For example, I know of no ethical theory holding that the individual should be *completely* honest with others in human interaction. Even if such honesty were possible, one could argue that it is destructive, and therefore unethical, to reveal all of our misgivings, hostilities, and affections toward others when first meeting them. It is possible, on the other hand, to provide survey respondents with a basically accurate statement on the scope and purposes of the research. They may not know much about survey research or the intricacies of data processing, but they can be given a fair idea of what they are getting into. This situation of roughly accurate but less than complete understanding is rather different

13. *Ibid.*, pp. 169-170.

14. James Gustafson, "Basic Ethical Issues in the Bio-Medical Fields," *Soundings* 53:151-180, 1970.

than one in which the investigator deliberately misrepresents a study by leaving out important information about how and why the respondent was chosen, as in Humphreys' research.

*Privacy*. Privacy is related to personal freedom in the sense that certain aspects of the self are seen as inviolable or subject to discussion only under the most restricted conditions. A crucial part of freedom consists of the capacity and opportunity *not* to reveal or even discuss certain beliefs, attitudes and behaviors. The question raised by *Tearoom Trade* and other social research is how far the social scientist can intrude into the inner reaches of the self without jeopardizing freedom. This problem is highlighted in the quotation by Nicholas von Hoffman at the beginning of this article.

The response to von Hoffman's criticism by the editors of *Trans-Action* is instructive. At first they are unwilling to take his charges seriously, and attempt to undercut them by an *ad hominem* counterattack.

> Von Hoffman seems to mean this to be a statement about the right to privacy in a legal sense, but it really represents a denial of the ability of people to understand themselves and each other in an existential sense. This denial masks a fear, not that intimate details of our lives will be revealed to *others,* but rather that we may get to know *ourselves* better and have to confront what up to now we did not know about ourselves.[15]

In other words, von Hoffman's concern about the privacy of others covers up a deep fear of his own unconscious aroused by Humphreys' data.

Later, however, they admit that the study does involve a conflict between two goods: the right to know and the right to privacy. They then offer several lines of defense for Humphreys' methods. First, Humphreys had as much right as anyone else to be in the restrooms since they were public. This is true enough, except that the point of *Tearoom Trade* is to show that tightly private interaction networks develop in public places. Second, those who frequent tearooms run the risk "that they have among them people

15. Horowitz and Rainwater, "Sociological Snoopers and Journalistic Moralizers."

who have ulterior purposes. . . . The fact that in this instance there was a scientific rather than a criminal or sexual 'ulterior motive' does not necessarily make it more hideous or more subject to criticism, but perhaps less so."[16] This is certainly damning by faint defense. Third, it is Humphreys' obligation as a sociologist to pursue the truth, to create countervailing knowledge about homosexuality (against the police), and to demystify "the shadowy areas of human experience." Presumably these ends justify the means chosen, though the authors do not say precisely why or how far they would extend such legitimizing power. Fourth, the law itself is vague on the definition of privacy and incidents constituting invasions of privacy. Until such definitions are clarified, Humphreys' research should not be criticized for invading privacy. One might counter by pointing out that changes and clarifications in the law are usually brought about in *response* to debate and criticism. In short, it is hard to escape the conclusion that, whatever the current state of legal definitions of privacy, Humphreys intruded much too far into the lives of the men he observed and studied. From now on tearoom participants must be on the alert not only for blackmailers and policemen, but for sociologists in voyeur's clothing.

*Misuse of Information.* One of the greatest fears plaguing any conscientious social scientist is that information collected with good intentions or given him in good faith by others will be used against them or bring them harm. The data collected by Humphreys could have been used either for purposes of blackmail or criminal prosecution. During the process of data-collection and analysis the master list of names was stored in a safe-deposit box, and then was later destroyed. (One would conclude from reading *Tearoom Trade* that the master list was still in the safe-deposit box. I learned about its destruction only through personal correspondence.) A critical problem with these and other social science data is that they enjoy no legal protection or privilege. This situation arises, of course, with hundreds of sociologists, social workers, newspaper reporters, and others who possess potentially damaging information. However, Humphreys was running unusual risks by collecting

16. *Ibid.*

the kind of data he did. This is one of the few social scientific studies which would have lent itself directly to a grand jury investigation. Homosexuality, especially in public restrooms, is clearly a more sensitive and explosive subject than many of the topics on which social scientists collect potentially damaging data. Also, its sensitivity and potential harm to respondents were heightened by the fact that it dealt primarily with one city.

A second and equally grave problem is the anxiety produced among the individuals studied by the fact that *someone knows*. Probably some of the men are aware that they were studied as a result of the publication of *Tearoom Trade*. Moreover, unless they have read the book, they may not know of the precautions taken with the data and, even if they did, they would not know that the master file containing their names had been destroyed. Thus some may rightly wonder whether Humphreys or someone else will somehow reveal their indiscretions and thereby damage or destroy their reputation. It might be objected that the social scientist should not be responsible for the irrational fears of those he studies. My reply is that any conscientious professional person *must* be concerned about the anxiety he creates in people as a result of his work. This concern should be especially great when a researcher imposes himself on others for his own ends, without their knowledge. The men in the tearoom did not, after all, *ask* to be studied or helped.

## Social Research and the Society

The intrusions of social research are commonly justified by the benefits it brings to the larger society. The census and sample surveys, for example, play a vital role in supplying governments with data needed for economic and social planning or action programs. However, social research must also be set in the context of a rising tendency to collect more data on individuals and groups, and increasing sophistication in the storage, retrieval, and analysis of these data. The growing prevalence of such research has raised doubts about the conventional liberal assumptions concerning the inherent value of information. These assumptions are clearly reflected in the *Trans-Action* editorial defending the research by Laud Humphreys.

Sociologists have tended to assume that well-intentioned people fully accept the desirability of demystification of human life and culture. In the age of Aquarius, however, perhaps such a view will be recognized as naive.[17]

The only indictment seems to be among those who are less concerned with the right to know than they are with the sublime desire to remain in ignorance. In other words, the issue is not liberalism or conservatism or privacy vs. publicity, but much more simply and to the point, the right of scientists to conduct their work as against the right of journalists to defend social mystery and private agony.[18]

The logic here is amazingly facile: the more information we have about society, the happier we will be. Those who collect it are contributing to the alleviation of social misery; those who oppose it force the oppressed to live on in agony. While some degree of demystification may contribute to human freedom, it seems absurd to assume that extreme demystification produces social bliss. Men in every age—including the social scientists of the present—need illusions to be free, if only the illusion of destroying the illusions of others.

Another possible reactive effect of social research is to reinforce the tendency of individuals to be wary and to live "for the record." Arthur Miller states one side of the problem as follows:

As the populace becomes increasingly aware that a substantial number of facts are being preserved "on the record," people may start to doubt whether they have any meaning apart from the profile in the computer's files. As a result, they may begin to base their personal decisions, at least in part, on whether it will enhance their record image in the eyes of third parties who have control over important parts of their lives.[19]

17. *Ibid.*
18. *Ibid.*
19. Arthur R. Miller, "Personal Privacy in the Computer Age: the Challenge of a New Technology in an Information Oriented Society," *Michigan Law Review* 67:1150, 1969.

Complaints along these lines have already been lodged against the secret files maintained by federal agencies on political dissenters. The kind of research carried out by Humphreys raises a similar problem: an increased fear among ordinary citizens that someone, be he a social scientist or a credit checker, is watching. An important part of human freedom is the ability to withdraw into our home or other private domain and feel that we will not be observed. To the extent that social scientists engage in covert observation, however noble the cause, this freedom will be reduced. It is only in a totalitarian society that one must constantly look over his shoulder or check under his bed to be sure that he is not being observed and heard. The social scientist will say, of course, that covert observation is still rare, and that it is often justified by the higher cause it serves, such as helping homosexuals. However, this argument can be applied with equal force by the FBI, salesmen posing as survey researchers, and credit checkers entering suburban homes under various guises. Everyone feels that *his* cause is of paramount importance, and that the abuses wrought by *his* intrusion are minimal. At this stage we must be concerned not only about the impact of the single intrusion, but also with the cumulative effects of thousands of acts of prying on the quality of human life.

## The Researcher and the Research Professions

Humphreys' study further raises the question of the balance between the freedom of the individual researcher and that of his colleagues in allied professions. We might draw an analogy between social research and the growth of industry. Both make use of scarce resources, and both may create environmental pollution preventing further expansion. The resources consumed in social research include money, personnel, public tolerance, and the good will of the participants—all of which are finite. Just as the emission of industrial wastes can pollute rivers, lakes, and the atmosphere, so can the abuse of social research contaminate the environment for other users. The most common and harmful abuses are the sheer overexposure of the public to all types of research, and illegal activities, deception, misrepresentation, or other offensive behaviors on the part of researchers.

Viewed in this context the net effect of Humphreys' study on the research environment is likely to be negative. Undoubtedly public reaction to *Tearoom Trade* will be strongly affected by the subject matter and the way in which the findings are presented. Many readers, finding the whole topic revolting, will channel their distaste against the author and sociology in general. Indeed, Humphreys invites this reaction by lacing the text with graphic detail that does not seem to be called for by his scientific goals. Even so, I would strongly defend Humphreys' right to study this topic, however controversial it might be. My objections are not to the topic but to the tactics. Humphreys, however, sets himself above considerations of appearances and public opinion.

> Concern about "professional integrity," it seems to me, is symptomatic of a dying discipline. Let the clergy worry about keeping their cassocks clean; the scientist has too great a responsibility for such compulsion.[20]

Recent experience with field interviewing suggests that this "public be damned" attitude is producing a growing backlash against social research. Field directors of large survey organizations in the United States report that it has become increasingly difficult to obtain a high response rate in central city areas. The reasons for this situation are complicated, but fears of deception and misrepresentation, or sheer fatigue with surveys, are certainly part of the problem. A study in the United States shows that as of 1964, 250 communities in 34 states had passed legislation restricting the activities of survey interviewers.[21] The degree of control varies from complete prohibition to the requirement that interviewers register with local law enforcement officials. It is reasonable to expect that the greater the nuisance value of social research, and the more social scientists are perceived as untrustworthy, the more difficult

20. Humphreys, *Tearoom Trade,* p. 168.

21. Rome G. Arnold, "The Interview in Jeopardy: a Problem in Public Relations," *Public Opinion Quarterly,* 38:120, 1964.

it will be to carry out any kind of field study. Indeed, a *lack* of concern for professional integrity may spell the death of field research.

There is always a danger that remarks such as these will be interpreted as a plea for safe, bland, non-controversial research. A sharp distinction can be drawn, however, between research which is controversial or offensive to the public because of its subject matter, and studies which create ill-will, suspicion, and resentment because of Machiavellian methodology. C. Wright Mills carried out a great deal of research which was offensive to political conservatives because of its subject matter and conclusions, but to my knowledge he never engaged in deception or misrepresentation. Social scientists have not only a right but an obligation to study controversial and politically-sensitive subjects, including homosexuality, even if this brings down the wrath of the public and governmental officials. But this obligation does not carry with it the right to deceive, exploit, or manipulate people. My concern with backlash centers primarily on the alienation of ordinary individuals by research methods which leave them feeling that they have been cheated, deceived, or used. If social scientists set themselves and their methods above society, they must be prepared to take the consequences. The brief history of the social sciences suggests that it is abuses of ordinary people, such as research subjects, rather than political controversy *per se* which generate pressures for legal restrictions on research.

## Conclusions

We come, then, to the most basic question of all about Humphreys' study: should he have done it? The author himself asks:

> Are there, perhaps, some areas of human behavior that are not fit for social scientific study at all? Should sex, religion, suicide, or other socially sensitive concerns be omitted from the catalogue of possible fields of social research.[22]

Most of us in the social sciences would answer no, but these are the wrong questions. The real issue at stake is not whether male homo-

22. Humphreys, *Tearoom Trade,* p. 167.

sexuality or any other subject should be studied, but whether the methods used are ethically justified. In other words, does the end justify the means in social research?

Humphreys clearly feels that *his* ends justify the means he used. These ends, aside from the usual aim of increasing scientific knowledge, center about improving the lot of homosexuals in American society. One way to do so, he argues, is to gather data which can be used as a countervailing force against police repression of this group. He does not make explicit, however, how this knowledge will benefit the individuals in question, nor does he consider the hypothesis that it could be used by the police to improve their means of control. But perhaps his most basic argument is that increased knowledge about homosexuality will stir a concern in the larger society and perhaps lead to changes in present repressive laws and practices. He writes:

> We are not, however, protecting a harrassed population by refusing to look at them. At this very moment my writing has been interrupted by a long distance call, telling me of a man whose career has been destroyed because he was "caught" in a public restroom. . . . The greatest harm a social scientist could do this man would be to ignore him. Our concern about possible research consequences for our fellow "professionals" should take a secondary place to concern for those who may benefit from our research.[23]

The author's concern for the suffering individual is admirable, but his logic and ethics are not. Several assumptions in this passage are particularly dubious. First, the notion that social scientists do positive harm to suffering individuals by *not* studying them suggests a rather inflated sense of professional self-importance. I also wonder if the tearoom participants would agree that they would have been harmed by being left alone. Second, what is the factual basis for assuming that *Tearoom Trade* will ultimately alleviate the risks and suffering of male homosexuals in public restrooms? While this book has apparently been well-received in homosexual circles, my impression is that a widespread reading by the larger public might well produce negative rather than positive results.

23. *Ibid.*, p. 169.

But even if we grant that this research will ultimately help homosexuals, we come back to the very basic question of means and ends. Should every social scientist who feels that he has a laudable cause have the right to deceive respondents about the nature of surveys, engage in covert observation, and resort to other kinds of trickery? Should the same rights be extended to credit-checkers and the FBI, or do social scientists have special rights in the society? If a right-wing social scientist felt that the type of sociology practiced by Humphreys and advocated by his defenders constituted a threat to individual rights, and that these social scientists themselves needed help, would he be justified in sending covert observers to spy on their private lives? Whose causes are the right causes in social research? Neither Humphreys nor the editors of *Trans-Action* address themselves to these questions. They take the righteousness of their causes for granted, and assume that all men of good will should do likewise.

In sum, there are three ethical objections to the research tactics reported in *Tearoom Trade*. First, the researcher took advantage of a relatively powerless group of men to pursue his study. Had Humphreys passed as a voyeuristic gardener or chauffeur for a prominent family he would have been subject to legal and other kinds of retaliation. The men in the tearooms could not fight back. A critic might argue that Humphreys' subsequent acceptance by homophile organizations, including his election to a position on the National Committee for Sexual Civil Liberties, testifies to the fact that he did not exploit the people he studied. However, the men he studied are probably not represented in these organizations because of the covert nature of their activities. Even if they were, one could still object to the manipulation and deception of research subjects for whatever end. Second, through his research tactics Humphreys reinforces an image already prevalent in some circles that social scientists are sly tricksters who are not to be trusted. The more widespread this image becomes, the more difficult it will be for any social scientist to carry out studies involving active participants.

The third and strongest objection is that the use of deception, misrepresentation, and manipulation in social research encourages the same tendencies in other parts of society. A democratic nation is ultimately built upon respect for constitutional processes and restraint in the use of means. If one group arrogates to itself the right to use non-constitutional means for advancing its ends others will do likewise. The same lesson applies to the social sciences. If we claim that our causes justify the use of deception and manipulation, those advocating contrary causes will apply the same logic to their choice of means. When the issue of wiretapping first came before the Supreme Court some forty years ago, Justice Brandeis warned against the damage that would be wrought by letting the government violate the law in the name of the law. He also warned that the doctrine of the end justifying the means would bring terrible retribution to the country. About the same time Aldous Huxley wrote, "The end cannot justify the means for the simple and obvious reason that the means employed determine the nature of the ends produced." Social research involving deception and manipulation ultimately helps produce a society of cynics, liars and manipulators, and undermines the trust which is essential to a just social order.

# Impersonal Sex

Myron Glazer

WHEREIN HUMPHREYS DISGUISES HIMSELF TO OBSERVE HOMOSEXUALS IN PUBLIC BATHROOMS AND IN THEIR HOMES, COMES UNDER FIRE FROM JOURNALISTS AND SOCIAL SCIENTISTS ALIKE, AND IS VIGOROUSLY DEFENDED BY COLLEAGUES ADVOCATING COMPLETE FREEDOM OF RESEARCH.

LAUD HUMPHREYS' research is a prime example of the use of disguised observation and led to a heated debate on the appropriateness of such methods. In pursuing his doctoral work at Washington University at St. Louis he studied the nature of homosexual relations between men who had been total strangers prior to their brief intimate encounter. Humphreys observed such meetings in park bathrooms ("tearooms"). Since a lookout is extremely useful to watch for police or other unfriendly strangers, the researcher was able to assume a role that provided both an identity and a key observation post. From his guard position, Humphreys watched hundreds of acts of fellatio and made careful, systematic records of some fifty interactions. With the assistance of an actual participant, he also gathered another thirty accounts. These gave him sufficient

Reprinted from *The Research Adventure: Promise and Problems of Field Work,* by Myron Glazer. New York: Random House, 1972, pp. 107-108, 110-116, 119-120, 123-124.

data to analyze the nature of the contact that occurred in the bathroom stalls.

For a more complete analysis, however, Humphreys wanted to collect information on the socioeconomic characteristics, family relationships, and psychological motivations of the participants. The attempt to collect these data created a new set of obstacles. Humphreys' resolution posed another array of ethical issues. Since most of the men entered and left the "tearoom" quickly, there was little opportunity for casual conversation that might be transformed into an interview. Humphreys pursued a complicated, disguised, and effective procedure in order to question them later. He traced automobile license numbers to locate the men's home addresses; allowed a year to lapse, changed his hair style, manner of dress, and car to avoid recognition; and only then introduced himself as a researcher involved in a study of community health patterns. Humphreys successfully interviewed these men in their own homes without, according to him, their ever being aware that he knew of their "tearoom" visits. To the best of Humphreys' knowledge, his presence seemed to pose no threat to them or their families, which was of crucial importance to the researcher. . . .

Soon after the completion of his dissertation, officials at Washington University at St. Louis began to raise serious questions about the methodology. Charges were levied that the disguised observations violated the stipulations of Humphreys' grant from the National Institute of Mental Health regarding the protection of subjects. The Chancellor of the university informed the NIMH of these concerns and asked that another grant largely earmarked for Lee Rainwater, Humphreys' dissertation adviser, be held up pending an investigation. Although this grant was later awarded and the university investigation of Humphreys dropped, these events were exacerbated by departmental tensions that, according to Humphreys, allowed the university administration to "clip the wings" of the sociology faculty.

The conflict between the sociology department and the university administration was publicized by a local newspaper. Humphreys relates the reactions of some of the men whose active help he had secured in his study:

By the next day, several of my cooperating respondents had phoned to ask if they were in any jeopardy. I assured them that no one was in danger of exposure, that all data containing any possibility of identification had been burned. When the furor arose, I had carefully destroyed all tapes and portions of the interview schedules that contained occupational and other traceable information. At first, I hid the master list in a safe-deposit box nearly a thousand miles distant. Eventually, after committing that to memory, it was also destroyed. They seemed fully satisfied with my assurances, and I asked them to pass the word around the local tearooms. I then set about to contact each of the remaining cooperating respondents. Subsequent contacts with these men, as well as with several others who later came to realize their role as subjects in my research, have left me confident that they remained unscathed by the negative publicity my work received.[1]

Yet it is crucial to emphasize that Humphreys' respondents knew full well that he had no legal means by which to keep the potentially explosive data from falling into the hands of police or other authorities. Humphreys' informants were totally dependent on his shrewdness. Social scientists, I would stress, are vulnerable to subpoena and, unlike physicians, lawyers, and clergy, cannot promise their respondents any legal immunity.

The subsequent publication of Humphreys' work in *Trans-Action* created another storm of controversy and became a topic of heated debate among social scientists, journalists, and other interested readers of the popular and prestigious social science journal. Nicholas von Hoffman, writing in *The Washington Post* (reprinted in *Trans-Action*), accused Humphreys of the same kind of blatant invasion of privacy as police are often charged with. There are certain areas of personal life, according to von Hoffman, that are simply not the domain of the "snooping" social scientists. Von Hoffman discounted the precautions that Humphreys had taken to protect the identity of the men and asserted that Humphreys' material could have been used for blackmail.

Irving Louis Horowitz and Lee Rainwater, two social scientists most directly responsible for *Trans-Action,* and closely associated

1. Personal correspondence between Laud Humphreys and the author dated February 24, 1971.

with Humphreys' work at Washington University at St. Louis, wrote a stinging retort to von Hoffman and all critics of unrestrained social science inquiry. They maintained that the crucial issue centers on the right of the researcher to cast light into social areas hitherto covered by ignorance and darkness. The history of scientific research, they argued, is replete with instances in which investigators have been condemned for delving into what some considered private and sensitive areas. They commended Humphreys' scrupulous care in protecting the identity of those he studied and reiterated that, unlike policemen or journalists, social scientists are rarely interested in exposing particular individuals to public scorn or legal prosecution. On the contrary, the desire to generalize is the primary rationale for scientific research. Horowitz and Rainwater praised Humphreys for his courage in undertaking such pioneering research and argued that his findings could contribute to enlightened social policy.

There has been a great deal of controversy among social scientists about the appropriateness of Humphreys' research. Many lend support to the arguments put forth by Horowitz and Rainwater. A few have denigrated Humphreys as a mere pornographer because he described homosexual activities in clear detail. Certain associations are too private or unpleasant to publicize, the detractors seem to maintain. Personal revulsion, however, is not of primary concern. More pertinent questions concern the scientific relevance and ethical implications of Humphreys' study.

Did he select an important problem area? Humphreys reports that a high percentage of police arrests occur among those frequenting public men's rooms and yet nothing is known about these men, their background, work, and family life. Were Humphreys' methods directed toward careful collection of reliable data? His essay reveals a meticulous and sophisticated respect for social science research procedure. Did his work illegitimately infringe on the rights of those observed? Here, as I see it, the answer is far more complex and must be divided into the two major phases of the approach Humphreys followed. His first encounter with the men occurred in a *public* bathroom. He had as much right to be there as any of the participants. Indeed, as the lookout, he took the same risks as those he observed. Arrest, harassment, and physical violence could have been his lot.[2]

The situation was markedly different, however, in the second stage of the research design. Here Humphreys visited the men in their own homes. He watched them prepare barbecues, have their evening drinks, and converse with their families. Humphreys was an invited outsider. He took no personal risk by being there, but his presence did pose a potential threat to the men and their families. Humphreys' account is the only one available, and we do not know whether any of the respondents were frightened by the researcher's home visit. There has been no follow-up inquiry to alert us to any anxiety that they may have suffered as a result of the coverage that the research has received in the mass media.

Humphreys' decision to pursue the participants to their homes was a momentous one. He obviously believed that the blatant deception that he practiced was justified by scientific and policy returns. While it is difficult to evaluate this claim, it is apparent that social scientists assume a great responsibility when they deny respondents the rights of voluntary participation. What motivated Humphreys to utilize a method that he knew would raise the gravest ethical questions? The search for the answer provides important insight into the nature of the research craft.

2. Other field workers have suffered serious personal violence while conducting their research:

A Cornell graduate student said today she was clubbed by a policeman as she tried to film a police attack on demonstrators outside the Conrad Hilton Hotel here on August 28, 1968.

Testifying at the Chicago conspiracy trial, Mrs. Sarah Diamant said she came here during the Democratic National Convention to take films for her doctoral dissertation comparing 19th-century abolitionists with current student activists.

She said she, her husband and another Cornell student were filming and tape recording events in front of the Hilton Hotel when policemen charged into the demonstrators' rank, "beating people and pushing people up against buildings."

"I saw one policeman rushing toward me," she said. "I motioned toward the microphone in my hand. I thought he would understand. But he hit me with his club around the neck and shoulders." [From *The New York Times*, December 11, 1969, p. 43. © 1969 by The New York Times Company. Reprinted by permission.]

Humphreys' own views on this issue merit full presentation and careful consideration. It is important to emphasize that Humphreys saw his own work as part of a long-standing tradition in American sociology. He clearly identified his professional reference groups, which, he felt, gave full legitimacy to his investigation. Like the social scientists who "bugged" the jury room, Humphreys' decision was very much influenced by many members of the profession. Humphreys was deeply enthusiastic about his graduate school experiences and their influence on him:

The years from 1965 to 1968 were wonderful ones at Washington University. Not only did we have a faculty that ranged from Al Gouldner and Jules Henry on the left to Bob Hamlin on the right, but a number of the great minds of the discipline were in the middle. The first two years I was there we had an unbelievable colloquium series. Each speaker would stay for two days of formal and informal discussion with the students. The first year we had Howie Becker, Erving Goffman, Talcott Parsons, Kai Erikson, Marty Lipset, Robin Williams, Everett Hughes. Next year, as I recall, we had Richard Flacks, Herbert Marcuse, Oscar Lewis, Gideon Sjoberg, B. F. Skinner, Al Cohen, and Ed Friedenberg. The atmosphere was one of constant intellectual challenge and stimulation, very rough and tumble. Everything developed in conflict. One *had* to defend his own views, long before he knew what they really were. We were expected to be original, imaginative, and controversial.

Now, in such an environment, there are no taboo topics or forbidden strategies. The only things condemned were irrelevance and dishonesty. Rainwater and Horowitz were my mentors. Lee Rainwater played a major role as my research director. It was he who suggested, kept pushing, and supported me in three major strategies: the use of systematic observation forms ("simple observation is not adequate; it must be disciplined and systematic"), sampling by means of recording license numbers, and structured interviews of the participant sample.

My sociological reference group was clearly of the naturalist-ethnographic-underdog school. Because of my background in the ministry, Becker was more of a hero than Goffman. I saw myself as an inheritor of a tradition from Mead and Simmel, the Chicago School, Dollard, the Lynds, William F. Whyte, Becker, Polsky, Goffman—but also of an anthropological tradition of Malinowski, Firth, Oscar Lewis, Jules Henry, and Elliot Liebow. Along with this tradition, I also saw myself as part of another—not quite so cool and somewhat more committed: Marx, C. Wright Mills, Paul Goodman, Friedenberg, Harrington, Horowitz, Christian Bay.

There is no question but that I see myself connected with (and sometimes pulled apart by) two very vital and legitimate sociological traditions. On the other hand, I do not make a good "party man." I can't think of a time I have ever been in the mainstream of anything. The cutting edge, yes—mainstream, no. For as long as I can remember, I have been a boundary tester. There was plenty of precedent for my research strategies; but Rainwater, Horowitz, Pittman—all of my advisers—and I agonized over every move, every step of the research. Nick Demerath and Helen Gouldner, among others, had serious doubts about my publishing the results. So, to be honest, I knew damned well that I was going out on a limb. But I also knew there would be those holding a net below when the limb was sawed off.[3]

Humphreys' prediction was not entirely without merit. His former professors and many of his colleagues ardently supported him when he was criticized for the subject and methods of his research. He was also honored by the Society for the Study of Social Problems when his book received the C. Wright Mills award as a major contribution to the study of critical social issues.

Yet other social scientists are far less sanguine about Humphreys' methods. Daniels, whose research on the military was discussed earlier, is particularly worried about the lack of ethical standards governing professional behavior and the resultant danger that faces unwary respondents or consumers. Her subsequent study of psychiatrists did not leave her any more reassured:

I have very grave doubts about the argument that we should rely upon Humphreys' personal sense of honor, ethics, or professional discretion, no matter how well developed these traits are in him. The point of a professional control structure is to obviate the necessity for depending upon individual integrity so entirely. In my opinion, no one in the society deserves to be trusted with hot, incriminating data. Let me repeat, *no one*. And that is because we should not have to rely upon the individual strength of conscience which may be required. Psychiatrists, for example, are notorious gossipers about the more "squidgy" aspects of

3. Personal correspondence between Laud Humphreys and the author dated February 24, 1971.

patient life. They feel free to talk over details with associates because of their collegial relationship and mutual understanding of the rules of confidentiality.

O.K. So they mainly just tell one another. But they *sometimes* tell wives, people at parties, you and me. And few of them would hold up under systematic pressure from government or whatever to get them to tell. I understand there are many victims of the McCarthy era who are now heartily sorry that they told their psychiatrists about radical political interests. The issue is not that a few brave souls *do* resist. The issue is rather what to do about the few who will not? I think it is better to tell no one. And better to entrust no one (outside of the priesthood and people trained all their lives to hold up under secrets) with any "hot" material. There is *nothing* in our training—any more than in the training of psychiatrists, no matter what they say—to prepare us to take up these burdens.[4]

I need not completely subscribe to Daniels' harsh critique of contemporary professional ethics in order to point to the dangers inherent in Humphreys' research procedures. By his own account, he was willing to take risks and suffer the consequences for probing into the most private areas of human relationships through the use of most controversial methods. My conversations with Humphreys convinced me of his extraordinary courage and ability to withstand condemnation and abuse. Yet these very characteristics make him a poor model for others to emulate without the most painful self-scrutiny. There are few social scientists who have such personality strength and commitment to the underdog. There are even fewer who combine these characteristics with Humphreys' research expertise. There are almost none who are also so completely assured of the ultimate importance of their efforts.

While admiring Humphreys, I know that I could not pursue such research myself and would attempt to dissuade others from such a path. The dangers to respondents, to the researcher, and to the precious sense of respect for the privacy of others seem too great for the returns. Had Humphreys faltered, had his data been secured by police officials or unscrupulous blackmailers, Humphreys would have been branded a rogue and a fool. He can now legitimately

4. Personal correspondence between Arlene Kaplan Daniels and the author dated July 30, 1971.

reject these epithets. Others, particularly those whom we hope to help by our efforts, should not be put in such jeopardy except with their explicit consent. . . .

The perceptive field worker is always faced with certain ethical problems. For some researchers these questions are particularly grave. Have they been justified in consciously accumulating material through the total ignorance of those who provide it? At what point has an inappropriate infringement of privacy occurred? Humphreys and his defenders argue that no area should be neglected by social scientists just because of its sensitivity. Others who hold the same views have undertaken pioneering research in human sexuality but have gained the permission of the subjects. The issue is not only the sensitivity of the subject matter but also the nature of the methods used to examine it.

Uniform standards do not and probably cannot exist. Every profession relies on the internalization of ethical precepts by its members, the sanctioning power of professional organizations and public officials, and, of course, the weight of public opinion, which may directly affect the offending practitioner. There are grave questions as to the general effectiveness of these safeguards on professional conduct. Their efficacy in the shadowy areas of social science ethics may be even more uncertain.[5]

Many of those engaged in social science field work continue to tread a thin line. Their critics outside of social science often accuse them of disrespect for basic human rights. Their colleagues, at times, raise questions about the actual or potential harm they may cause others. These colleagues maintain that trust and respect are the crucial components in a research relationship. The researcher, they argue, must convince others not only that he is worthy of their support and that he can appreciate their reluctance to assist him, but also that he is at least competent to protect them from ridicule. Respondents, these colleagues continue, should be warned of any possible danger and should be the ones to make the choice about participation. When they refuse, as they sometimes will, the social scientist should, and usually can, find alternate respondents.

5. For a perceptive and critical discussion of the problems of disguised observation, see Kai T. Erikson, "A Comment on Disguised Observation in Sociology," *Social Problems,* 14 (Spring 1967), 366-373.

Social scientists who employ disguised methods of data collection insist, on the other hand, that these are perfectly permissible as long as they are utilized by competent and committed researchers. Bias, they argue, can often best be reduced when others are unaware that they are being observed. The social scientist must, of course, employ proper safeguards to protect the identity of unwitting respondents, but he would be derelict in his search for knowledge were he to neglect crucial areas of social life because of the resistance of respondents or the condemnation of colleagues or interested others.

The arguments will continue. Individual cases will, no doubt, be settled on their own merits. Often the relative power of involved groups will be the deciding factor as in the jury hearings. Social scientists are reluctant to set closely delineated lines to regulate their own behavior. They desire the flexibility to choose their own methods according to the nature of the research and their personal proclivities. This makes open and probing debate all the more essential. Social scientists are, justifiably, reluctant to spare others from intensive analysis. They must expose their own procedures to the same rigorous scrutiny. Honest reporting of methods and continuous debate among colleagues and students are essential for those engaged in the research adventure. Social scientists who use disguised techniques must stand ready to defend themselves before a wide array of critical audiences.

An ominous new ingredient has now entered the controversy. The recent disclosures of widespread military surveillance of civilians, the ever-growing use of phone tapping, and the burgeoning data banks on millions of American citizens gravely undermine the rights of free expression and privacy. For their own interest, social scientists should be among the staunchest defenders of these rights against the would-be censors and controllers. Social scientists should be scrupulously careful about contributing to the fast-growing reservoir of suspicion and distrust that plagues the United States in the closing decades of the twentieth century.

# Retrospect: Ethical Issues in Social Research

Laud Humphreys

WHEN I BEGAN graduate work in sociology at Washington University in June of 1965, I had already acquired one graduate degree and ten years of experience as a parish priest in the Episcopal Church. Largely due to my intense involvement in the Civil Rights movement of the early 1960s, I found myself increasingly at odds with vestries and bishops and disenchanted with the church as an effective instrument for promoting the social change that I thought essential for dealing with the problems of individuals.

I was not long in discovering that sociologists have their own prejudices, a common one being a strong distaste for those who leave the ministry to build a career in the social sciences, the so-called "refugees from the parsonage." Whatever justification there may be for this anti-clerical bias, it involves one false stereotypical image, that of the clergyman as a naive, other-worldly individual who lacks knowledge of the streets. When my first graduate professor, in discussing a proposed research project, urged me to study the gay bars of St. Louis, I took it as a serious challenge. "Get out of your sheltered tower," she advised. "Get out in the streets and get your hands dirty!"

In the twenty years since my mother's death, I had been "out in the streets" more than I cared to remember: first, as a delinquent kid in dust-bowl depression Oklahoma; then working my way through college as a newspaper reporter; later in mission work in Chicago slums and such "Wild West" towns as Cripple Creek, Colorado; finally, in the sit-ins and protest marches of the movement for black liberation. The suggestion that I engage in some tough ethnography I took as a challenge to my identity as a person and a nascent social scientist.

The early stages of this research were largely motivated by that original challenge. As tearoom behavior came into focus, however, the obstacles often seemed too great to overcome. I frequently considered changing my dissertation topic or even moving out of the deviance field into my second major area, medical sociology. However, events in the spring of 1966 assured the continuation of my research into impersonal sex: I was granted a predoctoral fellowship for research in homosexual lifestyles, and I was introduced to David, the necessary informant.

Chronicals of field research bear repeated testimony to the central role of a key informant. Both Whyte[1] and Liebow[2] tell us of the importance of Doc and Tally to their respective projects. I should like to provide similar praise for David, the informant who facilitated this research, but I fear that comments approaching a full disclosure of his vital role might reveal his identity.

The danger of exposing David to stigma illustrates a unique problem that plagues any account I attempt of my research. I would tell many tales of warmth and humor about the interaction between my respondents and myself. Some became lasting friends of my family, and my sense of the identity of nearly all of them goes far beyond a code number on an interview schedule. But now, as in writing the book, I must suppress the sort of anecdotal material that makes the "Appendix" of Whyte's *Street Corner Society* so

1. William Foote Whyte, *Street Corner Society,* (Chicago: University of Chicago Press, second edition, 1955).
2. Elliot Liebow, *Tally's Corner* (Boston: Little, Brown, 1967).

appealing. With much caution and removing all identifying tags, I told everything I could in the original manuscript. Each time I start to involve another person, to provide a human account of how a nameless research subject became a cooperating respondent, I risk exposing that person to stigmatization. Thus I return to talking about myself and my reaction to individuals who must remain faceless and anonymous, as if the impersonality of tearoom sex has to be duplicated in every description of those who participate in that furtive ritual.

Most reviews of *Tearoom Trade* did not surprise me a great deal. My greatest pleasure came from the consistently favorable reaction of the gay press, and the attacks from positivist devotees of survey research were expected. Von Hoffman's comparison of me with Attorney General Mitchell, odious as it was, gained some ironic value when I was later arrested, tried, and imprisoned under Mitchell's authority for destroying a photograph of Nixon during a draft board demonstration in 1970. But three reviews really stung by accusing me of lacking compassion for my respondents. Typical of these is one that appeared in *Issues in Criminology,* written by Barry Krisberg:[3]

> One feels a tremendous sense of uneasiness while reading Humphreys' ethnography or, in fact, the ethnographies of other "hip sociologists" such as Howard Becker, Elliot Liebow, Ned Polsky, or the grand master, Erving Goffman. Perhaps the root of the dis-ease is that one senses that the sociologist appreciates his deviant subjects but is not compassionate with them. To be compassionate, it seems to me, requires that the researcher understands the fundamental passion or suffering of his subjects. This lack of sensitivity to human suffering leads the "hip sociologist" to ignore important dimensions of the social problem which he is describing.

After noting that the book won the C. Wright Mills Award of the Society for the Study of Social Problems, he continues:

> It is not hard to imagine how Mills, the great radical sociologist, would have responded to such an irony. The moral relativism of the hip

3. Barry Krisberg, "Tearoom Trade," in *Issues in Criminology* (Winter, 1972).

ethnography would in Mills' terms be evidence of "moral cowardice." Compassionate analysis of the victim or consequences of social injustice seems central to Mills' radical perspective.

About the time Krisberg's review appeared in print, my second book, an analysis of the gay liberation movement, was published.[4] Krisberg and others who objected to the "clinical," "hip," or "dehumanized" nature of my tearoom sociology have not reviewed *Out of the Closets,* but I suspect some of them might find its style more to their liking. In that work, however, I was free to discuss "the fundamental passion or suffering" of my respondents, chiefly because they were overt gay activists whose identities I did not need to protect. In that study the liberation of my subjects liberated the researcher; whereas the anonymity and lack of commitment of the tearoom participants forced me to write of them in a cool, dispassionate manner that some readers interpreted as a lack of concern.

Given that my primary ethical concern in the study was to safeguard respondents from the many dangers that might have attended their exposure, I can only hope that those who read the book and this retrospect will understand the necessity for ellipses and cautious reporting on my part. If that means I must be labeled as "cool" or "hip," I find it preferable to being destructive.

## Ethical Criticisms

With these considerations in mind, I must direct the reader back to the first four chapters of the book for the bulk of what can and should be said regarding my research strategies. I shall concentrate here on some of the ethical questions that have been raised. In doing so, it is not my intention to counter all of the objections raised by von Hoffman, Warwick, and others, but I shall try to recall how ethical concerns appeared to me and how I dealt with them in the field.

As noted in the "Postscript" to the main text, I suffered little from doubts or hesitation about observing sexual acts in the tea-

4. Laud Humphreys, *Out of the Closets: The Sociology of Homosexual Liberation* (Englewood Cliffs, N.J.: Prentice-Hall, Inc., 1972).

rooms. These were, after all, public restrooms, and my role, a natural one in those settings, provided extra protection for the participants. In my nonsexual way, I was a true participant. Erikson's excellent "Comment on Disguised Observation" was published toward the end of my systematic observations but summarizes, after the fact, my feelings about this stage of the investigation:

> Some of the richest material in the social sciences has been gathered by sociologists who were true participants in the group under study but who did not announce to other members that they were employing this opportunity to collect research data. Sociologists live careers in which they occasionally become patients, occasionally take jobs as steel workers or taxi drivers, and frequently find themselves in social settings where their trained eye begins to look for data even though their presence in the situation was not engineered for that purpose. It would be absurd, then, to insist as a point of ethics that sociologists should always introduce themselves as investigators everywhere they go and should inform every person who figures in their thinking exactly what their research is all about.[5]

Erikson appears to be referring primarily to research in those places of daily concourse where the social scientist plays a natural role not engineered for the purposes of his study. It does not seem an unfair extension, however, to follow the same principle in public settings where the sociologist steps into a natural role, particularly when that unobtrusive role is not central to the action observed. It may provide some insight into my lack of doubt about the ethics of my observations to know that I spent an hour discussing my research with Erikson at about the same time his paper on ethics was published. Neither of us recall that he raised any ethical objections at that point; we were both more interested in the nature and quality of the data being gathered.

Warwick makes an issue of my use of a hidden tape recorder for recording observations while seated in my automobile. He assumes that "the point of this procedure was to avoid the possibility that those frequenting nearby tearooms would discover his true identity." The truth of the matter is that I covered the recorder with a pasteboard box for two reasons: to avoid tempting thieves, and to avoid giving passersby the impression that I was a policeman. My

5. Kai T. Erikson, "A Comment on Disguised Observation in Sociology," *Social Problems,* Vol. 14, No. 4 (Spring, 1967), p. 368.

reasoning was much more in the cops and robbers line than cloak and dagger. Although I used a less portable tape recorder on a number of occasions to interview fully informed and consenting respondents, I did not do this in my automobile. In addition, I find transcribing from tape (a task I could not entrust to others in this research) a terribly time-consuming operation. I tried using a notebook, and then a clipboard, in my car, but despaired of that method of note-taking after a couple of near accidents while making notes on the park drives. Actually, a number of the conspiratorial machinations attributed to me by reviewers were no more than mundane solutions to problems of research technique.

## Legal Problems

Much more serious are some of the legal objections to my field work. Along with a number of questions about the protection of my respondents, all of which I believe were well answered, the Chancellor of Washington University argued that I had committed numerous felonies in the course of my research. He was not successful in having my degree revoked on this basis, but he did terminate both my teaching contract and my participation in a research grant. By observing, perhaps facilitating, and failing to report some 200 acts of fellatio, was I not guilty as an accomplice to the acts? Stated in that form, the answer may appear obvious. Strangely enough, I don't think the question even occurred to me until late in my research.

In retrospect, I have tried to probe my conscience about this apparent disregard for the law. The only answer I have found, if not totally satisfying, is of some criminological interest. Some might call it a case of "improper socialization." There are many laws I have never had any intention of obeying, including most of those governing victimless "crimes" against "public order." When I conform, which is most of the time, it is only because I have no interest in committing a certain act or because I fear the possibility of being caught at it. I remember my terror when counselling at a summer camp in Colorado upon finding that I had violated the law by picking columbines to decorate the tables of the mess hall. The priest in charge of the camp made me throw them all out for fear of being caught and bringing shame upon the institution.

To be raised in prohibition Oklahoma, where all the social drinkers in the church regularly voted for the sheriff who promised to crack down on bootleggers, is to be brought up in contempt of certain kinds of law. As a state legislator, my father was most diligent in promoting the passage of Sunday "blue laws." He also helped establish a law school in the attic of the State Capital so that blacks would not have to be admitted to the University. I am one of those people who have been officially "rehabilitated" by months in jail and years on probation, yet I still have utter contempt for a number of statutes on the law books.

If I did commit felonies in the course of my research, it never occurred to me that I was wrong in doing so. Had I been prosecuted and convicted, I would have been "wrong," at least in a sociological sense; but it would have been impossible for a prosecutor to prove that any particular act observed took place at any particular time and place between specified individuals. Now that the statute of limitation has run out, I can address this matter with some bravado.

My self-assurance fails, on the other hand, in the face of another objection raised by von Hoffman, Glazer, and Warwick. The latter expresses it with frightening directness: "This is one of the few social scientific studies which would have lent itself directly to a grand jury investigation." In the wake of front-page publicity, fostered by members of the administration and faculty at Washington University soon after the completion of this research, I am surprised that no such investigation followed. Even with the care I took to safeguard my data, I spent some weeks early in the summer of 1968 burning tapes, deleting passages from transcripts, and feeding material into a shredder. Memories of that time of panic have helped me understand, though not approve, the procedures of some White House conspirators in the Watergate cover-up.

As I pondered during sleepless nights what I would do to protect my respondents if called to court, my resolve was to plead the Fifth Amendment and risk contempt citations rather than reveal the identity of a single tearoom participant. There was no question in my mind that I would go to prison rather than betray the subjects of my research. My lawyer, my advisers, and I spent some time discussing these matters, and I now realize they were not as placid as I was about the prospects. Since those days of uncertainty, however, I have spent three months of a Federal sentence in a county jail and am no longer so certain that I could have withstood the pressures of the criminal justice system.

There was little danger either to researcher or respondents in the observation of sexual encounters between individuals whose identity was unknown. For those subjects who knew the nature of my research and freely consented to participate in it, the ethical and legal responsibilities were at least shared and reciprocal, though no less pressing on the researcher in protecting the confidentality of his data.

With these considerations in mind, I am forced to agree with my critics regarding that part of my study in which I traced license numbers and interviewed respondents in their homes. At the time, although troubled and cautious about my research strategies, I justified them in much the same terms as I have outlined on p. 42. It seemed that I was interviewing subjects in the least disturbing and least dangerous manner possible. I now think my reasoning was faulty and that my respondents were placed in greater danger than seemed plausible at the time.

I know when my change in thinking on this matter took place. Two events occurred while I was an inmate of Albany County Jail in the spring and early summer of 1972. The first mail I received in prison was a copy of Glazer's *The Research Adventure,* giving me the opportunity to read and reflect upon it over many hours. (Later, I passed this book around to fellow inmates and a few guards as part of my policy of informing everyone at the jail of the sort of research they might expect of me while incarcerated.)

The second event brought home some dangers of research. I was called out to the visiting room one afternoon for a conference with two inspectors from the New York State Police. They had learned (probably from students in my course in Field Research Methods who were policemen on leave) that one of my students was doing research in certain bars where Albany's drug and prostitute traffic was believed to center. As the result of aggressive reporting in a local newspaper, a Grand Jury had been called to investigate these establishments. The inspectors wanted to know the identity of my student, along with any notes or recollections I might have of his findings. Fortunately, I had no notes and only a faulty memory, but I could not avoid identifying the student. He had a bad memory, too, I suppose, for he was never called to testify.

Since then, although I remain convinced that it is ethical to observe interaction in public places and to interview willing and informed respondents, I direct my students to inform research subjects before interviewing them. Were I to repeat the tearoom study, I would spend another year or so in cultivating and expanding the category of willing respondents into which the "intensive dozen" fall. Perhaps the sample of participants would not be as representative as in the original study, if I were limited to these methods, but the richness of data gained would certainly surpass those obtained from the interview schedules. Perhaps by these means I could discover, as Rainwater urges in his Foreword to this book, more about "the personal significance to the participants of their homosexual behavior."

Years have passed since I studied the tearoom encounters and those who enact a hidden portion of their lives in them. There is no reason to believe that any research subjects have suffered because of my efforts, or that the resultant demystification of impersonal sex has harmed society. The scandal called Watergate has reached its glorious climax, perhaps leaving the nation somewhat humbled. Among the lessons we should have learned is the need for each of us to make frequent ethical self-examinations—and this applies to research as well as to politics and business. But we also need to learn the danger of secrecy and of maintaining illusions. Warwick states that "men in every age—including the social scientists of the present—need illusions to be free." I shall always disagree with that romantic statement. We are in desperate need of knowledge to be free.

Somewhat chastened by the controversy surrounding my study of the tearoom trade, I remain proud of the work done. I often wish other sociologists would give more attention to some of my substantive findings that I believe provide an increment of understanding of social behavior in our society. At the same time, I realize that serving as a focus for ethical debate is no mean contribution. Above all, I know that this study is increasingly cited by attorneys seeking acquittal for clients arrested in public restrooms. What began as a relatively uncomplicated ethnography of the gay community grew in complexity as the logic of research took hold, and ended as much in a quest for justice as for knowledge alone.

# Index